Marion A. Bilich, PhD
Susan T. Bonfiglio, MSW
Steven D. Carlson, MDiv

Shared Grace
Therapists and Clergy Working Together

Pre-publication
REVIEWS,
COMMENTARIES,
EVALUATIONS . . .

" **S** *hared Grace: Therapists and Clergy Working Together* provides a very personal and revealing look at the collaboration between therapists and clergy in the treatment of a woman suffering from dissociative personality disorder. Their story is unique in that it portrays the ways in which their mutual respect for one another's discipline influenced and changed their approaches to the woman they treated. Throughout the text, the authors interject their own personal reflections on the issues raised in the course of their collaboration. The Benevolence Model' of treatment that they propose honors both the theological and clinical perspectives it employs. At times their reflections and treatment approaches challenge standard clinical practice and orthodox theological interpretation. In so doing, they call upon clinicians to establish authentic therapeutic relationships and clergy to demonstrate the theological principles they espouse. This book offers an exciting model for collaboration and treatment."

Homer U. Ashby Jr., PhD
Professor of Pastoral Care,
McCormick Theological Seminary

More pre-publication
REVIEWS, COMMENTARIES, EVALUATIONS . . .

"This creative and provocative work provides a paradigm for facilitating the healing of persons in a multidisciplinary manner. Utilizing basic theological maxims as a foundation, the book illustrates the manner in which therapists and clergy can implement 'The Benevolence Model' of healing, which benefits both those being healed as well as the healers. This work is an essential read for all therapists and clergy who are interested in the cooperative and holistic healing of those entrusted to their care."

Robert H. Albers, PhD
Professor of Pastoral Theology,
Luther Seminary,
St. Paul, Minnesota

"This book highlights collaboration between therapists and clergy members on behalf of a person who experienced childhood abuse and neglect. In terms of structure, it is well organized, with a clear focus on intervention as defined by The Benevolence Model. The chapters are presented in a logical fashion and the transition between each one is smooth thanks to chapter introductions and summaries. The authors' writing style is crisp and lively with quotations and examples from a case study that runs throughout the book. All terms are defined in a concrete fashion. The references and resources included at the end of the book are both extensive and helpful."

Carolyn J. Tice, DSW
Associate Professor
and Department Chair,
Department of Social Work,
Ohio University,
Athens

"This book will be a beneficial addition to the libraries of therapists (psychologists, social workers, psychiatrists, and counselors) and clergy/spiritual leaders as well as educators of these disciplines because it explains the step-by-step process for therapists and clergy to collaborate respectfully with one another. The book consists of an in-depth case study for working collaboratively with survivors of severe childhood abuse. While this case study is insightful, it is important to remember that knowledge is transferable and therefore many of the strategies and approaches can be successfully used with other problems clients may present."

Leola Dyrud Furman, PhD
Associate Professor,
Department of Social Work,
University of North Dakota

"In *Shared Grace,* Marion Bilich, Susan Bonfiglio, and Steven Carlson join forces to explore interprofessional collaboration. Although their main focus is on childhood abuse, the book offers a lot of applicability to other issues that confront people in therapy and pastoral counseling. The book is dedicated to developing an understanding of psychological, spiritual, religious, and theological issues as they affect people. One major strength of the book is the authors' use of 'experience near.' The authors anchor their observations in clients' clinical stories/data, which they explore to highlight the need for interprofessional collaboration. The practical guidelines presented throughout and the resources at the end of the book make it user friendly for clinicians and clergy. Indeed, this is a must-read and practically useful book grounded in clinical and theological experience."

Hugo Kamya
Professor of Social Work,
Boston College Graduate School
of Social Work

The Haworth Pastoral Press®
An Imprint of The Haworth Press, Inc.

Shared Grace
Therapists and Clergy Working Together

THE HAWORTH PASTORAL PRESS
Religion and Mental Health
Harold G. Koenig, MD
Senior Editor

New, Recent, and Forthcoming Titles:

Shared Grace
Therapists and Clergy Working Together

Marion Bilich, PhD
Susan Bonfiglio, MSW
Steven Carlson, MDiv

The Haworth Pastoral Press®
An Imprint of The Haworth Press, Inc.
New York • London • Oxford

Published by

The Haworth Pastoral Press®, an imprint of The Haworth Press, Inc., 10 Alice Street, Binghamton, NY 13904-1580

Quoted material from *Lion and Lamb* by Brennan Manning, 1986, is reprinted by permission of Fleming H. Revell, a division of Baker Book House Company, Grand Rapids, Michigan.

Cover design by Jennifer M. Gaska.

Library of Congress Cataloging-in-Publication Data

Bilich, Marion.
    Shared grace : therapists and clergy working together / Marion Bilich, Susan Bonfiglio, Steven Carlson.
        p.   cm.
    Includes bibliographical references and index.
    ISBN 0-7890-0878-5 (alk. paper)—ISBN 0-7890-1110-7 (pbk. : alk. paper)
    1. Adult child abuse victims—Pastoral counseling of—Case studies. 2. Abused women—Pastoral counseling of—Case studies. 3. Multiple personality—Patients—Pastoral counseling of—Case studies. 4. Adult child abuse victims—Counseling of—Case studies. 5. Abused women—Counseling of—Case studies. 6. Multiple personality—Patients—Counseling of—Case studies. 7. Psychotherapy—Religious aspects— Christianity. I. Bonfiglio, Susan. II. Carlson, Steven, 1959- III. Title.

BV4463.5 .B55 2000
261.8′327—dc21
                                                                                    99-462143

CONTENTS

Acknowledgments

Many people helped us over the years, as we prepared the manuscript for this book. We would first like to thank Michael Hardin for getting us all together and for teaching us about a theology of love and grace. Jim Smollon has been a part of our work since the beginning, and we thank him for his participation in all aspects of our collaboration. We want to thank Sarah Jane Freymann, Warren Purkel, and Judith Rabinor for their help in rewriting earlier drafts of the manuscript. We would also like to thank Warren Purkel for giving Marion a kidney, because without that gift, this book never would have been completed.

ABOUT THE AUTHORS

Marion Bilich, PhD, is a licensed psychologist in private practice on Long Island, New York. She holds a doctorate in clinical psychology from the Fielding Institute in Santa Barbara, California, and a master's in social work from Columbia University. She is the author of *Weight Loss from the Inside Out: Help for the Compulsive Eater* and numerous clinical and research papers in professional journals. Dr. Bilich is nationally known for her work on eating disorders and has presented workshops throughout the country on eating disorders and on the inclusion of spirituality in the treatment of women who have been abused.

Susan Bonfiglio, MSW, is a certified social worker on Long Island, New York. Under the auspices of the Peninsula Counseling Center, she directs the Meeting Place Clubhouse, a psychiatric rehabilitation program that teaches vocational, interpersonal, and social skills to individuals with chronic mental illness. She holds master's degrees in social work from Adelphi University and in mental health counseling from C. W. Post.

Steven D. Carlson, MDiv, is a pastor who works with youth in Sacramento, California. He received his master's degree from the North Park Seminary in Chicago, Illinois. He is co-author, with Dr. Bilich, of "Therapists and Clergy Working Together: Linking the Psychological and the Spiritual in the Treatment of MPD," which was published in the *Journal of Christian Healing*.

Chapter 1

Our Story: Beginnings

The beginnings of all things are weak and tender; we must therefore be clearsighted in beginnings.

Michel de Montaigne

INTRODUCTION

Roberta has been tormented by memories of severe sexual and physical abuse all her life. Her father had sexually abused her repeatedly throughout childhood. He would often torture her as well—tying her up, sticking objects into her body, locking her in closets. At the age of fourteen, her teacher, a trusted friend of the family, had also tried to sexually abuse her. Unable to tell anyone about her abuse, Roberta had felt frightened, confused, and guilty for years. As she grew into adulthood, she became increasingly depressed and anxious, turning to drugs and alcohol to ease the pain of her memories. She reached out in desperation to her religious community, hoping to find some relief from her pain, but she remained riddled with doubts about a God who would have allowed such horrible abuse to happen to a child. At the age of thirty-five, determined to heal from the effects of her abuse, Roberta has recently entered therapy. Roberta and her therapist work well together, but the therapist's experience is somewhat limited and she is unable to explore Roberta's spiritual questions and doubts in any depth.

Roberta had turned to her minister for spiritual guidance in the past.

Minister: Roberta has become so dependent on her therapist. It seems that all the therapist is doing is making her more dependent. There is no healing. They're bringing up old issues that are so painful. Can't they work on getting beyond that? To grow, it seems she should be able to get beyond the pain. I don't understand why Roberta doesn't hear what I'm saying about forgiveness. Why isn't she open to this? She used to seek out my spiritual guidance. Now all she wants is my friendship, and she's not interested in hearing what I have to say about God. In fact, when I did share with her that she needs to turn back to God, seeking her direction from God, she slammed the phone down on me. I'm sitting here in pain, asking God what I did wrong. How can I help this person without feeling so frustrated? Everything I say seems to make it worse!

Therapist: Roberta has been talking to a minister who has been telling her that she should not dwell on the past. Rather than encouraging her to deal with her emotions, he is just telling her to pray and to read the Bible more. I wish that she would stop talking to this person, because he's only confusing her. He's only making her feel worse—more guilty. I don't understand how God enters into this anyway, because Roberta must get past the emotional pain of her childhood to go on. I don't know what to do. All I want is to help Roberta, but as long he is pulling her in another direction, I feel as if I'm fighting a battle with one arm tied behind my back!

Both the therapist and the minister want to be helpful, yet each has experienced only frustration, pain, misunderstanding, and confusion when faced with the work of the other. Poor Roberta. She is caught in the middle between two people she admires—two people upon whom she is depending in her healing journey. Is there any way for the therapist and the minister to get past the preconceived notions they have about each other's work? Could they call a truce? Is it even possible that in the service of helping this survivor of severe abuse they might learn to work together in a true collaboration? What if the therapist and minister are of different religions? Could they still work together?

Yes. We know that such a collaboration is possible, because that is what happened to us. This book recounts our experience—a collaboration between Marion Bilich, a Jewish psychologist, and Steven Carlson, a Christian minister—as we worked together helping a woman we call "Teresa" heal from the effects of her severe abuse. Teresa was a young woman with dissociative identity disorder (commonly known as multiple personalities). Not long after her alter personalities revealed themselves in therapy, Teresa asked Marion to speak with her pastors. She wanted Marion to explain to them about some of the psychological and emotional issues involved in healing from her abuse. Her spiritual life was important to her, and she wanted her pastors to be included in some way in her psychotherapy. Marion contacted the senior pastor, Michael Hardin, unsure of what kind of input he could have in her work with Teresa. However, she remained open to the possibilities. Thus began a collaboration that profoundly affected the lives of all involved. Susan Bonfiglio, our other co-author, is a social worker. She provides a unique perspective as a member of the support group established by the senior pastor of the church to provide a support system for Teresa within her church community.

> **Marion:** We are well aware of the controversy in the field of psychology as to whether dissociative identity disorder actually exists, and if it does, how rare it is. In addition, we are aware of the problems with recovered memories. Increasingly, therapists have been accused of planting false memories in their patients through suggestions and hypnosis. At the outset, I would like to clarify a few points. First, let us deal with the issue of recovered memories: Teresa never forgot her abuse. Though she repressed details of some of her abuse through the creation of different identities, Teresa remained aware throughout her life that she had been horribly abused during her childhood. She remembered many horrible incidents of being abused by her mother, an uncle, and a cousin, although the worst experiences of abuse were relegated to her alters.
>
> Second, never did I suggest to her that she might be suffering from dissociative identity disorder until I had evidence. She had been in therapy with me for two years before she

began revealing the details of her abusive childhood. As her story unfolded, I began to suspect she might have multiple personalities, especially when she told me about "lost years," years of her life she could not remember having lived. I consulted with several mental health professionals experienced in the field of dissociative disorders. However, I did not make a diagnosis, nor did I discuss my suspicions with her, until one of her alter identities "came out" to talk to me. It was only then, as the alters appeared one by one that a diagnosis of dissociative identity disorder was made.

We also want to emphasize that true dissociative identity disorder may be rare, and that not all people with a history of severe and sadistic childhood abuse will have multiple identities. Although the person we describe in this book turned to alternate identities to cope with her abuse, this does not mean the book will not have relevance to therapists and clergy who work with abused women who do not have this disorder. In fact, the collaboration between therapist and clergy need not be limited to helping women who have experienced severe childhood abuse. We believe that therapists and clergy can work together collaboratively to help any individual suffering from trauma, and physical, emotional, or psychiatric illness. Our work with Teresa provides an example of how such collaborations can be undertaken, but you need not limit yourselves to work with survivors of abuse alone.

This book demonstrates how our collaboration offered Teresa a deeper, richer experience than any traditional psychotherapy alone could have accomplished. We describe how *all* involved—therapist, minister, survivor, and the members of Teresa's support group—grew spiritually, emotionally, and professionally through the work together. However, this book is more than a mere recounting of our personal experiences. It provides guidelines and suggestions for others who want to undertake such an endeavor. We have interviewed many therapists and members of the clergy throughout the country and have included their experiences as well. In addition, we have developed "The Benevolence Model"—a spiritual model that we believe transcends any particular religion and provides a common framework out of which therapists and clergy of different backgrounds can work together. This book is also a deeply personal story about how four people came together and how their interactions changed their lives forever.

Collaboration between therapist and clergy is about putting aside ideological and theological differences in the service of helping survivors heal from the effects of their abuse. It endeavors to bridge the gap between psychology and religion, breaking down the walls between the two disciplines so that people can work together effectively. Collaboration can take many forms—from open communication and dialogue, to frequent consultation, or to an equal partnership designed to provide the survivor with the emotional, psychological, and spiritual support she needs to heal.

Since our own collaboration focused on work with a survivor of severe childhood abuse who was suffering from a dissociative identity disorder, we have devoted a great deal of material to describing work with survivors of abuse. However, we do not mean to suggest that all severely abused people are dissociative. Nor do we believe that collaboration between therapist and clergy should be confined to work with such individuals. It is our hope that you will consider collaboration as a means of helping many types of individuals who are suffering—those with mental illness, severe physical disorders, or physical handicaps, for example. We look forward to hearing from other therapists and clergy about how their own collaborations helped people deal with all kinds of difficult life problems.

This book is aimed at three groups:

1. *Therapists and other mental health professionals.* Those therapists involved in the treatment of people who were severely abused in childhood may be especially interested in this book, because we focus on work with such individuals. However, as we pointed out, therapists involved in working with individuals suffering from any major physical or emotional problem— trauma, catastrophic physical illness, severe psychiatric illness—may also be interested in the benefits of collaboration with clergy. Especially in this era of time-limited managed mental health care, therapists are looking for ways to extend the therapy of people with serious emotional and physical

problems beyond the twenty-session limits. Collaboration, as we will see, can provide opportunities to do so.

2. *Ministers.* The book will be helpful to ministers who want to offer spiritual guidance to those in their congregations who are suffering from severe physical, mental, or emotional problems. It will be especially helpful for those ministers who work with women healing from the effects of severe abuse, since the actual collaboration described in detail in the book focuses on a woman who had been severely abused in childhood. (We use the generic term "minister" to refer to all types of clergy—rabbi, priest, pastor, nun, etc.)

3. *Survivors of severe abuse who want to add a spiritual dimension to their psychotherapy.* Although this book focuses on the collaboration between therapist and minister, it is also a story about how one woman was able to heal from her severe childhood abuse, through the inclusion of a spiritual dimension to her therapy. Including spiritual dimensions can enhance the healing process and profoundly alter the way one lives one's life.

We have chosen to refer to therapists using the female pronoun, "she," while ministers will be referred to as "he." Similarly, survivors of abuse will be referred to as "she." We are aware that many therapists are male, that clergy are often female, and that many survivors of severe childhood abuse are males. However, for convenience and consistency, we chose to use these pronouns to represent therapists, ministers, and survivors, as they match the genders of the authors and the subject of this book.

Undoubtedly, the process of psychotherapy for survivors of severe childhood abuse is a difficult and demanding one for both therapist and survivor alike. Robert Kluft, a psychiatrist who works with multiple personality and other dissociative disorders, has described the experience of the therapist as one of "bewilderment, exasperation, and a sense of being drained" (Kluft, 1984b, p. 51). Therapists in private practice are often isolated and alone as they struggle to help the survivor deal with memories of horrible abuse. Often the therapist has sole responsibility for the care of the survivor. Therapists and other mental health professionals might welcome collaboration—a shared responsibility, a true partnership—with a member of the clergy. This book will provide therapists with specific guidelines toward establishing such a collaboration.

Many therapists working with severely abused individuals have found traditional therapy limiting in its focus solely on the cognitive, emotional, and intrapsychic aspects of experience. Furthermore, survivors of severe abuse often pose spiritual and existential questions with which the therapist is ill prepared to deal. Moshe Torem, psychiatrist and past president of the International Society for the Study of Dissociation, has written that "listening to and being with survivors of trauma makes us confront some crucial questions about life and death and fundamental dilemmas about good and evil: Why are innocent, defenseless children abused and tortured? . . . Why did God allow this to happen? Why did God not rescue me when I prayed for help? Why does evil exist?" (Torem, 1993, p. 1).

Psychotherapists are generally educated as scientists in programs that emphasize interviewing techniques, listening skills, data collection, diagnosis, and treatment methods. Few have training in dealing with existential issues of life and death, good and evil. Torem points out that some therapists feel so threatened by these issues that they often avoid dealing with patients who raise such questions. "Our patients present us with fundamental issues, and if we are willing to face our helplessness, confusion and lack of knowledge, we risk exposing our imperfections, and, thus, our humanity. Science, which has become a God-like discipline for many clinicians, has not been a source of answers for such questions. The existential issues raised by our patients expose the weakness of the scientific method as a philosophy that will provide us with solutions to all problems. We have been taught by our professors that every problem can be solved by designing the ideal scientific study with data collection, double-blind testing, and statistical analysis. Not so, my friends. Science has its limits" (Torem, 1993, p. 1).

Survivors of severe abuse have also decried the limits of a scientific psychotherapy that excludes spiritual dimensions. A plea from a woman with multiple personalities illustrates this point:

> I wish therapists could feel more comfortable with discussions about religion and God. After all, many MPD victims are linked to ritual abuse. Yet therapists are often afraid to say the "G" word in therapy. I have a really skewed idea of God and need to come to terms with my religious beliefs in order to get well. I want my therapist to be with me in my struggle. (Grace, cited in Cohen, Giller, and Lynn W., 1991, p. 110)

Based on a survey of clinical psychologists, Shafranske and Malony (1990) concluded that 60 percent of clients often express themselves in religious language. Mental health professionals can no longer afford to ignore their clients' religious and spiritual lives. Yet while many therapists long to add a spiritual dimension to their work, they often lack the knowledge or training necessary to deal with such issues effectively in psychotherapy. A survey of over 400 clinical psychologists found that only 5 percent had religious or spiritual issues covered in their training programs (Shafranske and Malony, 1990). Collaboration with members of the clergy, as described in this book, can provide therapists with the guidance and training they lack.

Recently, several prominent mental health professionals have begun urging collaboration between therapists and clergy. Psychologist Andrew J. Weaver and psychiatrist Harold G. Koenig have noted the large body of research supporting the relationship between religious commitment and mental health (Koenig, 1995; Weaver, Koenig, and Ochberg, 1996). In the treatment of women who have been severely abused, inclusion of clergy in the therapeutic process is finally being recognized as valuable. Psychiatrist Elizabeth Bowman and pastoral counselor William E. Amos have concluded that by including clergy in the treatment of individuals with dissociative disorders, therapists can be assured that their patients' spiritual needs are met, that therapeutic neutrality is maintained, and that "therapeutic tasks are dealt with more rapidly and competently than either therapist or clergy could accomplish alone" (Bowman and Amos, 1993, p. 52). Psychologist Christopher Rosik (1992) also suggests ways for therapists and clergy to work together within a religious setting to help individuals with DID. It appears that collaboration between the mental health profession and members of the clergy is an idea whose time has come. This book will help therapists take steps to establish a working relationship with members of the clergy. In addition, the book examines some of the spiritual questions and issues that may surface in psychotherapy with survivors of severe abuse, and we have also provided guidelines to help the therapist when confronted with such existential issues as good and evil.

Ministers, too, will benefit from such collaborative efforts. Although they have the training and knowledge to deal with spiritual questions, clergy have often had little preparation for dealing with the special needs of members of their congregation who were severely abused as children or who suffer from mental illness. Yet, people in distress often turn first to clergy. A survey by the National Institutes of Mental Health reported that clergy are more likely than psychologists and psychiatrists to have a person with a psychiatric diagnosis seek their help (Hohmann and Larson, 1993).

Besides the serious emotional problems such individuals may have, survivors of abuse may have strong spiritual doubts and questions because of their abuse. They are likely to hold dysfunctional or distorted images of God based on their experiences with their earthly parents. Ministers need to be aware of the special spiritual and emotional needs of such individuals. Collaboration with the therapist offers clergy an opportunity to learn more about these special needs. In addition, rather than feeling that he is working at odds with the therapist, the minister can become actively involved in integrating spiritual and religious issues into the survivor's psychotherapy.

Survivors of severe childhood abuse face many obstacles in their healing journey. They may have to be patient with those who want to help. Therapists are just beginning to learn how to include a spiritual dimension in their work. Ministers may have had little training in dealing with survivors' problems. This book will not only provide both therapist and minister with guidance on how to work together in the interest of the survivor, but should also help *the survivors* bring a spiritual dimension into their healing. The chapters on support groups and on healing interventions will also help extend the therapy outside the therapist's office and into the survivor's everyday life.

Throughout the book, there are sections in which each of us chose to speak individually. Sometimes, one of us wanted to add personal reactions, experiences, or perspectives. Other times, we wanted to clarify a particular point. These passages are presented separately in extracted text. Though Teresa did not participate in the writing of this book, she did read the manuscript, and has chosen to comment on how various aspects of our work affected her personally. Most of those comments are presented by "Justin," one of her alters. Justin's comments have added both a richness and a unique perspective to the book.

As beginnings are important, the first chapter sets the stage, providing necessary basic information toward understanding our work with Teresa. After we briefly examine some basic terms and some clinical and spiritual premises upon which our work was based, we will review Teresa's background and how we each became involved in her healing journey.

BASIC TERMS

Severe Childhood Abuse

Although not a clinical term, the term "severe childhood abuse" is used in this book to describe severe and persistent physical, emotional, and sexual abuse of children. This type of abuse involves sadistic torture and infliction of extreme pain. Examples of severe abuse include being locked in dark closets for long periods, being forced into prostitution at a very young age, having insects and/or snakes placed on one's body while being tied up or left in a dark, enclosed space. Typically, more than one method of abuse is used by an abuser over a period of years.

Post-Traumatic Stress Disorder

This condition consists of a group of symptoms that develop because of exposure to an extremely stressful, traumatic event—an event that is out of the ordinary, expected experience of the average person. Such events would include witnessing a murder; being the victim of violent physical assault; being severely abused sexually, physically, or emotionally; or witnessing and/or participating in atrocities of war. People suffering from post-traumatic stress disorder report feelings of intense persistent fear and anxiety; persistent reexperiencing of the trauma; nightmares; avoidance of any stimuli associated with the trauma; a numbing of emotional responsiveness; and a heightened startle response. Symptoms usually appear within three months of the trauma, although delays of months or even years may occur before symptoms appear (American Psychiatric Association, 1994). Individuals who have been severely abused in childhood will often present themselves for treatment suffering from post-traumatic stress disorder.

Dissociation

Dissociation refers to changes in a person's consciousness or sense of identity. Dissociation is a common occurrence in life and, in itself, is not pathological. Most clinicians see the process of dissociation as existing on a continuum, ranging from everyday types of dissociation (daydreaming or total absorption in a film) to the formation of alternate identities. If you have ever experienced driving a car and suddenly realized that you have not been paying attention to your driving for the last five minutes, yet continued to drive the car successfully, then you have experienced a form of dissociation. People who have gone through a severe trauma will often report having dissociated during the event. For example, research on the effects of the San Francisco earthquake of 1989 has demonstrated that many people dissociated during the earthquake. Some felt detached from the experience. They described feeling as if they were in a dreamlike state or that they were watching a movie of the events. Some even reported out-of-body experiences. Clearly, dissociation serves a protective function, defending against the horror of traumatic events (Bliss, 1984; Kluft, 1984b; Putnam, 1989). Similarly, children who have been abused will often report having dissociated during the abuse. They relate that they "left" their bodies or that they were pretending to be somewhere else.

Dissociative Identity Disorder (DID)
(formerly, Multiple Personality Disorder [MPD])

Instead of using the more well-known term multiple personality disorder (MPD), we will refer to dissociative identity disorder

(DID)—a term not yet generally known outside the psychiatric community. As of 1994, with the publication of the *Diagnostic and Statistical Manual of Mental Disorders* (DSM-IV), the official name of MPD was changed to DID to reflect current clinical thinking about the disorder. In the interests of accuracy, we will use the term DID to describe what was popularly known as multiple personality disorder. DSM-IV describes the essential feature of DID as the presence of two or more distinct identities or personality states that recurrently take control of the individual's behavior. This condition is generally recognized to result from severe childhood sexual and/or physical abuse. Just as a child will tend to dissociate when faced with traumatic events, such as physical or sexual abuse by a parent, a child faced with horrible, torturous abuse will likely dissociate to a greater extent. For example, a parent might be holding a gun to the child's head, and the child might "go somewhere else" to avoid the experience. It is understandable how a young child might create another identity to handle the abuse—somewhat like creating an imaginary friend—an alternative identity who would experience the abuse and then return inside, leaving the primary identity with no memory of the horror that just occurred. Such a form of dissociation might allow the child to survive the incident and continue to function in the world without going mad or committing suicide. The DSM-IV (American Psychiatric Association, 1994) states that a dissociative identity disorder results from a failure to integrate the various aspects of one's identity, memory, and consciousness. Each alter or personality is experienced as having its own distinct history, self-image, and identity, including its own name. Usually, a primary identity carries the individual's given name and may be unaware of the existence of the alternate identities or alters. This primary identity is referred to as the *host*. The other alters usually have different names and characteristics that contrast with those of the host. Alters may differ from the host in age, gender, vocabulary, general knowledge, interests, and abilities. Alters, too, may deny awareness of the other identities, or they may be aware of the existence of the others but may be critical, hostile, or in conflict with them.

Keeping these definitions in mind, let us briefly examine some basic premises that informed our own collaboration, helping Teresa heal from the effects of her severe childhood abuse.

BASIC CLINICAL AND SPIRITUAL PREMISES

Although in the collaborative case described in this book, the psychologist and the ministers came from different religious backgrounds, certain common beliefs about both spirituality and dissociative disorders formed the basis of their work together.

Clinical Premises

1. *We view DID not as an illness, but a survival tool.* We maintain that dissociation is for many the healthiest adaptation that a child could have made to severe and horrible abuse. Richard Lowenstein, a psychiatrist known for his work with dissociative disorders, has stated that DID patients do not typically demonstrate a true process thought disorder. He points out that the personality organization of such patients is frequently a unique form, based more on dissociative and post-traumatic factors rather than on any borderline or psychotic structure (Lowenstein and Ross, 1992). Psychotherapist Valerie Heller has suggested the term "dissociative *reaction*" rather than "dissociative *disorder*" (Heller, 1999, personal communication). For the purposes of this book we have chosen more commonly used terms, though clearly Heller's term better reflects our understanding of dissociation.

At the base of DID is a worldview based on the abused child's experiences—a worldview that includes violence, sadistic torture, and hatred. The model of the world presented by the abusers is one of terror and unpredictability. The adoption of dissociative defenses was perhaps the healthiest and most functional alternative a young child could find. That is not to say that the behavior of a person with DID is not dysfunctional at times, but that this dysfunctional behavior was developed in response to a highly abusive environment. Part of our work with survivors of severe abuse is to show them that although their dissociation was functional during childhood when the abuse was taking place, it is no longer functional or necessary. For instance, using dissociation to deal with stress can lead to problems with memory. As an individual dissociates during situations fraught with extreme emotion, parts of the individual become disconnected and separated from the whole. Aspects of life are then handled only by a *part* or *fragment* of the individual's total personality, blocking off one's full capacity. Finally, we do not claim that all people with DID are *healthy*. Although some individuals possess psychotic and abusive alters, not *all* those with DID exhibit such pathology. In other words, the act of dissociating, even to the point of creating multiple identities is not in itself evidence of mental illness.

2. *As we do not consider DID an illness, we focus on healing from the effects of abuse, rather than on treatment or cure.* Healing in this context includes helping the abused individual develop a new worldview based on experiences with loving people. We make no claim that the establishment of good loving relationships is a sufficient condition for successful psychotherapy. Rather, it is a *necessary* condition for complete emotional and spiritual healing—the kind of healing most needed by survivors of severe childhood abuse. Any psychotherapy that focuses solely on the cognitive, emotional, and psychological components of growth, ignoring the spiritual and relational aspects, is incomplete at best, ultimately shortchanging the survivor in her quest for wholeness and healing.

3. *We believe that no matter how damaged a person may have been by her abuse, even if the abuse occurred in a religious setting or involved religious leaders, a core of spirituality can be tapped within the individual.* For many survivors this spiritual core can be found through the establishment of loving relationships and through a fearless examination with both the therapist and the minister of such difficult questions as "Why does God allow such terrible things to happen to children?" and "Is the universe friendly?"

Spiritual Premises

Through our own collaboration we slowly developed a set of spiritual principles that guided our work. Our attempt to articulate and further develop these principles in turn facilitated their implementation in our work with Teresa. We developed what we term The Benevolence Model—a set of principles that transcends any particular *religious* beliefs we held individually, but which were consistent with the *spiritual* beliefs we held in common. We will briefly describe the principles in this chapter, but Chapter 3 is devoted entirely to a more in-depth examination of each of the basic premises of the model. Before we describe the principles, we would like to make two important points. First, although we were able to find common spiritual ground out of which to work, that does not mean that *all* therapists and clergy must find the same or even any common spiritual model for their work. The challenge for the minister is *not* to try to convince the therapist of any particular religious or spiritual belief, but to put aside differences so that some common ground can be found. The therapist, in turn, must focus on understanding the survivor's spiritual and religious world to be helpful. For example, let us take the case of a Jewish therapist working with a Catholic survivor. If Jesus is important to the survivor, the therapist's task is to try to understand how Jesus is important in the survivor's life—what Jesus means to this person. An attempt by a Jewish therapist to understand Jesus' meaning in the life of another says nothing about that therapist's faithfulness to her own religion, but speaks to her willingness to be of service to another. The therapist need not engage in a theological discourse, but in an exploration of the foundation of this person's spiritual and religious beliefs and how those beliefs influence her life.

Our second point deals with any possible limitations of The Benevolence Model. Though we believe (based on our experience and the opinions of others who reviewed our work) that the premises transcend any particular religion, we are basically familiar only with Judaism and Christianity. If any of the basic premises are inconsistent with the religious beliefs of anyone reading this book, we do not mean to offend. Similarly, when we relate the premises to Judaic and Christian writings and traditions, we do so because these are precisely the traditions with which we are most familiar.

The Benevolence Model

1. *God is love.* This is not meant as a trite statement. We must strive to go beyond a purely intellectual understanding of that statement to an *experience* of that love that is God. Through meditation, prayer, through our experiences with human love, even through mystical experiences, we come to *know* on a deep level what it means to say that "God is love." Since God is love, God is not to be viewed as a punitive parent to be feared, nor as a cruel master mercilessly seeking revenge on those who disobey the commandments—images of the divine that many of us unfortunately still hold. Many of us get fidgety and uncomfortable at the mention of God as

love. For the Jewish therapist or member of the clergy, especially, this principle might seem too "Christian," evoking images of the Church and Jesus. However, this first principle is actually consistent with most religions, Judaism and Christianity included. In terms of our model, it is in essence a *spiritual* rather than a *religious* principle. If this first principle still makes you uncomfortable, bear with us a bit. We will explain the concept that "God is love" more fully in Chapter 3.

2. *God loves us.* We are loved by God no matter what we do or say, and we can derive our sense of self-worth from God's acceptance of us. Since the nature of divine love is beyond human comprehension, people have created a number of human images to convey a sense of the depth and enormity of God's love for us. God has been conceptualized as a Father, a Mother, a lover, and a Creator. Yet God's love cannot be "captured" by any one image. These images are merely metaphors that help us get beyond an intellectual understanding of divine love.

3. *God's love is unconditional.* If God is love, then it follows that this love is unconditional. It is difficult for many of us to believe that God loves us unconditionally, because we tend to hold God to *human* standards. Since most of us have difficulty loving people who have hurt us or "sinned" against us, we cannot truly understand a divine love that surpasses our human shortcomings.

4. *God's forgiveness is always available to us.* Although God's forgiveness is always available, we often turn away from it, believing that we are unworthy of that forgiveness. Yet, if God's love is truly unconditional, then it follows that divine forgiveness is always available to us. This point is an important component in the healing of women who have been severely abused, because often they blame themselves for their abuse.

5. *We are called to love God, ourselves, and others.* We are called in this life to love God, but we must also love others. As we reach out in love to our friends and family, we must also reach out to those in need, those who are different from us, even to those with whom we disagree. In addition, we must also love ourselves, treating ourselves with the same love and respect we extend to others. As we come to truly believe in God's unconditional love and forgiveness of *every* human being, we begin to become more forgiving and loving of

ourselves. And, as we become more loving and forgiving of ourselves, we extend that love to others.

6. *We were created to be in relationship with one another.* We each
have something to give, and it is through relationship with others that
we can see our value and what we have to give. Furthermore, it is
through relationship with one another that God's love enters the
world.

7. *Love transforms and heals.* Love, which reaches us through
relationship, is the force that ultimately leads to healing of past
wounds and transforms the pain into compassion and wisdom. The
therapist comes armed with knowledge, theories, and practical techniques aimed at helping the survivor overcome her abusive past.
The minister similarly is armed with spiritual wisdom and biblical
knowledge. Both are important healing forces. Yet, the true healing
factor is the love they bring into the life of the survivor.

These spiritual premises constitute a model of loving which is radically different from the one in which most survivors of severe abuse
have been raised. In Chapter 3 we will explore the premises in depth.
In Chapters 4 and 5, we examine in detail how we were able to use
The Benevolence Model in our collaboration to enhance the psychotherapeutic process and promote emotional and spiritual healing.

TERESA'S STORY

Since our own collaboration was intended to foster the healing of
one individual, Teresa, we will present some background information
about her life and how she came to enter therapy with Marion. Details
of her life have been altered to protect her anonymity, but the essential
elements of her abuse are presented as they were reported.

Teresa is a thirty-five-year-old divorced woman who works as a
nurse in a local community hospital. She is a recovering alcoholic
and cocaine addict, heavily involved in a twelve-step program. She
had no children with her ex-husband, and is currently living alone.
She entered therapy five years ago because she had bulimia, having
binged and purged daily for many years. She chose Marion as her
therapist because she had read her book on compulsive eating and
had decided that Marion's nondiet approach appealed to her. For

one year, they worked solely on the eating problem, touching only briefly on other problems in Teresa's life.

Then, slowly, as she came to trust Marion more, Teresa began to reveal a history of repeated violent and sadistic acts of abuse during her childhood. From her earliest memories she had been brutally abused and terrorized, physically, emotionally, and sexually, first by her mother, and later by an uncle and his son. For six months a story of severe abuse unfolded, as Teresa increasingly recounted more sadistic and violent memories of her childhood. Teresa described being given enemas by her mother and then locked in closets with instructions "to hold the enema in." Failure to hold in the enema would result in extreme punishment. Other times, Teresa would be locked overnight in a dark closet infested with insects. The uncle had repeatedly tied up Teresa in his basement, sticking objects into her vagina.

> **Marion:** One day, while discussing a particularly horrifying incident of torture, Teresa suddenly became silent, her eyes vacant, her face emotionless. When she began to speak again, the voice was not Teresa's, but sounded flat and mechanical. She appeared to be unaware of my presence, and stated repeatedly, "I am the voice that lives inside the life form." I kept talking to her, assuring her that she was safe and that no harm would come to her. After some time, Teresa became quiet again. Then, after a few seconds, the Teresa I knew "returned." She seemed disoriented and confused. Looking at the clock, she seemed surprised as she said, "It was just three o'clock. Now the clock says 3:15. How did that happen?" It was at that point that my suspicions were confirmed. Teresa had DID.

That day in Marion's office, the "others inside," Teresa's alters, had sent out "Robot" to meet her—a test to see how Marion would handle the situation. (Refer to Appendix A for a list of Teresa's alters.) Robot was the alter who acted as a central station, an emotionless machine who could continue functioning—and in turn keep the system functioning—even in the face of the horrible acts of torture and abuse with which they were faced daily. Based on Marion's reaction to Robot, the "others inside" had decided that she could be trusted, and that they could reveal themselves to her. Over the next few months, one by one, other alter identities emerged, each with different memories of abuse.

Terry was competent, intelligent, funny, and well educated. She was the alter who went to work each day, functioning as an adult in the outside world.

Monica, aged nineteen, was an alter whom Marion had been told by the others "had a mouth like a truck driver." She had been prostituted by the mother at a young age. Extremely intelligent, secretly spiritually oriented and well read, she hid her "soft side" from everyone (inside and out) behind a rough exterior. Monica was not getting along with the others inside. She was the alter who held the anger, rage, and resentment about the abuse. She was also the one who was acting out—going to bars and picking up men, often prostituting herself.

Brian was a shy, sensitive, but self-effacing eighteen-year-old boy with interests in music. He was very protective and loving toward the "children inside." Both Brian and Monica had been the victims of the mother's favorite game—a form of Russian Roulette in which she would hold a loaded gun to their heads, telling them that there was one bullet inside. After taunting them for some time, she would pull the trigger.

The "children inside" included Sarah and Sandy who were five and six, respectively. The mother had sexually abused and tortured them, putting sharp objects, crayons, and ice into their vaginas. They would hold onto stuffed animals when they "came out," cautious of Marion, but so in need of nurturing and love that they looked forward to spending time with her.

Then, after many months, Mimic emerged. Like Robot, Mimic believed himself to be a computer, but his function in the system was entirely different. He had apparently been created in response to the mother's attempts to "program" Teresa with commands. The "Mother"—as Teresa's mother was called by all the alters—had convinced Teresa that she was subhuman and would often chain her to the wall using a dog choke collar, forcing her to eat large quantities of dog food. She would also force Teresa to kneel in submission and kiss her feet. Teresa had been taught that she was a member of a lower class and that she was not worthy of associating with members of a higher class. During these "training sessions," the Mother had used a variety of hypnotic and brainwashing techniques, as well as drugs, as she attempted to convince Teresa of her subhuman status and the need to obey the Mother's commands. We do not know if the Mother intentionally created an alter, or if this alter was created by Teresa to experience the abuse of the "training sessions," but apparently, an alter named "Mimic" had been created—an alter whose sole purpose was to carry out the Mother's commands. Mimic would relentlessly punish the others as he carried out his "programming." (He was called "Mimic" because he could successfully imitate or mimic any alter in the system.) Some basic beliefs with which Mimic was programmed included:

1. Mimic is an inferior life form.
2. The inferior life form is not permitted to look into the face of its "Superiors."
3. If the inferior life form makes a mistake, it must kneel, confess the mistake, and request punishment.
4. The inferior life form is not permitted to have feelings, wants, or needs.
5. The inferior life form will trust only the Mother.
6. The inferior life form exists at the Mother's discretion.

During the two years of therapy with Marion, Teresa had continued to be abused by the Mother physically, sexually, and emotionally (without Marion's knowledge). When the Mother realized that Teresa was involved in a successful psychotherapy, she tried to sabotage the therapy by programming Mimic (again using hypnotic and brainwashing techniques) with specific instructions about how to relate to Marion. These commands apparently were aimed at establishing a connection between the abusing mother and the therapist. These commands included:

1. You must kneel to Dr. Bilich.
2. Dr. Bilich has the power to punish you.
3. You exist at the Mother's discretion. You exist at Dr. Bilich's discretion.
4. Punishment will result every time you interact with Dr. Bilich.

Although Teresa's personality system contained over twenty alters, Mimic's story is especially important, because it is Mimic who ultimately became the most important alter involved in the spiritual and emotional healing of Teresa. At first, he could barely speak or look at Marion. He alternated between fearing Marion's imagined power and fighting her. His first words to her, in a machinelike, unemotional voice, were "You have met the enemy." Whenever any of the alters interacted with Marion in a session, he would later punish them—making them eat dog food or hurt themselves. Mimic expressed no human personality traits. He truly believed himself to be merely an emotionless machine, a computer with specific programming to be carried out.

OUR COLLABORATION BEGINS

Not long after the alters revealed themselves in therapy, Terry asked Marion to speak with the senior pastor of Teresa's church. The alters wanted the pastor, Michael Hardin, to be a part of their healing. A meeting with Reverend Hardin was arranged in which Marion informed him about Teresa's multiplicity. In that first meeting, Marion explained some basics about what was then known as multiple personality disorder (the etiology, symptoms, and treatments). She reviewed some of the specifics of Teresa's background of abuse.

A second meeting was set up in which Michael could meet several of Teresa's alters. Michael seemed excited about his possible involvement in Teresa's therapy, and, eager to learn everything he could about DID, he asked for reading material.

A week later, Michael had already met many of the alters. He continued to meet weekly with Marion for several months. During those sessions, Marion "supervised" his work with Teresa in terms of how each encounter affected the therapy. Michael in turn began teaching Marion more about Christianity and what it meant to Teresa. Michael began to include Teresa more and more in the life of the congregation, urging her to participate in church activities. At that point, Steven, who was an associate pastor at the church, was only peripherally involved. He had been informed of Teresa's multiplicity and was kept current on Michael's activities with her, but he had little involvement with Teresa directly. Michael suggested forming a support group consisting of members of his congregation. Marion and Teresa discussed this possibility in their sessions, reviewing the possible benefits and difficulties in revealing her multiplicity to people in her church. In the end, Teresa decided that such a support group would be a good idea. In putting together the members of the support group, Michael chose people he believed had the maturity and motivation to be part of a solid support network for her. He wanted them to be "authentic role models and friends of each of the personalities" (Hardin, 1991, p. 11). A meeting was set up so that the members of the support group could meet with Teresa, Michael, and Marion to discuss their involvement in Teresa's healing. During that meeting, several of Teresa's alters "came out" to meet the group members. Marion and Michael answered the many questions that arose about Teresa's background and history of abuse and about multiple personality disorder in general. Susan was a member of this support group, and her background in social work with a psychiatric population was invaluable. Marion and Michael also made themselves available to group members in the months that followed, answering any questions that arose. Marion maintained contact with several members regularly for some time. Briefly, this group (which will be described in greater detail in Chapter 7) served not only as a support system when Teresa was in crisis, but some members became real friends to Teresa. The support group provided a significant resocialization experience for her. Severe childhood abuse had seriously impaired Teresa's abilities to interact with people socially. Trips to the zoo, the ballpark, and the movies with members of the group were helpful in teaching her about what people do together in the "normal" course of life.

Steven had *some* involvement as a member of the support group, but his real participation in the collaboration began when Michael went on vacation for an entire month, and he had to take over full responsibility for the church. Marion and Steven began meeting regularly to coordinate their efforts. Marion not only taught Steven about DID, but also gave him practical information about how to deal with abreactions, flashbacks, and persecutor personalities. ("Persecutor personalities" are alters within the personality system who believe it is their function to hurt and punish the other alters. They are sometimes responsible for episodes of self-mutilation or suicide attempts. Mimic would be considered a persecutor personality.)

Steven discussed spiritual issues with Marion, both to teach her and to inform her of what he was working on with Teresa. It was around these spiritual issues that a true collaboration developed. Marion was working on challenging the belief system instilled by the Mother—a belief system based on hate and lack of worth, based on terror in an unpredictable world. However, a purely cognitive approach can be limited when applied to severely abused people such as Teresa, in that such an approach leaves the client without a model or worldview to replace the rather comprehensive but disturbed one learned from the abuser. Through the collaboration of pastor and therapist, a new model based on love was presented to Teresa and her alters both in therapy and in the outside world. Both through words and actions, we presented Teresa with a radically different worldview on which to build a new belief system about herself and her place in the world. The model that guided our work and which we presented to Teresa is described in Chapter 3, titled "The Benevolence Model." In Chapters 4 and 5 we explain how we implemented this model in our work with Teresa.

As Marion continued working with Teresa in therapy, Steven began meeting regularly with Mimic. Mimic was the alter the others in the system felt was most in need of help. For months, discussions took place almost daily between Steven and Mimic about God and Jesus. Sometimes, Steven would just "hang out" with Mimic. He taught Mimic how to use a *real* computer, emphasizing the differences between Mimic and the computer and pointing out that Mimic was not really a computer. As they would work together on the computer, Steven would point out that Mimic was *more* than his programming. Marion, in turn, worked with Mimic in therapy on why he had needed to see himself as a computer. Mimic eventually discovered that he had chosen to "be" a computer so that he would not have to feel the pain of the abuse and the pain associated with hurting the others inside. Marion was also working with Mimic on changing the programming he had received from the Mother—from that of a persecutor personality to that of a protector of the others in the system. As Mimic began to see himself as more than a computer, Steven talked to him about God's love for him. He told him that we are *all* lovable in God's eyes. God's love in not conditioned on whether we are good or bad. God loves us, just because God *is* love.

Therefore, Mimic is loved by God. A most important point was that Mimic was indeed human and entitled to the same good things as every other human being. Steven emphasized that all people have value, therefore Mimic has worth and value. He would talk to Mimic of how Jesus reached out to the outcasts of society, those alienated from both society and themselves, and brought them back in relationship with others. Steven pointed to the many references, especially in the Gospel of Luke, to Jesus spending time with the lepers, the sick, and the lame (all outcasts of their societies), offering forgiveness and healing. This had particular meaning to Mimic, since he, too, saw himself as an outcast.

Steven also explained that since God made all people to be in relationship, it was through relationship with others that Mimic would discover his worth. Both Steven and Marion would often point to specific instances in which Mimic and the others inside had been helpful, loving, and caring to members of the congregation and to the people in the community through Teresa's work with her patients at the hospital. Steven would reinforce the notion that Mimic had worth because he had something to give others.

Susan, in her interactions with Mimic in the support group, helped Mimic develop a sense of "normalcy." By doing normal everyday activities with Mimic, she reinforced his humanity, his sense that he was like "everyone else."

The Mother (as Teresa called her mother) had created a closed relationship between herself and Teresa, limiting Teresa's interactions with others for fear she would learn that the Mother had lied to her. Steven worked to replace this view of relationships with an image of the Church as a human body, needing many people to function. It is through the interactions of *each* individual in a more "open system" that growth of that body could occur.

As Mimic came to see his humanity, he began to feel guilty for all the harm he had inflicted on the others inside. Steven taught Mimic that God forgives us unconditionally. In fact, God has given us the freedom to make mistakes, and it is through an examination of our mistakes that we grow. Freed to some extent from crippling guilt, Mimic was then able to examine his "mistakes" in his therapy with Marion and to glean from them important lessons about whom he wanted to be and how he wanted to behave in the future.

Besides discussing these spiritual issues, Steven gave Mimic a copy of *The Ragamuffin Gospel,* a book that Mimic found especially helpful. Two quotes had specific meaning to Mimic:

> To live by grace means to acknowledge my whole life story, light side and the dark. (Manning, 1990, p. 22)

> Grace strikes us when we are in great pain and restlessness. It strikes us when we walk through the valley of a meaningless and empty life. (Manning, 1990, p. 25)

These concepts contrast sharply with the commands the Mother had instilled in Mimic and the others about punishment for the smallest infractions. Extending this new model of a loving God to Mimic replaced the old worldview instilled by the Mother. Perhaps more important, it brought hope to Mimic and the others—hope that things could change, that there was love and forgiveness in the world. Hope is an essential component of the healing process. In addition, the new model of a loving God slowly became the basis for a new personality structure in the system.

Despite the obvious value of these discussions and readings for Mimic and Teresa and the other alters, words alone could not have counteracted the effects of the horrible abuse. Herein lies an advantage of the collaborative process. The Benevolence Model was *demonstrated* through the actions of Steven, Michael, Marion, Susan, and the members of the congregation involved in the support group—expanding the "therapy" to the world outside the therapist's office. We modeled the love we were trying to teach.

Simple acts such as Steve taking out Teresa's garbage were transformed into meaningful acts of love for Teresa who had been taught by the Mother that she was not even worthy of taking out other people's garbage. Brennan Manning has written that "to evangelize a person is to say to him or her: you, too are loved by God . . . And not only to say it, but really think it and relate it to the man or woman so they can sense it . . . *But that becomes possible only by offering the person your friendship,* a friendship that is real, unselfish, without condescension, full of confidence and profound esteem" (Manning, 1990, p. 22).

This passage had particular meaning to Mimic, since it was through his friendship with Steven that some of his greatest growth occurred. This relationship had an effect on many of Teresa's alters, but for Mimic especially, this friendship, freely offered, provided the foundation upon which he was able to transform his self-identity from that of a computer to a human being.

The relationship that developed between Steven and Mimic was healing not only because Steve was able to minister to the needs of a parishioner, but because it evolved into a give-and-take friendship, in which mutual sharing of feelings occurred. Slowly, over time, Steven was able to share with Mimic some of his experiences in life and his own emotional pain, thus giving Mimic the opportunity to "care" for *him* at times. This occasional "role reversal" gave Mimic a tremendous sense of his own worth, in that he realized he had something to offer to someone he deeply loved.

The issue of how much mutuality is beneficial in a helping relationship has long been problematic. Maurice Friedman has explained that "in the healing partnership one person feels a need or lack that leads him or her to come to the other for help and that the other is a therapist or counselor who is ready to enter a relationship in order to help" (Friedman, 1992, p. 189). In this case, both minister and therapist entered a relationship with an individual in pain. The question becomes: "In what way can each be most helpful to that individual in promoting healing?" The role of the therapist is strictly delineated, so that a minimum of self-disclosure takes place, especially in more traditional, psychodynamically based psychotherapies. Although the degree of mutuality in the therapeutic relationship differs depending on the individual therapist's orientation, basically, the relationship between the therapist and the client is asymmetrical. Marion was more self-disclosing than a traditional psychotherapist might have been, yet was ever mindful of the fact that she could be most helpful to Mimic by establishing a relationship with firm boundaries. In that way, Mimic could be cared for without having to consider the needs of the caretaker. Although, as a minister, Steven's role was also to help Mimic and the others heal from the abuse, he was less constrained by his role. As a minister, he had greater freedom to relate to Mimic with more fluid boundaries, providing Mimic with the opportunity to practice what it meant to be a friend, to be fully in relationship. If the aim was for Mimic to learn to be in relationship, in community, the relationships offered by *both* Marion and Steven were necessary. Herein lies one advantage of a collaboration between clergy and therapist. Mimic first needed to experience being cared for in a healthy way. The Mother had equated caring with torture and pain, having told Mimic "a mother's love is pure. No one will love you like I do." Marion, in the position of the therapist, was able to counteract Mimic's experience with the Mother, providing a strong, secure base. However, to truly grow, Mimic needed to be involved in a relationship in which there would be mutual sharing of life's experiences and life's pain. This relationship was offered by Steven (and to some degree by Susan and the other members of the support group).

Marion did, however, break with the traditional psychotherapeutic practice of not seeing a client outside the office. Together with members of the support group, she attended a birthday party given by Michael in Teresa's honor. She also spent a day in Manhattan with Teresa and Steven. They traveled together on the Long Island Railroad (LIRR) into the city and spent the day visiting places and doing things that Teresa had never done before—things that a "normal" child would have experienced during a childhood on Long Island. Mimic was "out" for most of that day. They went to FAO Schwarz, a famous toy store on Fifth Avenue. (FAO Schwarz was the site of the scene in the movie *Big* where Tom Hanks' character played a giant keyboard with his feet.) They took a carriage ride through Central Park, and ate at an expensive ice cream parlor on Central Park West. Though Mimic felt unworthy of their attention and of being taken around the city, Marion and Steven kept reinforcing Mimic's right to enjoy life like anyone else. With much encouragement from Steven and Marion, Mimic was even able to walk through the lobby of the Plaza Hotel—quite a feat for someone who felt unworthy of even *being* in the presence of "people of a higher class."

Marion: Though some will criticize me for breaking the normal therapist/client boundaries by participating in a "field trip" with Teresa, this trip, and several other out-of-the-ordinary experiences, were pivotal in helping Teresa and the other alters

reclaim their humanity. It was as though years of therapy were
accomplished during this one trip. Initially, Mimic, in particular, had felt unworthy of my attention and time, but eventually
he came to understand that it was out of love for him that I
accompanied him and Steven to the city. Issues of worthiness
with which Mimic had been struggling for months were suddenly being dealt with on a deeper level. We had made a crack
in Mimic's belief system—a crack I believe would have taken
months or years to make had we not taken that trip together.

Not long after the trip, Mimic finally realized that he was human
after all. A most significant and moving ceremony took place at that
point in which Mimic took on a human name. The name "Justin"
had been suggested by Michael, who had explained to Mimic that the
Latin root for the name was "justice." Members of Teresa's support
group who attended were given an opportunity to talk about what
contact with Mimic had meant to each of them. We give a detailed
description of that ceremony in Chapter 8, "Healing Interventions."
    Clearly, the benefits of a collaboration between therapist and clergy
are many. Briefly:

1. *Collaboration adds a spiritual and religious dimension to the
   treatment process.* The presentation of The Benevolence Model provided Teresa with a psychological alternative to the
   worldview instilled in her by her mother. To the religiously
   committed individual, the inclusion of material from the Bible,
   through the use of metaphors, guided meditation, and story,
   added a new dimension to the treatment process.
2. *Collaboration allows both therapist and minister to model the
   love and caring inherent in their spiritual model.* Not only was
   spirituality discussed both inside and outside the therapist's office, but love and caring were being *demonstrated* and *modeled* through interactions with Teresa in her everyday world.
3. *Collaboration helps bring the survivor back into the community through the involvement of members of the church or synagogue in the healing process.* The establishment of a support
   group made up of members of the congregation can help counteract the social isolation experienced by so many who have

been severely abused. This involvement by others promotes healing on both psychological and spiritual levels.

4. *Collaboration broadens the support network for the survivor.* The inclusion of clergy in the therapy and the establishment of support groups provide a network of people who are available to support the survivor in times of crisis, lessening dependence on the therapist as the sole source of support. In addition, the social contact with the people in the community who also become involved in the survivor's healing provides opportunities for resocialization, opportunities to learn about normal human interactions in the social world outside the therapist's office. Through the mutual friendships that develop through such contact, the worth of the survivor is affirmed. These support people can also take part in ceremonies and rituals that affirm the survivor's humanity, worth, and importance in their lives.

5. *Collaboration broadens the scope of the therapy, creating a multidimensional approach.* For those who have been severely abused, traditional psychotherapy in the therapist's office once or twice weekly does not offer an experience comprehensive enough to effect healing at all levels—psychological, emotional, social, and spiritual. By adding the resources of the community to the therapeutic process, a more broad-based multidisciplinary and multisystemic approach can be taken.

6. *Collaboration counteracts some of the problems resulting from the present U.S. managed health care system.* Currently in this country, people with severe emotional or psychiatric problems are not receiving the level of care they need. From a practical standpoint, people either have no insurance coverage for mental health, or they have coverage that severely limits their number of sessions. It is not unusual for someone to receive only twenty sessions of therapy a year. For a survivor of severe childhood abuse, an individual suffering from a dissociative disorder, or for any person with a severe psychiatric illness, twenty sessions a year falls far short of their needs.

Imagine for a moment what it is like to tell a young woman whose life (and perhaps whose very identity) has been shattered by severe and persistent childhood abuse that she has used her twenty sessions for the year, and that she is now on her own. Any caring person would shudder at the thought of denying her the benefit of therapy. Short of seeing people who need long-term care for little or no money (which some therapists have been doing), the mental health profession increasingly has to rely on resources in the community to provide their patients with the level of care needed for healing. As we will demonstrate, collaboration between therapists and clergy allows such therapeutic contacts outside the therapist's office and beyond the constraints of managed mental health care, supplementing the limited number of sessions currently being authorized.

In sum, we believe that a collaboration between therapist and clergy offers the survivor a deeper, richer experience than any traditional psychotherapy could offer. As we will see in the next chapter, children who have suffered from severe abuse differ from other people in significant ways. Therefore they require a more comprehensive approach to "treatment." In this day of managed care and mandated short-term psychotherapy, when survivors of severe abuse are often allotted only a few sessions of therapy a year, collaboration between therapist and clergy can offer the survivor her only chance at deep emotional and spiritual healing.

Chapter 2 focuses on healing and therapy and on therapeutic issues specific to those who have been severely abused in childhood. In the chapters that follow we present more details about our own collaboration—what we did, obstacles and problems we encountered, mistakes we made, the effects the collaborative work had on each of us emotionally and spiritually. We also provide guidelines for others who would like to begin such work themselves. Remember that it is not necessary to agree with everything we present. We are presenting only guidelines. The essential ingredient that underlies our successful collaboration, or *any* successful collaboration for that matter, is the willingness to be open to new ideas, diverse viewpoints, and different value systems. Provided we each remember that we, as helping professionals, are vehicles through which God's love comes into the life of the survivor, we can overcome any obstacle and work together in the service of those in need.

Chapter 2

Healing the Effects
of Severe Childhood Abuse

*The Spiritual Quadrant is the one that opens you up and that
leads to healing, physically and emotionally.*

Elisabeth Kübler-Ross, MD

*"It is the relationship that heals" is the single most important
lesson that the psychotherapist must learn.*

Irving Yalom

*Our beliefs sit there like a pair of sunglasses through which we
see the world. We're so used to seeing through those sunglasses that we don't know we're wearing them.*

Joan Borysenko, PhD

Every mental health professional operates within a model of human behavior and with a set of rules about how to change behavior
that follows from that model. The basic beliefs that underlie a
therapist's model may be conscious and well articulated or largely
unconscious and unstated. In any case, the model—the set of principles that together form a comprehensive belief system—shapes
every aspect of that individual's thoughts and actions in therapy—
how she perceives the client's problems, how he behaves toward the
client, the goals of therapy (and who sets them), even the kinds of
boundaries or limits that are set on the therapy relationship.

For example, let us contrast two different models of psychotherapy—the psychoanalytic model and the humanistic model. Relationship is central to both models, as change and growth are viewed as

resulting from the relationship between client and therapist, but each model differs greatly in its statements about *how* the therapy relationship produces change. Psychoanalytic therapy focuses on *analyzing* the therapy relationship. The psychoanalytic therapist offers interpretations to foster self-exploration and insight into early emotional wounds, and suggests that the client's thoughts and feelings about the therapist result from a transference of feelings toward significant others from early life onto the therapist. Since the psychoanalytic therapist takes a neutral stance in the therapeutic encounters—neither too warm and loving nor cold and withdrawn—the client's feelings about the therapist are believed to be largely projections to be examined and explored. Change and growth come from this analysis of the transference. The humanistic therapist, on the other hand, sees the relationship itself as healing; hence the therapy relationship is not the focus of exploration. Change in the client is believed to occur because that client is in relationship, perhaps for the *first time*, with someone who is willing to listen to her empathetically and relate to her authentically. Therefore, the relationship is not viewed as a vehicle through which transference can be analyzed, nor does the therapist remain neutral and detached. Rather, the therapist is supposed to be "engaged" and "authentic" in the therapy session without imposing her own values or thoughts on the client.

Both the humanistic and the psychoanalytic models stress the importance of relationship, but each is based on a different set of belief about how the therapy relationship brings about change and growth in the client. As a result of the differences in these basic beliefs systems, the very behavior of the psychoanalytic and the humanistic therapist during a session will differ markedly.

Since one's therapy model is so important in determining what happens in therapy, and since, as Joan Borysenko (1994) has pointed out, our beliefs are like sunglasses through which we see the world, we want to be clear about some of *our* basic beliefs—the beliefs about therapy and healing from the effects of severe abuse that informed our work. Keep in mind as you review our basic premises that you need not agree with our views on healing, on therapeutic boundaries, or on the limits of therapeutic neutrality in order to utilize the collaboration model we present in later chapters. We present our basic assumptions at this time because we believe it is important to clarify one's own position at the outset. Hopefully, our presentation will spark some thinking on the part of the reader, as it would be helpful for therapists and members of the clergy reading this book to examine their own basic beliefs about both spirituality and psychotherapy before undertaking their own collaboration.

> **Marion:** As you read over our basic assumptions, remember that this book is not intended as a comprehensive manual for the treatment of people suffering from multiple personalities, nor does it aim to describe a new type of treatment for survivors of severe abuse; it is a book about how therapists and clergy can collaborate in helping such people heal. Nor have we included all aspects of Teresa's psychotherapy in this chapter. Therefore, our presentation of the basic beliefs will be brief and limited to those principles we feel are important to an understanding of our work. Since a successful psychotherapy includes many factors that we will not discuss here, an annotated bibliography at the back of the book (see Appendix B) will provide the clinician with resources for learning about treatment of severe abuse and dissociation.

BASIC ASSUMPTIONS ABOUT THERAPY

Our Emphasis Is on Healing Rather Than on Cure

As we stated Chapter 1, people who have suffered from severe abuse in childhood are not necessarily mentally ill, but they carry deep wounds with them into adulthood. Therapy for such individuals requires something more involved than what is often referred to as *symptom-relief* by behaviorally oriented therapists or *cure* by psychodynamically oriented therapists. It requires what we have termed "healing." Healing is a natural process that unfolds when the right ingredients are made available to an individual. In medicine, many doctors will admit that they can never really *cure* a patient. They can only provide the patient's body with the tools it requires to heal itself—medicine, surgery, bed rest. Given the right environment and the right tools, the body can often effect a cure. Consider another example—that of the seed. A seed contains the potential, the know-how, to grow into a plant, but it cannot grow unless it is supplied with the right environment and tools, i.e., water, light, soil, and food. The human being, like the seed, has the innate capacity to grow, and, like the doctor's patient, each human being has the innate capacity to heal. All that is needed are the right tools and the right environment. When working with a survivor of severe abuse, a human being suffering from severe psychic wounds, the therapist and the minister have the opportunity to provide the survivor with the tools and the environment she needs for her own healing.

> **Marion:** I realize that our position on healing and therapy is likely to spur some controversy, particularly among therapists who follow more traditional models of psychotherapy, but keep in mind that we are by no means implying here that it is necessary to throw out the *science* of therapy. Good training as a psychotherapist arms the mental health professional with the tools needed to help the person heal. While working with Teresa, I used my skills as a therapist in many ways, among them to challenge her cognitive belief system, to deal with flashbacks and abreactions, and to help her find new ways to deal with life's stresses and pains other than by dissociating. Yet, to facilitate the deep healing from the severe abuse of her childhood that Teresa sought, I had to offer her more than a set of skillful psychotherapeutic interventions.

Healing Is a Process

Cure often implies a one-time or at least a short-term intervention that is applied to the patient to rid her of her symptoms. Healing usually implies a gradual change over time. Fundamental change at the most basic level of one's belief system—the kind of change of which the survivor of severe abuse is most in need—cannot be accomplished quickly. It is a gradual process in which the survivor slowly gives up the childhood core beliefs she has held about herself and her place in the world, and replaces them with new core beliefs based on her therapeutic experiences and relationships as an adult.

We Stress the Importance of Relationship
in the Healing Process

One of the most important things the therapist and the minister can bring to the survivor's healing journey is that of *relationship*. Relationship is like the container and the soil in which the seed is planted so that it may grow into a healthy plant.

Some psychoanalytic therapists will argue with our idea that the relationship itself is healing, accusing us of ignoring the importance of the transference. Yet even the object relations analyst, Fairbairn, pointed out that "you can go on analyzing forever and get nowhere. It's the personal relations that is therapeutic." Furthermore, he held that psychoanalytic interpretation is not therapeutic *per se,* but only as it expresses a personal relationship of genuine understanding (Guntrip, 1975, p. 155). Similarly, Harry Guntrip believed that psychotherapy is a "process of interaction . . . the personalities of two people working together toward free spontaneous growth" (Guntrip, 1975, p. 155).

This understanding of relationship in therapy has relevance to our work with survivors. Psychologist Philip Kinsler has stated that "it was in relationships that abuse has harmed our clients, and I believe it is in the restorative relationships that they recover." Furthermore, he adds, "a good therapy relationship for the severe abuse survivor creates an environment that *through its very nature and quality* counteracts these lessons, and teaches other, more helpful ones" (Kinsler, 1992, p. 166). Though we do not agree with everything Kinsler stated in his controversial paper, we are in agreement about the centrality of the relationship and the "special" needs of the person who has been severely abused in childhood. By "special" we do not mean the therapist's overinvolvement in the client's life nor a radical restructuring of therapeutic boundaries, but rather a more engaged, active stance than might be found in traditional therapies for less severe problems. Although the therapist may work cognitively on challenging the belief system instilled in the survivor as a result of the childhood abuse, this approach alone is not sufficient to counteract such a far-reaching, comprehensive system of beliefs. It is through the relationship with the therapist and the minister (and any other people involved in the healing) that the lessons learned from the abuse can be counteracted and new lessons learned. We therefore see a need for a comprehensive, multidimensional approach that addresses the spiritual as well as the emotional, cognitive, and behavioral levels of the client's life. Collaboration between therapist and clergy can offer such a comprehensive approach.

We offer a word of caution. While the therapist or the minister may offer a healthy, healing relationship to survivors, there is no guarantee that this relationship will be used constructively in the service of their healing. Some people are not ready to receive it, no matter how hard others try to bring love and healing energy into their lives. We must offer the relationship in the hope that it will be of use, but we must also be prepared for failure. Each survivor has her own timetable.

We Stress the Importance of Love in the Healing Relationship

Psychiatrist M. Scott Peck (1978), has taken a rather unorthodox and controversial stand on the nature of the therapy relationship—a stand with which we wholeheartedly agree, and which was demonstrated in our work with Teresa. Going out on a limb in his bestselling book, *The Road Less Traveled,* Peck emphatically states that the essential ingredient of successful, deep, and meaningful psychotherapy is love. He explains that there is nothing inappropriate about a patient coming to love a therapist who has truly listened to her, accepts her nonjudgmentally, has refrained from using her to gratify her own needs, and has been instrumental in alleviating her suffering. Not all the feelings a patient has for the therapist are unconscious projections from earlier relationships. In other words, loving feelings toward one's therapist are not necessarily merely evidence of transference. Similarly, Peck maintains, it is not inappropriate for the therapist to develop feelings of love toward the patient as they struggle together, over time, to help the patient grow. In fact, Peck goes as far as to state that for the therapy to be successful, it is essential for the therapist to love a patient. In a successful therapy, Peck believes, the therapeutic relationship will become a mutually loving one.

There are strong prohibitions in "mainstream" psychotherapy communities against displays of caring by the therapist. Psychologist Irene Stiver explains that caring about patients has often been viewed as something that *gets in the way* of effective treatment. Stiver (1991) attributes these prohibitions against expressions of caring as coming from two major assumptions underlying traditional models of psychotherapy:

1. *The belief in the need for neutrality and distance in the therapy relationship.* To be helpful (and presumably to foster the development of a healthy transference), traditional therapy models require the therapist to be objective, nonemotional, and relatively impersonal.
2. *The belief that growth and change can occur only if the therapist does not gratify the patient.* Stiver points out that the experience of frustration and learning how to tolerate and respond to deprivations in therapy is seen as valuable and therapeutic.

Many therapists, especially those who believe in a psychoanalytic model, would view expressions of caring toward the patient as gratification of their infantile dependency needs. It is our contention that survivors of severe abuse have already experienced more than enough frustration and deprivation, to say the least. What they need from a therapist, what they need from any human being, is genuine caring expressed through loving relationships.

Some therapists have difficulty with the use of the word "love" in the context of therapy. For some, love has sexual or romantic connotations. Because of the strong feelings that can develop between therapist and survivor as a result of the intimate nature of their relationship, sexual attractions can occur. Some therapists caution against emotional intimacy in the therapy relationship to avoid the development of such feelings. Yet, such feelings are natural and in themselves not dangerous or destructive to the survivor *provided that they remain unexpressed or at least unconsummated.* Sexual relations with a patient are not only unethical and even illegal in most cases, but are harmful to the survivor. Besides the usual constraints, the therapist must remember that this individual was most likely sexually abused by someone who was supposed to care for her, a trusted adult, a caretaker who was supposed to have her best interests at heart. Since therapists are putting themselves in the position of trusted caretaker, *no* sexual contact should be involved in the relationship, not even after the termination of the therapy.

Some therapists object to the use of the word "love" in the context of therapy with survivors, because that word carries intense emotional meanings for those whose perpetrators used so-called love as a justification for their abuse (Olson, 1992). They claim the use of the word "love" can lead to misconceptions by the survivor. We believe that the concept of love that was perverted because of the abuse needs to be redefined for true healing to take place. Ignoring the issue by not mentioning the word in therapy only serves to perpetuate the problem. Survivors need to have the concept of love redefined, reframed, so that they can understand what healthy love in the real world is about. They also need an *experience* of healthy love. What better way to learn about the true nature of love than through involvement in loving, caring relationships?

Some Degree of Mutuality Is Present in a Successful Therapy Relationship

Contrary to traditional views of the need for strict rules about therapist neutrality and distance, we contend that *complete* neutrality is neither possible nor desirable in the healing relationship. Despite all efforts to appear neutral, the therapist cannot help but reveal a lot about herself just from her nonverbal reactions to what the client is saying— from the look in her eyes, to the barely perceptible involuntary shudder, to the inflection in her voice as she speaks in response. Although therapists must continuously monitor and examine their own countertransference reactions, they would be foolish to think that their clients remain completely unaware of them.

Although many therapists may disagree with us on our basic principle of the need for love in the therapy relationship, most who have had extensive experience working with dissociative disorders will agree that traditional views on the need for total therapist neutrality must be modified when working with people who were severely abused in childhood. Robert Kluft, director of the Dissociative Disorders Program at the Institute of Pennsylvania Hospital, and one of the most prolific writers and researchers in the field of dissociative studies, has suggested that the therapist take a warm and flexible therapeutic stance when dealing with people who have multiple personalities (and therefore have experienced severe abuse in childhood). He writes "MPD often results in part because people who could have taken action to protect a child did nothing. *The therapist can anticipate that passivity, affective blandness, and technical neutrality will be experienced as uncaring and rejecting behavior, and that the therapy is better served by taking a warm and active stance that allows a latitude of affective expression*" (Kluft, 1993b, p. 97). He suggests that several compelling reasons support this advice. The first is that trauma victims often perceive relative remoteness in the therapist as the therapist attempting to distance herself from them and their shameful circumstances. The second deals with the issue of transference in the therapeutic relationship. Since the patient's transference is likely to include a view of the therapist as a dangerous and hurtful person (such as those in authority who abused her in the past), "if the therapist has not been relatively real, the patient may have more than the usual amount of difficulty seeing the therapist through his or her projections, and the patient may, in the grips of powerful emotions, be unable to distinguish past and present and behave toward the therapist as if he or she were an enemy the patient has to attack in order to be safe" (Kluft, 1993b, p. 97).

So, not only is it impossible to maintain a stance of complete neutrality in the therapy session, but such a stance is not necessarily conducive to promoting emotional growth in survivors of severe abuse. Our contention that the therapist needs to love the client in order to be helpful implies some degree of involvement and mutuality in the therapy relationship. Traditionally, psychoanalytic concepts of the therapy relationship have been shaped by theories that view the completely independent, autonomous, and self-reliant individual as the healthiest. The role of the therapist is thus to promote the individual's growth in this direction. Any degree of emphasis on mutuality in the therapy relationship would be viewed as promoting dependence rather than autonomy and would not be in the interest of the patient. More recent views of psychotherapy stress the interdependence of human beings and growth through connectedness. The work of psychologists at the Stone Center in Massachusetts is most notable here, and although it focuses on *women's* psychological development, we believe the theory of growth through connection has relevance to both men and women who are survivors of severe abuse. According to this theory, traditional models of "human" development have been formulated by males and reflect male values of autonomy and separation. When applied to women's emotional growth, however, these models do not accurately reflect what happens.

Psychologists at the Stone Center have proposed that women grow not by breaking away from their families, becoming completely autonomous human beings, but *through* their connections with significant people in their lives. Therefore, rather than stressing independence and separation from others as an endpoint, a therapeutic goal signifying psychological maturity, these psychologists recommend a focus on enhancing the client's ability to engage in healthy relationships. It is our contention that a major goal of therapy for all survivors, male and female, is to be able to engage in healthy relationships—relationships that acknowledge the essential interconnectedness of *all* human beings. It is through participation in healthy relationships that the client truly grows emotionally, psychologically, and spiritually.

Any therapy that has as its focus growth through participation in healthy relationships will stress some degree of mutuality in the therapy relationship, though of course there are some limitations on how much mutuality is optimal. Judith Jordan of the Stone Center claims that in a good therapy both people are affected, and that both client and therapist grow through a relationship of mutuality. However, Jordan cautions, in several ways the therapy relationship is not a fully mutual relationship. In therapy, one individual discloses more, having come into the relationship expressly to be helped by the other, to be listened to and understood. Jordan has stated that "the client's self-disclosure and expression of disavowed or split-off experiences, in a context of nonjudgmental listening and understanding, forms a powerful part of the process" (Jordan, 1991b, p. 95). To facilitate this process, the therapist and client create a contract that puts the client's subjective experience at the center. They then agree to attend to the therapist's subjective experience only insofar as it may be helpful to the client. Within this context, "there can be real caring that goes both ways. There is an important feeling of mutuality, with mutual respect, emotional availability, and openness to change on both sides. And the experience of relation-ship, of mutuality often grows in therapy" (Jordan, 1991b, p. 95).

Some mental health professionals will argue that a focus on any degree of mutuality in the therapy relationship exploits the client or is too self-gratifying. Jordan suggests that in part this view conforms to an old therapy model based on scarcity, power, and hierarchy. She argues that this is exactly the model most clients carry in their heads, which makes it so difficult for them to attend to their own needs. In practice, Jordan claims, people discover that in giving to others they feel enlarged: "In expanding the relationship and our understanding of it, both members are enriched. If we honor the notion of a relational self-identity anchored in the world of human connection, interaction, and interdependence, and want to assist patients in expanding their sense of personal aliveness and wholeness in relationships, we must be ready to expand our own awareness and openness in the therapy relationship" (Jordan, 1991a, pp. 288-289).

We agree with Jordan about the need to expand our experience of the therapy relationship to reflect an understanding of the relational aspects of growth. One of our goals is to help the survivor develop a self-image as a person interconnected with other human beings. One of the best ways to accomplish this end is through a relation-ship in which both the therapist and the client are open to growth and change through their interactions with each other. Yet, the rela-tionship cannot be fully mutual, in that the focus of the interactions is always to further the growth of the *client*. Although some degree of mutuality is desirable, and although the therapist cannot help but grow from an involvement with the client, this focus on the client's growth remains the guiding force of the relationship. One of the ad-vantages of a collaboration between therapist and clergy is that it allows for differential degrees of mutuality in each of the survivor/helper relationships. We will discuss this point in more detail later in this chapter.

Importance of the Spiritual Dimension in the Healing Process

Sometimes religious people will question the need for psycho-therapy. Some have criticized therapy for focusing too much on the *individual* and *individual needs*. Psychotherapy is viewed as mak-

ing people too self-absorbed and self-centered. "Where is God in
this process?" many ministers have asked us. Carroll Wise, a pastoral counselor who views psychotherapy as a *religious* process has
explained that when a minister asks where God comes into the process, he is

> expressing his own lack of understanding of the religious pro-
> cess. Here God is thought of as an external Being who some-
> how penetrates the individual with healing power. There is a
> strong sense of dependency in this concept. Rather, God
> should be thought of as already present within any process in
> which self-revelation, the search for the truth about the self, or
> genuine growth toward love and faith are experienced. As the
> person becomes more aware of his inner strengths he under-
> stands that he is using resources that he did not create, that he
> finds them within. They are part of God's creation in the nature
> of man; they are also a means of grace and healing. The task of
> the pastoral therapist is that of helping persons discover the
> healing forces that God has placed within him, and then to
> symbolize that experience in ways that are meaningful to him.
> The pastoral therapist should be aware that when he is dealing
> with the depths of a person he is participating in an experience
> of profound religious significance. (Wise, 1983, pp. 162-163)

If the aim of intensive psychotherapy is to discover the true self
that lies under all the hurts and fears, under all the defenses against
hurt and pain, then that true self would be the *Self*—the road to the
divine within us. When all the hurts and fears are put aside, we
discover the Self that is connected to God. Doing God's will at this
point becomes synonymous with our own will. So, good psychotherapy only brings us *closer* to God. Furthermore, true inner healing
implies change at both psychological and spiritual levels. Working
through our emotional issues frees us up to focus on our spiritual
development; letting God into our lives helps soothe the pain of our
suffering and allows us to grow emotionally and psychologically into
the people we were meant to be. Matthew Linn, Sheila Fabricant, and
Dennis Linn have expressed similar sentiments: "God has built into
us patterns of emotional development, stages which we go through
in developing as a healthy mature person. Hurts can interrupt this

process and cause us to remain stuck in development. The grace of healing builds upon a natural process of growth, and the effect of prayer is ordinarily to mobilize and strengthen this process" (Linn, Fabricant, and Linn, 1988, p. 13). Thus spirituality and psychotherapy are different aspects of a whole, a divine plan to foster human growth. The survivor allows God's natural healing into her life through many means, among them prayer, meditation, and involvement in loving relationships with both clergy and therapist. Rather than being at odds with each other, the therapist and the minister can view themselves working *together* to do God's work and as vehicles through which God's healing love comes into the life of the survivor.

Just as some clergy are skeptical of the value of psychotherapy, many therapists decry the inclusion of spiritual issues in psychotherapy, viewing any discussion of spirituality as an imposition of the therapist's values on the client, or dismissing the importance or even relevance of spiritual issues in the therapy process. Although the spiritual dimension is not necessary to healing for *all* survivors of severe abuse, we believe that for many complete healing and a sense of inner peace cannot be attained without its inclusion in the therapeutic process.

Numerous studies have demonstrated that religious commitment is associated with mental health and physical well-being. In addition, an increasing number of people who have no affiliation with organized religion have expressed interest in spiritual issues. Books and movies on spirituality abound. In a time when the American public has so overwhelmingly endorsed religion and spirituality, therapists can no longer afford to ignore the part religious and spiritual values play in the lives of their clients.

EFFECTS OF SEVERE CHILDHOOD ABUSE

Now that we have delineated some of the basic beliefs that informed our own work, let us turn to a brief examination of some psychological, emotional, and spiritual effects of severe abuse on children. Any efforts to help in the healing of such individuals as adults must take into account the effects their childhood experiences had on their lives.

Social psychologist Ronnie Janoff-Bulman (1992) has studied the effects of trauma on adults—traumas such as rape, natural disasters, and life-threatening illnesses. The psychological disequilibrium that results from such trauma, she argues, stems from a shattering of their most basic assumptions about the world—assumptions that the world is benevolent and that the self is worthy. Basic assumptions about the world and one's place in it are formed in early life. Traumatic events in adulthood have the ability to shatter them completely, leaving the individual with a sense of disequilibrium and ground-lessness. If such traumatic experiences have such devastating effects on adult survivors, can you imagine the profound and pervasive impact severe emotional, physical, and sexual abuse would have on a small child? A child has not yet even formed basic assumptions about the world and her place in it, and, as she begins to attempt to understand her world, she will base her assumptions about the workings of the world on her experiences of abuse. Carolyn Holderread Heggen, in writing about the effects of sexual abuse on human beings, describes sexual abuse as "a violation of the body, of personal boundaries, and of trust. It destroys a sense of personal, individual value. It objectifies persons—treats them as objects, as things. No wonder sexual abuse is sometimes called "murder of the soul" (Holderread Heggen, 1993, pp. 27-28).

Psychologist Philip Kinsler has suggested that we can understand the effects of severe abuse on a child by thinking about what lessons that child would have learned about life—lessons about the meaning of life, about other people, about the self, and about relationships (Kinsler, 1992, p. 167). Keeping this concept of lessons about life in mind, we can attempt to understand severe childhood abuse on a deeper level than the merely intellectual by imagining what it would be like to be a small child thrown into such a terrifying situation. Take a few moments to think about the following exercise. Be prepared, though; this exercise can be rather upsetting.

Can you imagine what it would be like to be an infant, totally dependent on your parents for meeting your physical and emotional needs? Can you imagine what it would be like if those parents treated you in cruel and sadistic ways? Is it possible to imagine that you are lying in your crib and your mother comes into the room and begins to stick pins into your body? Can you imagine being three years old, afraid of the dark, and your father walks into your room with a rubber bag and a long tube extending from the bag? Is it possible to imagine how you would feel as he puts the end of that tube into your rectum filling you with icy cold liquid, then puts you into a small, dark closet and locks the door, warning you to "hold in" the icy cold liquid or else "bad things will happen to you"?

Can you imagine what it would feel like to be six years old and your mother is holding a revolver to your head, explaining that there is one bullet in the gun? Is it possible to imagine how you would feel as she pulled the trigger? Can you imagine what it would feel like to hear that she is doing this to you because you are a bad person and deserve to die?

Can you imagine being eight years old and your father informing you that you must go into the bedroom and have sex with one of his friends? Is it possible to imagine what it would feel like as this man, reeking of alcohol, began to touch your child body? Can you imagine what it would feel like to hear that this horrible experience is happening to you because you *want* it to, that you are just a slut?

Could you imagine the cumulative effect such experiences would have on your sense of safety in the world? On your self-image? On your ability to trust? On your sense of hope for the future?

For many of us, it is very difficult to believe that anyone, especially a parent, could treat a child so cruelly. As horrible and perhaps unbelievable as each of these scenarios may appear, each one actually happened to a survivor of severe childhood abuse. Children who are severely abused live in a perpetual nightmare; and, as one might imagine, the effects of such experiences are profound, touching on every aspect of their existence. Let us look at what the clinical and research literature has taught us about the emotional, psychological, and spiritual effects of severe abuse. Again, remember that we are not presenting a comprehensive manual for the treatment of dissociative disorders. We aim here to discuss those effects of severe abuse that are of interest to therapists and ministers who are working together.

Trust Issues

Erik Erikson postulated that the first developmental task in life is to develop a sense of *basic trust,* a sense that the world is good and that people in that world are trustworthy. He has defined basic trust as "an essential trustfulness of others as well as a fundamental sense of one's own trustworthiness" and has proclaimed it "the most fundamental prerequisite of mental vitality" (Erikson, 1968, p. 96). Basic trust also implies that one's basic needs will be met by others. The infant, having developed this sense of trust, can predict that she will be fed when she indicates she is hungry and comforted when she is frightened. Developmental psychologist Patricia Miller explains that babies develop trust in themselves from the feeling that others accept them and from increased familiarity with their own bodily sensations and urges. This faith in oneself and the world, she adds, "corresponds to religious faith in the 'cosmic order' of the universe" (Miller, 1983, p. 166). Similarly, Matthew Linn, Sheila Fabricant, and Dennis Linn have pointed out that just as unloving parents can distort our image of God, those moments when we have given or received parental love can heal our image of God. "The child whose earliest experiences of crying out at night are followed by being gathered up in the arms of a loving father, or who is fed at the breast of a mother whose eyes convey 'you are uniquely precious in all the world'—such a child, whose immediate reality has been trustworthy, will become an adult who can have faith in an Ultimate Reality" (Linn, Fabricant, and Linn, 1988, p. 45). The development of basic trust thus relates to a capacity for spiritual and religious faith as well. Failure to establish trust leads to a distorted image of God. There may be a belief that God cannot or will not care for the individual. There might be great anger at God for allowing the abuse to take place. The concept of God might even be totally rejected.

While some degree of mistrust is necessary to human survival in order to detect impending danger or distinguish between dangerous and safe people, when mistrust wins out over trust, the child will tend to become frustrated, socially withdrawn, untrusting and suspicious of others, and will exhibit a severe lack of self-confidence. People who have been severely abused in childhood have experienced a frustration of their most basic needs for comfort and safety. Some are denied food while they watch parents eat. Others have been force-fed various substances (such as dog or cat food, garbage, and human feces) or have been subjected to daily enemas. Most children never know when the next bout of abuse will occur. They live in constant uncertainty. Eliana Gil, in her marvelous book for survivors of abuse, *Outgrowing the Pain,* has stated that it is easy to understand why trust becomes a major issue for adults abused as children: "If when you cried, sometimes you were fed, and sometimes you were beaten, you cannot develop trust or learn to expect consistent nurturing responses. You either learn to stop crying, or take a risk each time and see what happens. To stay safe, most adults abused as children stopped taking chances, and expected little from others" (Gil, 1983, p. 33). One can only imagine the effects on the child's self-image and sense of trust in others when the child's mother and/or father have participated in this kind of cruel physical, emotional, and sexual torture. The sense of mistrust of others and oneself must be overwhelming. Perhaps the only way such a child could survive would be to split off memories of the abuse, allowing one portion of the self, an alter ego, to exist with no conscious knowledge of the horror perpetrated by the parents upon her. The rest of the alters, retaining memories of the details of the abuse, would thus exhibit a lack of the most basic sense of trust in the self, in others, and ultimately in God. Such is often the case with people who have multiple personalities (Kluft, 1993a).

Those whose sense of basic trust was damaged by severe abuse are likely to have difficulty establishing and maintaining intimate relationships and in reaching out to and making use of helping individuals, such as therapists and clergy. After all, if they could not trust their parents, can they trust anyone? They will also tend to be hypervigilant, expecting bad things to happen to them at any moment. To such individuals, the world appears to be a very dangerous place.

Self-Esteem Issues

Just as those severely abused in childhood will have issues with trust, so will they experience great difficulty forming a healthy self-image and developing self-esteem. They may blame themselves for the abuse and believe that they are inherently bad. Often the abusers have reinforced this notion throughout the survivor's childhood. One survivor described her feelings of self-blame:

> I always thought that I was the problem, that I had done something terrible which I couldn't remember but for which I was being punished by having to carry around this terrible pain in my heart. Whatever I had done was surely the reason for my long history of depression, eating disorders, self-abusive behaviors, and broken relationships. (Holderread Heggen, 1993, p. 31)

Some children find it easier to blame themselves for the abuse than to admit to themselves that their parents, the very people they depend upon for their most basic needs, have betrayed them. Carolyn Holderread Heggen has explained that self-blame decreases the child's sense of powerlessness and vulnerability. The child knows that it is impossible to change her world or the adults in it; but she may find some hope in believing that if she could somehow be different (smarter, more attractive, better behaved), she could prevent further abuse (Holderread Heggen, 1993). For other survivors, there may have been merely a questioning of "why me?" and a conclusion, in the absence of any information to the contrary, that the reason the abuse occurred is that they must have done something to bring it about.

This tendency toward self-blame has grave consequences for one's sense of self-esteem. The beliefs about one's inherent badness and responsibility for the abuse, coupled with guilt and anxiety, lead to a shamed sense of self—a sense that the self is unlovable, deserving of abuse from others, and unworthy of care and positive attention (Courtois, 1988).

Christine Courtois has pointed out that survivors of severe childhood abuse may project this shame onto their therapists, expecting the therapist to hold them in the same contempt they have for themselves and to behave toward them as the abusing family did in the past. They will tend to feel undeserving of the therapist's attention and caring, and fear that sooner or later the therapist will discover their secret—that the abuse occurred because of something about them. They expect a reenactment of the lack of protection and the blame experienced during their childhood. One survivor described her feelings:

> I'm on familiar terms with feelings of blame and shame. I always thought I'd be blamed if anyone found out. Even when I started seeing my therapist, I had that "edge of the chair" feeling that she would surely blame me. Obviously, she never did. I'm sure I would have accepted it, maybe angry as hell, but nonetheless accepted it. I've always believed that I was guilty, that it was all my fault. (Courtois, 1988, p. 217)

Interpersonal Issues

Related to problems with trust of others and self and to low self-esteem, problems in interpersonal relationships abound in those who have been severely abused as children. Children who have been severely neglected tend to become shy, withdrawn adults with strong dependency needs or hostile, angry adults who claim they "don't need anybody." In either case, they will tend to have few friends and thus a poor social support network. Those who have been sexually abused will tend to eroticize relationships throughout their lives, leading to problem relationships and vulnerability to further abuse and victimization. Often, such individuals will allow themselves to be abused in adulthood, thinking that this is the only kind of treatment they deserve. Survivors will tend to have difficulty maintaining intimate relationships, never allowing anyone to get too close to them. Several research studies have found that heterosexual survivors remain unmarried in disproportionate numbers when compared to a nonabused control group (Courtois, 1988).

These problems in interpersonal relating make it difficult for the survivor to establish close, trusting relationships with a therapist or a minister. There may be a "push/pull" phenomenon in which the survivor reaches out to the therapist or minister in desperation and then suddenly pulls back or runs away when she feels too close.

Emotional Issues

Generalized anxiety and a constant state of fear are common emotional issues faced by those who have been severely abused.

Profound depression is also common. This depression may include feelings of utter hopelessness for the future, suicidal ideation and/or attempts, and various self-damaging behaviors, such as cutting oneself with razor blades or burning one's skin with cigarette butts. Alcohol and drugs may be used excessively in an attempt to self-medicate the anxiety and depression and to shut out the memories of the abuse. A common defense of those who have been severely abused is dissociation. Initially, this defense is a positive way to escape the horrors of the abuse in a young child who is powerless to protect herself or prevent the abuse. However, as that child grows into adulthood, she may come to rely on dissociative defenses even when they are no longer necessary. She may learn to dissociate when she feels *any* negative emotion—anger, fear, frustration—in normal, everyday life situations. Her dissociation may then begin to cause problems for her, as she has difficulty remembering things that happened to her in her daily life, experiencing as well problems with concentration, and an increasing inability to handle stressful situations.

Spiritual Issues

As we have seen, those who have survived severe abuse in childhood often have grave questions about the nature of the God who would allow such horrible things to happen to young, innocent children. They may feel abandoned by God. Some may come to doubt the very existence of God. Many are left with a sense that life is meaningless, and that the purpose of life is merely to survive, even if it means surviving at the expense of others.

GOALS OF TREATMENT

Again, we do not aim to describe a treatment manual for survivors of abuse, but we seek only to delineate some of the goals of treatment that arise out of what we know about the effects of the abuse and which relate to a collaborative effort between therapist and clergy. Both therapist and minister must aim to create an environment that counteracts the messages and lessons about self, others, and God learned in childhood. We have identified the following five goals.

1. *Building trust in oneself and in others.* As we explained in our examination of the effects of abuse, severe childhood abuse radically affects the most elementary developmental task of the infant—that of developing a basic sense of trust in oneself and in others. Survivors come into adulthood never having successfully negotiated this critical phase. Although trust issues are important in all therapeutic relationships, they are especially important and often troublesome when working with survivors of severe childhood abuse. The process of developing trust in the therapist or minister is a long and difficult one for the survivor, with many twists and turns, ups and downs. Therapists and clergy alike must be prepared for much testing and acting out. Psychologist Philip Kinsler has pointed out that many of the difficult behaviors encountered in working with DID patients (dependency demands, rages, destructive acting out) can best be understood as attempts to deal with basic mistrust (Kinsler, 1992). Keeping this in mind helps those involved in working with such individuals weather the many storms.

The most important way in which the therapist and minister can foster the development of trust is to be trustworthy themselves. Consistency, honesty, empathetic listening—all convey to the survivor over time that at least some people can be trusted. Survivors are usually extremely sensitive to nonverbal cues. If they are lied to or are treated in any way dishonestly, they will perceive it immediately. Those involved in working with survivors must be on their toes constantly, and must maintain consistency and honesty in the relationship. We must be willing to admit our mistakes when we make them, never pretending that we are always right or that we have all the answers. Similarly, promises must never be made to the survivor unless they can be kept.

Although it may be difficult at first for the therapist or minister to trust a person who is acting out—perhaps using drugs and alcohol excessively, prostituting herself, or mutilating herself daily—it is essential that we attempt to find *some* area of the survivor's life in which our trust in her can be demonstrated. As the helping professional is able to demonstrate at least some level of trust in the survivor, the survivor will slowly begin to realize that she can trust *herself.*

2. *Creating a sense of safety in the world.* As we have discussed, the survivor feels unsafe in a world in which terrible things can happen at any moment. Generalized anxiety and the symptoms of post-traumatic stress disorder are likely to be present. It is generally acknowledged in the field of treatment of dissociative disorders that the first stage of therapy must concern itself with the establishment of a sense of safety for the survivor. Robert Kluft has compared the models for the treatment of DID as described by three of the leading clinicians in the field. He has found that all three follow the same sequence of stages, beginning with an attempt to maximize safety and communication. Kluft explains that "in the first or safety phase, there must be a prioritization on creating an atmosphere of safety in the therapy, and an anticipation of what will be necessary to make the next phase [the examination of the trauma memories] safe as well. Consequently the treatment is governed by what I call Belafonte's law: 'House built on a weak foundation, it will fall! Oh, yes! Oh, yes! Oh, yes!' " (Kluft, 1993b, p. 89).

3. *Creating a new worldview.* Just as horrible emotional, physical, and sexual abuse in early childhood has a profoundly negative effect on the development of a sense of self and on the ability to trust, such abuse can have a disastrous effect on the formation of a worldview—a sense of what the world is all about and how it functions. The use of cognitive/behavioral techniques to help change the dysfunctional thinking that arises from early abuse is not enough to effect change, since the most fundamental assumptions about the workings of the world have been tainted by the abuse itself. The very fabric of the survivor's existence is woven with the threads of horrible abuse. A new worldview that encompasses cognitive, emotional, and spiritual aspects of the survivor's existence must be created. The therapist can provide the survivor with tools to evaluate her basic emotional and cognitive beliefs about the world, and the minister can provide her with guidance and information while she is developing a new spiritual outlook.

The creation of healthy boundaries by the therapist and the minister can go a long way toward creating a sense of safety for the survivor. Abusers violated sexual, physical, and emotional boundaries regularly, and in horrible ways. It is important for the survivor to learn that no such crossing of boundaries will occur when dealing with the helping professional. For example, some therapists refrain from touching a survivor—no hugs, no pats on the back—unless the survivor specifically asks to be touched. Some therapists will not touch a client who has survived sexual and/or physical abuse under any circumstances.

Sometimes the boundaries are established for the benefit of the therapist as well as the survivor. For example, when people with DID are in treatment, exploring their memories of the abuse, they may often experience crises and phone their therapists to receive reassurance that they will be okay. However, the therapist cannot be available to them twenty-four hours a day. The therapist might have to explain to the survivor that she cannot be available to talk at any hour of the day or night, that when she has to get up in the middle of the night to talk on the phone that she is likely to be sleepy and unable to work the next day. She might add that she is always available to take calls at certain hours. Not only would such a boundary help the therapist maintain a normal life, but it would demonstrate to the survivor that healthy people can say "no" and still care. Although the survivor may balk at the establishment of such a boundary, she may also feel a sense of safety, knowing that the therapist will take care of herself and will not be overwhelmed by the survivor's dependency needs.

4. *Enhancing a sense of self-worthiness.* Since survivors are likely to be self-blaming or at least to feel unworthy of being loved, nurtured, and cared for, one goal of treatment is to help them develop a sense of self-worth. The survivor's worthiness is demonstrated through caring, empathetic interactions with the therapist and the minister over time.

5. *Development of life-coping skills.* Since the use of dissociative defenses associated with severe abuse can cause dysfunctional behavior in adulthood, the therapist and the minister can actively teach the survivor cognitive skills and behaviors aimed at negotiating life's ups and downs more smoothly. The survivor can be helped to develop self-soothing behaviors to comfort herself when she is in emotional pain. Robert Kluft has emphasized that therapy must be done *with* the survivor, not *to* her. He suggests that tasks, assignments, and activities can all be beneficial in helping the survivor learn new ways to cope with her world (Kluft, 1993a).

Chapter 3

The Benevolence Model

I saw that God never began to love us. For just as we will be in everlasting joy (all God's creation is destined for this), so also we have always been in God's foreknowledge, known and loved from without beginning. . . .

Julian of Norwich

God is love. This statement has been repeated so often that we may view it as trite or dismiss it as too simplistic. Yet this simple statement forms the basis of the spiritual model upon which all of our work together was founded. It was the application of this spiritual model that was responsible for the transformation of Mimic, (Teresa's alter who believed himself to be a computer, programmed to carry out the Mother's commands) into Justin, a loving and caring human being. Although the focus of our work together has been on helping Mimic/Justin heal from the abuse, all of Teresa's personalities, in varying degrees, were affected by this work and have begun their own healing journeys. In fact, the application of the principles of this spiritual model profoundly affected both the therapist and the minister professionally, spiritually, and emotionally. The impact of this work on both therapist and clergy involved will be discussed throughout Chapters 4 and 5.

As we explained in Chapter 2, one's own spiritual model is not always conscious and articulated, yet that model determines to a large degree how we view human nature, how we interact with other people, and even how we assign meaning to our lives. One's spiritual model determines even the most mundane, daily interactions with others. Perhaps the best way to illustrate this concept is by describing an encounter between Justin and a stranger in a store.

Justin had been waiting to pay for some purchases at the cash register. Suddenly, a woman walked up to the counter, placing her items in front of Justin's. The cashier attended to her first. The woman turned to Justin and said curtly, "You don't mind if I go ahead of you. I'm late in picking up my husband." She proceeded to pay for her purchases. Justin's first reaction was annoyance, feeling as though the woman was discounting him. He clearly had not been given a choice to let her go ahead of him. Then he reminded himself that this woman, like all of us, had a divine spark within her, though that spark may have been covered up by years of hurt and fear. He resolved to see beyond her egocentric behavior. He was finally able to see her inconsiderate behavior not as personal, but as coming out of her own woundedness and hurt in life. He thought to himself that this woman must be a very unhappy person if she felt she had to "run over" people like that to get what she wanted, and that she must not feel good about herself if she had to behave this way.

This understanding allowed Justin to respond to her in a non-angry manner. Rather than yelling at her for getting ahead of him in line, Justin quietly said to her, "I wouldn't have minded, if you had asked if you could go ahead of me. I would have been happy to let you go. But I did mind you pushing me out of the way as if I weren't important." Had Justin responded with anger, the woman would have become defensive and discounted what he said. How-ever, in response to Justin's more gentle statement, she became quiet and pensive. Finally, she said, "I'm sorry. I didn't mean to cut ahead of you. I was just late." It was the conscious and deliberate application of one of the basic premises of the spiritual model he had learned that allowed Justin to transform what would have been an unpleasant interaction between strangers into a positive experi-ence from which both could learn.

The experience was helpful to the woman because she realized how her inconsiderate behavior was affecting other people. Justin, who had been taught to believe he had no worth or rights, was affirmed in that he was able to stand up for himself without being hostile. As this interaction illustrates, one's spiritual model can form the foundation upon which we relate to others, even in the most mundane encounters. The clearer we are about the basic premises of that model, the more deliberate we can be in the application of those premises to everyday life. It was to that end that the three of us decided to articulate and more fully develop the basic principles underlying our own spiritual model.

Marion: I had always been somewhat spiritually oriented, although I had never clearly articulated my spiritual beliefs. I was brought up Jewish but had received very little formal religious training. Although I believed in God, I had only vague notions about the nature of God. When Steven, Susan, and I began working together, the only belief I knew we shared in common was that God is love. It was through my work with them and with Teresa and my efforts to write about our work that I began to conceptualize the spiritual model upon which I was basing that work. The articulation of my spiritual beliefs as presented in this chapter has been part of an ongoing process. As I thought about and wrote about spirituality, and as I discussed my growing awareness with Steven, I became more mindful of how my spiritual beliefs influenced my interactions with Teresa and with other people in my life. At the same time, as I became more aware of the operation of these beliefs in my life, the beliefs themselves became clearer, more fully developed, and a more conscious part of my everyday thinking.

Steven: I was raised in a Christian family, oriented around the Church, with the words "God is love" communicated to me from the time I was young. But I was never able to put that into an understanding of the concept of love, and what that really means. Through a relationship, I deepened my understanding of love and what it was like to love and to care about somebody, in that you could be so self-giving that you would give all of yourself to another person. I realized that this is the kind of love God has for us. He loves us that deeply. That understanding transformed my life. Having always walked with love in my life, it was not until I began working with Justin, learning of his severe hurt and pain, and the absence of that love in his life, that I could understand on a deep level what it meant to say that God is love. Through my work with Justin and the others, and through my discussions with Marion, I began to more fully appreciate how important the experience of that love is to our wholeness.

In this chapter we will look at some of the basic premises of The Benevolence Model, the name we have given the spiritual model on which we have based our work. This model evolved over time through our discussions and interactions with one another, and we will describe the process we used as we began to articulate the basic principles. The Benevolence Model is a spiritual model that is not tied to any particular religion. The specific way in which these principles were *implemented* in our work with Teresa was a Christian one because Teresa was Christian. Had she been Jewish or Islamic, the way in which we utilized and explained these principles in our interactions with Teresa would have differed, but the basic premises of our spiritual model would have remained the same. In our work with this survivor, the application of some of the basic principles has been made concrete through an understanding of Jesus Christ, since *Jesus had a special meaning to Teresa*. Therefore, one need not be a Christian to use the principles of the model we are about to present. Any therapist of any religion can apply the basic premises to their work with any client, regardless of that client's religion. A Jewish therapist could collaborate with a priest in helping a Catholic client heal from her abuse; a Christian therapist could work just as easily with a Jewish client, applying the basic principles of this model. We are aware of nothing in our approach that *violates* the basic beliefs of any religion.

> **Susan:** An experience I had at work illustrates the point that the principles of this model transcend any particular religious orientation. I am a social worker and director of a psychiatric rehabilitation program for the chronically mentally ill. Dana was an Orthodox Jew, a new member at the center. Initially, she wanted nothing to do with me because I was overweight. She felt that my being overweight meant that I was unable to deal with my own life, so how could I help her? She publicly expressed her reservations at a community meeting which I did not attend. The staff later told me what Dana had said, so that if she brought it up with me, I would be prepared. My feelings were a mixture of anger and frustration. I thought to

myself, "Here we go again. I have to deal with being over-weight in my life. I didn't want to have to deal with it at work." But for me to be most effective in my work with her, I had to find a way to get past her label of me. I had to help her see that I was more than my weight, and I had to get past my own feelings of being labeled.

Applying the principles of The Benevolence Model, I was able to overcome my anger. I was able to see her as a child of God, created in the image of God. Her inability to see me as anything beyond my weight reflected a cultural bias and per-haps a personal problem. My seeing her as a child of God allowed me to move past cultural delineations between people and any personal issues I might have about my weight. Since each of us is a manifestation of God's love in the world, I needed to focus on that aspect of Dana, rather than on her wounded behavior. She was projecting her own unhappiness onto me, and if I were to do the same, I would just be perpetu-ating this destructive cycle.

As a result of this shift in my perception of her behavior as I began to apply these principles, I was always warm and open in my interactions with her. We began to develop a relation-ship. One day, we even talked about my struggles with weight, and this helped Dana to see me as a person, as more than my weight. Once we moved beyond the physical, we were free to relate to each other on a deeper level, engaging in involved discussions about God and spirituality, despite the differences in our religious backgrounds.

This whole experience did not depend on Dana adopting or even accepting my basic spiritual model. It did not matter that she was Jewish or that I was Christian. It was a shift in my perception that made the difference in our interactions. It was an internal process. In fact, she was unaware of this entire process.

It is important to keep in mind that we are presenting in this chapter the spiritual model that we used in our work—a model that developed over time out of our work together and that reflects our similar spiritual belief systems. However, we make no claim that one must use this spiritual model to be effective. We present The Benevolence Model so that the reader will understand more clearly how we implemented our spiritual beliefs into our work together. Some may closely identify with all of the principles of the model and adopt it in their work. Others will be able to use only those principles that appeal to them, rejecting other principles as contrary to their own belief system. Some may reject our model entirely. The minister and the therapist need not even share the same belief system. What matters is that both the therapist and the minister are clear and open with each other about what they believe, and that they are able to consistently act out of those beliefs in their interactions with the client/parishioner.

Before presenting the basic principles of The Benevolence Model, we would also like to point out that research in the field of religion and psychology has supported the notion that a spiritual model such as ours has beneficial effects on the outcome of psychotherapy. Kenneth I. Pargament, a psychology professor at Bowling Green State University in Ohio, has conducted research on how people use religion to cope with major life stressors, ranging from illness to recovering from terrorist attacks. He has found that the type of religious expression people choose has a profound effect on their recovery. Pargament suggests that when you look more closely, you find certain types of religious expression that seem to be helpful and certain types that seem to be harmful (Clay, 1996). In several studies, Pargament has found that people who embrace what could be called a "sinners-in-the-hands-of-an-angry-God" model have poor mental health outcomes. On the other hand, people who embrace the "loving God," people who see God as a partner who works with them to resolve problems, have more positive mental health outcomes. They also tend to view difficult situations as opportunities for spiritual growth.

Let us now examine in more detail the basic premises of The Benevolence Model. Keep in mind that we have artificially divided our spiritual model into separate statements that reflect our spiritual beliefs, but in reality, the basic premises are not independent of one another.

PRINCIPLE ONE: GOD IS LOVE

Christians and Jews alike have had trouble with this simple statement and its corollary—that since God is love, then it follows that "God loves us." This difficulty has led Brennan Manning to lament that in his twenty-five years of pastoral experience he has found that "the stunning disclosure that God is love has had a negligible impact on the majority of Christians and minimal transforming power" (Manning, 1992, p. 153). It is as though the idea that God could love them is merely an intellectual concept and not a life-transforming belief. Similarly, when Rabbi David Wolpe, a lecturer in Jewish Thought at the University of Judaism in Los Angeles, stands up in front of Jewish groups and says "God loves you," the members of the audience wince and squirm (Wolpe, 1992). Yet, there is overwhelming support in both the Jewish and Christian scriptures for the notion that God is love and that God loves us.

Perhaps one reason we have such difficulty with the statement "God is love" is that the concept itself is beyond normal understanding, beyond words. For most of us, it is an intellectual concept with little practical relevance to our lives. Knowing at the deepest level of our being that God is love can come only from an experience of that love. We can think about it; we can write about it; we can talk about it; but the only way to truly understand it is to have the experience of God's love in our lives. As Blaise Pascal said, "It is the heart which experiences God and not the reason."

Mystics have sought a deep understanding of the nature of God. Theirs is not an intellectual pursuit, but one in which God is experienced. We tend to dismiss the experience of mystics because it does not fit into our traditional rational way of thinking. We may laugh at these people who seem to have their heads in the clouds, "hallucinating" visions of God's glory, out of touch with people and everyday reality. Yet, it is the mystical experience that often best captures the notion that God is love. We have much to learn from the mystics. One such mystic was Julian of Norwich, who lived in the late fourteenth century. In her book *Showings,* Julian described a serious illness at the age of thirty. During her illness she received sixteen dramatic revelations of God's love. She called these revelations "showings." Like most mystics, Julian saw God in everything.

She writes of her understanding of God as love: "So I was taught that love is our Lord's meaning. . . . In this love we have our beginning, and all this shall we see in God without end" (Julian of Norwich, 1978, p. 183).

There are those of us who, while by no means mystics, are given a one-time gift, an out-of-the-ordinary experience, in which we obtain direct knowledge of the nature of God as love. Mystical experiences are more common than most people think. Since the early 1970s, Andrew Greeley, a priest and sociologist, has been studying spiritual experiences among Americans. He has found that at least 35 percent of the people interviewed had some kind of powerful, spiritual experience that few had ever discussed with anyone else. Our country may in actuality be a nation of "closet mystics." Joan Borysenko, a noted researcher and author in the field of spirituality and health, has written that "fear of disbelief and ridicule, and in fundamentalist circles, fear of being denounced as a channel for the 'devil' all conspire to keep people in the closet about their mystical experiences" (Borysenko, 1990, p. 119).

Marion: Sometimes, the earthly loves we have can become springboards to experiencing divine love. I would like to relate an experience I had while working on this book that illustrates this point. I was riding home from New York City one afternoon on the Long Island Railroad. The train was fairly empty, and I was enjoying the quiet, using this time to think about things in my life. I was thinking about someone I love very dearly when the thought came to me: "If only you could love God with the same intensity and passion with which you love this person." Suddenly, I was given a glimpse of what it would be like to love God and feel God's love in the world. Everything around me—the train, the conductor, the other passengers, the trees and buildings we were passing by— everything in the universe was part of God's creation and had suddenly become infused with a blazing love that is beyond description. I thought of some of the unhappy people I had encountered that day and could feel only love and compassion for them. Tears streaming down my face, I could only marvel at what was being presented to me. I thought to myself, "This is how

Jesus saw the world every minute of his life." The feelings of God's love were so intense that I was aware that I could only sustain them for a short time. The experience lasted only a few minutes, but I will never forget it.

Some of us will have such one-time, intense experiences—mystical experiences, life-transforming experiences, conversion experiences. Yet, such experiences are not necessary to spiritual growth. We each have our own paths to understanding God's love. For many of us, our development is more gentle—an unfolding process of deepening our understanding. Some people do not value or appreciate their own spiritual experiences, because they have been using those one-time intense "conversion" experiences as a yardstick by which to measure their faith.

Deepening of faith does not have to be showy or dramatic. Although most of us will not experience God's love through any kind of mystical or out-of-the-ordinary experience, one way we can feel God's love is through our relationships with friends and family and even in our everyday interactions with strangers. God's love is manifested in the world through people. This concept will be further explored when we discuss one of the later premises, but suffice it to say that God's love, manifested through others, was the basis of all our work together and the real subject of this book.

Marion: Though I have described a one-time "mystical" experience in which I felt God's love directly, I do not mean to imply that my spiritual development was solely dependent on that one experience. Most of my deepening understanding of God's love has been part of a lifelong process and has come through my interactions with others—my family, my friends, even strangers. Even the experience described above was precipitated by my interactions and love for another human being. It is clear to me that the most growth occurs through such interactions over time, and those one-time intense experiences of God's love are gifts, helpful, but not necessary to the process.

PRINCIPLE TWO: GOD LOVES US

Since God is love, then God must love us. Such is God's nature. Support for this concept is found both in Christianity and Judaism. David Wolpe has written, " 'God loves you.' That phrase may strike the Jewish ear strangely, but it is authentically and originally a Jewish conception. The love of God for human beings is deep and rich in the Jewish tradition" (Wolpe, 1990, p. 70). God's everlasting love and caring for humanity is repeated again and again in both the Hebrew and Christian Scriptures.

Yet, despite the numerous biblical references to God's love for us, and despite any intellectual understanding we may profess of God's love, many of us have difficulty truly understanding the nature of that love. It is a love that surpasses all human understanding, and so, over the ages, we have created many images that convey metaphorically something about the essence of that love. Just as we have attempted to understand the concept of God by creating anthropomorphic images (despite our knowledge that God is not really human), we have also tended to characterize God's love in human terms. To that end, various anthropomorphic images have been used to characterize God's love. God's love is portrayed as that of Mother, Father, lover, Creator. These images are merely metaphors that help us get beyond an intellectual understanding of divine love, and as such, they capture some of the essence of that love. No one image, however, will capture all of the mystery of God's love.

> **Marion:** Since I doubt any of the three of us have the same concept of God, we each mean something different when we say God is love. I know that Steven's God concept is a more traditional religious one than mine. He sometimes laughs (good naturedly) when I talk about God as a force of Love in the universe, as though I were talking about something out of *Star Wars:* "May the Force be with you." However, I know that even if we conceptualize God differently, we both agree that God is love. This is the essence of our collaboration. We do not have to agree on all aspects of our spiritual model, nor have we always agreed on all aspects of our work together. As

long as we have remained open and accepting of each other's beliefs, we have succeeded.

PRINCIPLE THREE:
GOD'S LOVE IS UNCONDITIONAL

If God is love, then it follows that this love would be unconditional. Yet, many of us have great difficulty believing this to be true, perhaps because we are holding God to our human standards. As we discussed earlier, we tend to conceptualize God in our own likeness. Since most of us have trouble loving people who have hurt us or "sinned" against us, we cannot truly understand a God who is capable of loving people despite their obvious flaws and "bad" behaviors. We expect to be rewarded by God for our good behavior, for following the rules. We expect to be favored, as a human parent would favor the "good" child. But divine love is different from our human love. It cannot be quantified and cannot be earned by good behavior. Nor can we lose God's love by our bad behavior. Difficult as it may be to believe, we are loved by God with an unconditional love that surpasses all our human understanding, all our human experience.

Not only do we hold God to human standards, but the very words we use to describe God's unconditional love are often misleading and subject to our own human distortions.

Susan: When we try to understand the Word of God as expressed in the Scriptures, we are reading words written thousands of years ago in another culture and another language. These words have been translated and then interpreted through the filter of our present cultural usage of those words. We are actually reading an interpretation of a translation of the original text. (Of course, this view is contrary to that of the Archie Bunker School of Theology: "Everybody knows that God wrote the Bible in English.") As Marcus Borg has stated, "the 'lens' through which one views Scripture very much affects what one sees" (Borg, 1987, p. 160). For example, in Matthew 5:48 it is written "Be perfect, therefore, as your heavenly Father is perfect." John Jacob Raub has pointed out that the command to be perfect is not as difficult as it appears to be at first glance, because we have misunderstood the meaning of the word "perfect." He explains that the original biblical meaning of the word "perfect" was "complete" or "whole," but in contemporary English, the word has a different meaning entirely—implying flawlessness. He writes: "If we take 'perfect' in this English sense, we could very easily end up a compulsive perfectionist, forever trying for the impossible. Or else we would despair in the face of the demand; how could we ever be as perfect as God?" (Raub, 1992, p. 68). Instead, using the more accurate biblical meaning of the word, we can look at God's love as being "whole." Raub continues: "To be perfect like God is to relate to all as God does. We are to judge no one, exclude none from our good will. We, like God, are to let our blessings, our sun and rain, fall on the good and the bad alike, that is, we are to have a love which is complete and whole" (Raub, 1992, pp. 68-69). To me, when we say that God's love is perfect, it means that divine love is without judgment or expectation—in other words, it is unconditional. To strive for perfect love, as God's love is perfect, means to suspend judgment of others and to let go of expectations that they must meet in order for them to be acceptable to me. This is not an easy task!

Marion: Sometimes we confuse unconditional love with lack of expectation for the beloved. When Susan said that divine love is without judgment or expectation, she did not mean that God has no expectations for us. What she meant is that God loves us, whether or not we live up to those expectations! A human example would be the love I had for my own child as she was growing up. Although I loved her with all my heart, I still had expectations for her. For instance, if she lied to me— as little children often do to protect themselves—I would get very angry with her. I had an expectation that she be honest and truthful with me, and would become very upset if she betrayed my trust by lying to me. Yet never for one moment did I stop loving her—even when she lied. My love for her was unconditional, but that did not mean I placed no judgment on her behavior toward me. God's love for us must be similar.

Once we accept this kind of unconditional love into our lives, we can then derive our sense of self-worth from God's unending acceptance of us. Since God loves us unconditionally, we must learn to love ourselves the same way. As Macrina Wiederkehr has stated in her book *A Tree Full of Angels,* "it is time, then, for us to embrace this frail flesh of ours with love. . . . What was good enough for God to embrace must be good enough for us" (Wiederkehr, 1988, p. 85).

PRINCIPLE FOUR:
GOD'S FORGIVENESS IS ALWAYS
AVAILABLE TO US

Since divine love is unconditional, God loves us and forgives us our wrongs. This forgiveness is available to all humankind, no matter what their religion, race, or gender. This forgiveness is always available to us. It is *we* who turn away from the forgiveness that is offered. Let us look more closely at the nature of this forgiveness in an attempt to understand why it goes unrecognized or is even rejected as we travel through the ups and downs of our lives.

First, more so than the other principles in The Benevolence Model, this principle may conflict with the beliefs of some groups of religious people. The concept of divine forgiveness not contingent on some act of atonement or repentance may be unacceptable to some people. Some Jewish clergy and therapists may have difficulty with it, since, in the Jewish religion, God offers forgiveness but also demands justice. According to Rabbi Elliot Dorff, "forgiveness is not automatic. It has to be earned through the process of *teshuvah,* a return to proper behavior and relations with the injured party and with God" (Bradley, 1999, p. 29). Rabbi Leon Klenicki, director of the Department of Interfaith Affairs of the Anti-Defamation League, has expressed similar sentiments in his statement that "As a Jew I can forgive people only if they change—that creates an atmosphere of healing" (Bradley, 1999, p. 29). Some Catholics and Christians of other denominations may also balk at our notion of divine forgiveness without the need for atonement, confession, or repentance.

Recently, a Jewish psychologist who read the material in this chapter asked us, "Do you mean that you believe God would forgive *Hitler* for what he did?" We had to answer, "yes." When we think as humans it is difficult to believe that forgiveness would be offered to someone so hateful and destructive as Hitler, but God is not human, and we must not hold God to human standards.

Even some humans are capable of forgiveness beyond that which most of us feel capable. Psychologist Everett L. Worthington Jr. has written about his unusual experience in forgiving. He had just completed co-authoring a book on achieving forgiveness through empathy (McCullough, Worthington, and Sondage, 1997) when his mother was brutally murdered by an intruder. After an initial murderous rage, he realized that if he truly believed what he had written in the book, he had to put his ideas into action in his own life. So, he attempted to understand the murder from the murderer's point of view. He thought about the crime. The intruder, surprised that someone was in the house on New Year's Eve and frightened that she had seen him, had lashed out in panic, striking Worthington's mother three times with a crowbar. Worthington writes: "I felt I better understood what had happened. Whoever murdered my mom did a terrible thing. . . . Through empathy, however, I saw that he had lashed out in fear, panic, guilt, and anger" (Worthington, 1999, p. 31). Worthington thought about his own initial rage at hearing of his mother's murder. He thought about his desire to lash out at the murderer and beat him with a baseball bat: "I was willing to do what he did, only with more forethought, more naked malice than he. Whose heart is darker? I almost spoke aloud. When I saw the evil I was plotting, I was humbled" (Worthington, 1999, p. 31). Worthington was able to forgive his mother's murderer. Could we conceive of a God who is any *less* forgiving than this man?

Marion: I am reminded of a recent incident with one of my patients. A deeply religious woman, she was feeling guilty and shameful about having had an affair. She dearly loved the man with whom she had the affair, but had broken it off because she felt so guilty. She believed that God would never be able to forgive her this sin. She had a married daughter about twenty-six years old. I asked my patient, "If your daughter fell in love with another man and had an affair with him, how would you react? Would you be able to forgive her?" "Of course," she replied, "I would tell her I loved her and would try to comfort her. I would hope that she would realize it was wrong to continue the affair, but I would certainly forgive her." "Then," I asked, "is God going to be any less forgiving than you would be?" She smiled.

How can we expect God to be any less forgiving than the best of humans?

For many, this idea of God's forgiveness without our first repenting or atoning is still a difficult concept to swallow. Psychologist Warren Purkel has pointed out that although the Jewish and Christian Scriptures do speak of God requiring sacrifices, "Does this mean that God is *pleased* when we kill a sheep in God's name? Is that dead sheep intrinsically satisfying to God?" Not likely. "To think so," Purkel explains, "would be to imagine a very human kind of god-king such as Zeus from the Greek Pantheon" (Purkel, personal communication, 1999). It may be that God understands that it is *we* who need to sacrifice, atone, or repent, to forgive ourselves or be forgiven by others. It is unlikely that *God* requires such actions from us. As Rabbi Leon Klenicki (Bradley, 1999) pointed out, atonement or repentance is *healing,* but let us not confuse what is necessary for humans to heal and forgive, with what God would need.

Still, some will balk at our concept of God's forgiveness as it is presented in this chapter. No matter what one's religious beliefs, this principle can be applied within the context of individual faith systems. In working with a Catholic survivor who feels she needs God's forgiveness for acts in which she participated during her abuse (such as prostitution), one might want to talk about confession and penance. Similarly, in working with a Jewish survivor, one might emphasize the need for atonement. What is important is not that one agrees with us about whether God requires these acts or whether these acts are for *our* benefit. What *is* important is the notion that *God's forgiveness is always available to us.* Keeping this in mind, let us continue our examination of God's forgiveness, and why many of us have difficulty with this concept.

God's forgiveness often comes upon us unexpectedly; since we tend to hold God to conventional human standards of conditional love and conditional forgiveness. But once experienced, this forgiveness can transform our view of ourselves and others. Paul Tillich has eloquently described this concept in his book *The Shaking of the Foundations*. In the following passage, he refers to God's forgiveness as "grace," a term that encompasses the concept of God's forgiveness:

> Grace strikes us when we are in great pain and restlessness. It strikes us when we walk through the valley of a meaningless and empty life. . . . Grace strikes us when our own disgust for our own being, our indifference, our weakness, our hostility, and our lack of direction and composure have become intolerable to us. Sometimes at that moment a wave of light breaks into the darkness and it is as though a voice were saying: "You are accepted. You are accepted by that which is greater than you. . . . Do not seek anything; do not perform anything. Simply accept the fact that you are accepted." If that happens to us, we experience grace. After such an experience, we may not be better than before. But everything is transformed. (Tillich, 1948, pp. 161-162)

What an earthshaking concept—that we are forgiven the things we do wrong, without question, without having to do anything, without even having to ask! This means we are acceptable to God, and that we are truly loved unconditionally despite our many faults. Such an experience of acceptance and love could be truly transforming. And yet, we often reject this offer of grace. We resist the concept intellectually, and we fail to recognize or sometimes even reject the experience when it occurs in our own lives. Why would such a wonderful gift from God be rejected?

The reasons are many, and they manifest on all levels of our experience—personal and social. First, on the personal level, we sometimes fail to recognize the forgiveness that is being offered us. We are often so wrapped up in the difficulties of leading our lives that we do not take the time to let in God's ever-present grace.

God's grace, God's forgiveness, is always available to us, but we have to let it into our lives. An old Hasidic story told by Martin Buber illustrates this point:

> "Where is the dwelling of God?" This was a question with which the Rabbi of Kotzk surprised a number of learned men who happened to be visiting him. They laughed at him: "What a thing to ask! Is not the world full of His glory?" Then he answered his own question: "God dwells wherever man lets Him in." (Polsky and Wozner, 1989, p. 217)

To recognize and let in God's forgiveness is truly a life-transforming experience. A poignant and true story by Terry Dobson, recounted in Robin Casarjian's *Forgiveness: A Bold Choice for a Peaceful Heart,* conveys the power of forgiveness to transform our lives. The author of the story describes a turning point in his life that took place on a train in the outskirts of Tokyo. While stopped at a station, an extremely large and dirty laborer entered the train and began terrorizing the few people in the car. He was drunk and verbally abusive, and as he attempted to hit a woman sitting with her baby, the author thought he would have to come to the defense of those in the car with him. The author of the story was a tall, young man who had recently completed a long training in the martial arts. He recalled that his aikido teacher had always taught him that aikido is nonviolent and its techniques should not be used in public. "Aikido is the art of reconciliation," his teacher would say, "to use it to enhance one's ego, to dominate other people, is to betray totally the purpose for which it is practiced. Our mission is to resolve conflict, not generate it" (Casarjian, 1992, pp. 26-30). The author of the story had longed for a day when a legitimate situation would occur in which his martial arts training could ethically be put to use. He was very excited because such an opportunity had seemed to have arisen, as the drunken man continued to threaten the others on the train.

Just as the author was about to act, a little old man shouted, "Hey." Everyone turned to look at the old man who was smiling at the drunken laborer and indicated that he had a secret to share. He beckoned the drunken man to come over to him and talk. Though still belligerent, the laborer decided to approach this peculiar man to hear him out. The old man explained that like the drunken man, he too loved sake. The laborer's expression softened as he proclaimed his own love for sake. Then the old man smiled at him and said, "And I'm sure you have a wonderful wife," to which the laborer sadly replied, "I don't got no wife." Sobbing, the man explained that he had little in life. The little old man listened sympathetically and asked the laborer to sit next to him and tell him all about it.

Just then the train arrived at Dobson's stop and he had to leave. As he maneuvered his way out onto the platform, he turned back for one last look. He was amazed to see that "the laborer was sprawled like a sack on the seat, his head in the old man's lap. The gentleman was looking down at him kindly, a beatific mixture of delight and compassion beaming from his eyes, one hand softly stroking the filthy, matted head" (Casarjian, 1992, p. 30).

This incident powerfully illustrates how we can be transformed by the offering of forgiveness. The author of the story took a very common human stance—that there are good people and bad people, and that violence is justified in the service of protecting the good from the bad. The old man, however, took a stance toward the drunk that is very different from our normal way of viewing violent behavior. He knew that underneath the abusive behavior was a great deal of pain and woundedness. Rather than condemning this man for his violence toward others, he offered the man compassion, love, and forgiveness. Surrounded by this attitude of loving forgiveness, the drunk was able to drop his mask, and face the real pain that was underlying his violent behavior. He was transformed by the forgiveness.

> **Marion:** As this story illustrates, God's love and grace are often brought into the world through people. It is often through our interactions with others that we come to experience this love. When I think of my own experiences with the transforming power of love and forgiveness, I think of small incidents in my life this past year—incidents that on the surface would not appear significant, but which nonetheless constitute powerful illustrations of this transforming power of love. One such incident occurred at a shopping mall. My daughter and I had decided to stop for a snack at a shop that

sold fine chocolates. When we entered the store, the woman behind the counter was attending to another customer. Both my daughter and I noticed that the storekeeper looked unhappy and was speaking to the customer in a voice that could almost be called "nasty." Somehow, we felt sad for her in her unhappiness. When it was our turn, without thinking, I smiled at her and said hello. Something about that smile, an expression of caring from a stranger, transformed her. Suddenly, her face lit up and she smiled back. We chatted while she measured out the chocolate, and as my daughter and I left the store, we noticed that she looked genuinely happy. She was approaching her next customer with a smile. Not a life-transforming experience by any means, but the expression of caring by another had the power to change her outlook and mood. Because she was able to let in our caring, she no longer felt the need to be curt and nasty to others.

A second incident occurred not long afterward. I was about to take my seat on a plane and was putting my luggage in an overhead bin above my seat, when a woman began to yell at me: "That's my spot. You can't use that space!" She had shouted so loudly that everyone around us turned to look. My first reaction was to think: "Who does she think she is, telling me I cannot put my luggage in an overhead bin because she wants the space?" But then I thought about why this woman would yell at me like this, and I suddenly realized that only someone who was unhappy and hurting would overreact as she had. Any initial anger I might have had seemed to melt away and was replaced with compassion for her pain. Instead of reacting in anger, I just calmly told her not to worry—that the plane was not going to be full, and that there was plenty of room for all our luggage. After we sat down, I noticed that this woman was extremely nervous, especially when the plane was about to take off. It was then that I realized that she was nervous about flying, and this anxiety must have prompted her rude behavior toward me. About an hour into the flight, she turned to me and gave me a big smile. Calmer, now that the plane had leveled off, she was able to show her appreciation of my gentle treatment of her.

Both incidents illustrate the transforming power of love and forgiveness. The kind of love and forgiveness I had to offer these two women, however, are merely reflections of the even greater unconditional love and forgiveness that God has to offer us. The power of God's grace to transform our lives is beyond description.

To be truly life-transforming, our acceptance of God's forgiveness must reach a deeper level of our being than a mere intellectual understanding of the concept of grace. Imagine for a moment what it would be like to truly awaken to the reality of God's unconditional love and forgiveness—to awaken to the reality that we are accepted and loved beyond limit no matter what we have done with our lives, no matter how we have treated ourselves and others, and no matter whom we have hurt along the way. Through such a deep acceptance of God's grace, we could become again the little innocent children we once were. Like babies, we would not worry about our worth. We would not fear that we are unacceptable. In such a state of self-acceptance, we would be letting go of the concept that we are good or bad depending on what we do. There would be no sense of shame.

People who are truly self-accepting are self-loving, and out of that love comes an acceptance and love for others. Such is the joyful experience of those who live in the light of God's ever-present forgiveness or grace. In answer to the moralists who find grace to be a morally dangerous concept, Lewis Smedes has wisely written, "grace genuinely experienced is not really dangerous at all. What is dangerous is the wearisome, joy-killing heaviness of living without grace" (Smedes, 1994, p. 113).

PRINCIPLE FIVE:
WE ARE CALLED TO LOVE GOD,
OURSELVES, AND OTHERS

The Judeo-Christian ethic strongly emphasizes the importance of love for God and for all humankind. Out of the love of God flows love for our neighbors, but note that implicit in these commandments is that we love ourselves as well. To love our neighbor as ourselves implies a love of self. This self-love does not come easy for most of us—particularly for those who have been abused as children. In Chapter 4 we will explore more about how such self-love can be achieved.

Our greatest commandment, our task in life, is to learn to love God, ourselves, and others. We take this commandment to be the most important, since out of it flows all the others. This is what we are here for—to learn to experience and extend love.

A most important point is that God has given us free will—to choose to act out of that love or not. M. Scott Peck has explained that "to create us in His image, God gave us free will. To have done otherwise would have been to make us puppets or hollow mannequins. Yet to give us free will God had to forswear the use of force against us. We do not have free will when there is a gun pointed at our back" (Peck, 1983, p. 204). If we were to be rewarded by God for doing good deeds and punished for doing bad deeds, then choosing good would have no spiritual meaning. Like little children, we would be doing good in order to reap the rewards and avoid punishment rather than freely choosing to live in keeping with God's will. When one person aims to hurt another, God will not intervene to prevent it, because to do so would be to take away that person's free will. It could be no other way. God waits patiently for us to learn to love one another and to act toward one another only out of that love, but we have to choose to do so. However, while God will not intervene to prevent us from being hurt by others, God is always there to ease the pain when we are suffering. This notion of God being available to us in our suffering will be explored further in Chapter 4, but it should be noted here that this notion is as much a part of Judaism as it is of Christianity. David Wolpe, in his book *The Healer of Shattered Hearts,* makes this point: "For most Jews the notion that God suffers seems profoundly Christian. Indeed it stands at the very center of Christian theology in the image of Jesus on the cross. But it is an idea with deep Jewish roots, and its resonance for Christians should not deprive Jews of the opportunity of exploring its impact upon Judaism and Jewish life." Furthermore, he writes, no one suffers alone: "No matter how quiet or hidden the suffering, how silent the afflicted, there is One who not only knows of it, but likewise feels the pain. There are lives of quiet desperation, but no lives of solitary desperation, for all suffering is shared" (Wolpe, 1990, p. 127).

We believe God has given us free will with the hopes that we will freely choose to bring love into the world through our interactions with one another. When we choose not to act according to divine law, as so often we humans do, we cause suffering and pain for others. God cannot prevent this suffering and pain, but is always there to ease the suffering.

The implications of this concept of free will are far-reaching. No longer is mere external conformity to a law a true fulfillment of that law. Our actions toward others must truly be based in a desire to fulfill the purpose of divine law—to love God, our neighbors, and ourselves. An old Hasidic story emphasizes the importance of avoiding strict mechanical observance of the laws:

> On a certain Purim, when the Rabbi of Mogeilnica was reading the scroll of Esther, a young man stood nearby and said to him when the reading was over: "I fear I did not listen closely enough and perhaps skipped over one word or another while I was silently reciting the scroll with you."
>
> Later, the rabbi said to his friends: "There's your superpious man! All he cares about is doing exactly what is prescribed. But he whose soul is directed toward doing the will of God within the commandment, and clings wholly to God's will, may very possibly fail to do something of what is prescribed, but it does not trouble him. For it is written: 'In thy love for her wilt thou err constantly.'" (Polsky and Wozner, 1989, p. 221)

There is more security in a legalistic orientation. We feel assured that if we do the right things, we will be rewarded, and to avoid punishment, we need only avoid doing bad. But as Brennan Manning has pointed out, legalism is born of fear. In a frightening world, filled with violence, it is easier to believe that one need only follow a set of rules to ensure God's protection and safety than it is to accept that there is no protection from bad things happening. We are here to love and extend love no matter what happens to us. It is more difficult to live out of love than by a set of laws. John Powell has explained that "love will ask much more of us than the law could ever require. True love can never say 'I have done enough. I have now fulfilled all my obligations.' Love is restless, drives us on. Love asks us to walk many miles not demanded by justice or legalism" (Draper, 1992, p. 136).

PRINCIPLE SIX: WE WERE CREATED TO BE IN RELATIONSHIP WITH ONE ANOTHER

Just as we were created to be in relationship with God, we were created to be in relationship with one another—to live in harmony with one another, to love and be loved. Writer Chris Schlauch (1993) has used the term "holy regard" to refer to the concept of seeing the presence of God in each individual we encounter in our lives. Applying this term to The Benevolence Model described here, one might say that we are called to have a holy regard for all human beings, to see the spark of God's presence within each individual, no matter how hidden that spark appears to be. When we interact with all fellow human beings, no matter of what gender, religion, social class or race, whether they are "good law-abiding citizens," or "hardened criminals," we are to remember that God loves us all, and that a spark of God's love abides within each of us. In the Jewish mystical tradition, we are all called to "raise the divine sparks" that are trapped in all living things. These sparks are raised as we recognize them in others and by acknowledging the holiness in everyone and everything.

In Christianity, the emphasis is on Jesus Christ. Essentially the message of Jesus was that we are to love one another. Through both his words and behavior, he showed us how to treat one another with holy regard. The Gospel of Luke, especially, is filled with instances in which Jesus reached out to the marginalized and the oppressed— the crippled, the lepers, the prostitutes, the tax collectors—the people who were shunned by his society. Through his love, forgiveness, and healing, he brought people back into society, back into relationship with family, and back into relationship with themselves. All this centered in Jesus' self-giving love. Jesus' loving behavior toward others has provided us with a model of how to treat all our fellow human beings. This model for compassionate human caring has prompted Brennan Manning to exclaim, "what enormous potential for healing lies within the worship community! If what was said

earlier is true—that we can only experience the compassion and
unconditional acceptance by Jesus Christ when we feel valued and
cherished by others—then it is the parish family itself that effects
the healing of the self-hatred for the divorcees, drunks, scalawags
and social misfits burdened with emotional and mental disorders"
(Manning, 1982, p. 57).

Marion: It has been my experience that some Jewish therapists and clergy have great difficulty at the very mention of
Jesus' name, let alone the concept of using Jesus Christ as a
spiritual model. I have even heard it said that "it was in the
name of Jesus that millions of Jews have been persecuted and
murdered." And while it may be true that over the centuries
some Christians have perverted Jesus' teachings to justify violence and murder of the Jews, Jesus himself would never have
condoned such acts. Some people close their minds at the mere
mention of Jesus, because they consider him a Christian. Yet
remember that Jesus was not a Christian. He was a Jew. There
were no Christians in his day. One must not confuse Christianity as it was practiced over the past two thousand years with
Jesus Christ. It is important to separate the actions of some
Christians in the past from the loving acts and teachings of
Jesus Christ. This book is about breaking down the barriers
that separate human beings, about breaking down the walls
that we have built up between the religions, so that we can
work together in helping people heal. Try to keep an open
mind, rising above any preconceived notions or misinformation about Jesus in the service of helping others. I have found
that in my work with Christian clients, whether I personally
view Jesus as the Son of God is not important. What matters is
the meaning Jesus has for the client. I have learned to put aside
my personal views in the service of helping clients for whom
the concept of Jesus is healing. In addition, no matter whether
Jesus is viewed as the Son of God, he remains a model of love
and forgiveness that can be a source of guidance for all human
beings no matter what their religion. Stephen Mitchell has
suggested that in listening to what Jesus had to say to humanity we remember that "here, in the essential sayings, we have

works coming from the depths of the human heart, spoken from the most intimate experience of God's compassion: words that can shine into a Muslim's or a Buddhist's or a Jew's heart just as powerfully as into a Christian's" (Mitchell, 1991, p. 7).

The concepts of "holy regard" and treating one's neighbor with love have parallels in Judaism as well as Christianity. An old Jewish story related by Martin Buber illustrates this point:

> A disciple asked Rabbi Shmelke: "We are commanded to love our neighbor as ourself. How can I do this if my neighbor has wronged me?"
> The rabbi answered: "You must understand these words aright. Love your neighbor like something which you yourself are. For all souls are one. Each is a spark from the original soul, and this soul is wholly inherent in all souls, just as your soul is in all members of your body. It may come to pass that your hand makes a mistake and strikes you. But would you then take a stick and chastise your hand, because it lacked understanding, and so increase your pain? It is the same if your neighbor, who is of one soul with you, wrongs you for lack of understanding. If you punish him, you only hurt yourself."
> The disciple went on asking: "But what if I see a man who is wicked before God, how can I love him?"
> "Don't you know," said Rabbi Shmelke, "that the original soul came out of the essence of God, and that every human soul is a part of God? And will you have no mercy on him, when you see that one of his holy sparks has been lost in a maze, and is almost stifled?" (Buber, cited in Polsky and Wozner, 1989, p. 268)

While in Christianity one speaks of "Christ Consciousness" or treating others with the compassion of Christ, in Judaism, one might use the term "Torah attitude" or treating others "in a Torah manner."

We began this chapter on The Benevolence Model with the statement that God is love, and we are ending with the notion that we are vehicles through which God's love can be extended into the world. Before we turn to how our spiritual model was implemented in our work together, we close this chapter with one final story. The story has appeared in many versions, in several books, and has been attributed to many sources, from Hasidic Judaism to Eastern Zen philosophy. No matter what its original source, however, this story remains a powerful illustration of the principles of our spiritual model, and a fine introduction to the chapters on how its principles can be implemented in helping people heal from childhood abuse:

> There was a man, who after he died, was taken to see the afterlife. He was taken to a room filled with people sitting around a large table. The table was filled with food, but the people were all frustrated and hungry, because the spoons they had been given were all much longer than their arms. His guide explained, "This is hell." "That's terrible," the man exclaimed. "Show me heaven!" The guide agreed, and they moved on to view heaven, but much to the man's surprise, heaven looked almost identical to hell. There was the large table filled with food, and people with the same long spoons sitting around the table. However, these people were happy and well fed, because they had learned a most important lesson. The difference between heaven and hell was that those in heaven had learned to use those long spoons to feed each other.

Chapter 4

Implementation
of The Benevolence Model I:
Transforming Images and Experience

We have committed the Golden Rule to memory; Let us now commit it to life.

Edwin Markham

Now that we have explored the basic principles of our spiritual model, in these next two chapters we turn to the issue of how therapists and clergy can work together to implement these principles. The implementation of The Benevolence Model was not merely an intellectual exercise for us. We have attempted to *live* these principles in our lives every single day—though not successfully all the time, and by no means perfectly. These spiritual principles became a framework that informed not only our work with survivors but our everyday interactions with one another and with the other people in our lives. We continue to grow and change as we practice the lifestyle to which these spiritual principles lead. God's love within empowers each of us to live the principles of The Benevolence Model. We make this point of our ongoing attempts to *live* these principles, because if they had been merely intellectual concepts they could not have been implemented consistently and honestly in our work. By no means do we want to convey the impression that we have mastered all these principles and live completely "holy" lives, nor do we intend to convey a "holier than thou" attitude, but we are aware that any attempt to implement the principles of this spiritual model, or any spiritual model for that matter, must include more than an intellectual appreciation of the basic principles. It is important to keep this in mind, especially when working with survivors of severe abuse, who are often very sensitive to inconsistencies and dishonesty in the people with whom they interact.

In this chapter we will focus on how we were able to implement this model in our work with Teresa and how other therapists and clergy can work together in helping survivors heal from their abuse. Chapter 5 describes how the principles of the model can be utilized both in healing images of God and in helping to reframe issues in the survivor's life. Most important, however, the chapter focuses on "healing through relationship"—in other words, applying the principles of The Benevolence Model, both in word and deed, in ways that can transform the lives of all involved.

In this chapter we encounter an intersection between the psychological and the spiritual, as we integrate the spiritual principles of our model with the therapeutic goals of treatment. Briefly, reviewing the psychotherapeutic and spiritual goals of treatment for survivors of severe abuse as described in Chapter 2, we aim to:

1. Build trust in oneself and in others
2. Create a sense of safety in the world
3. Create a new worldview
4. Teach life-coping skills
5. Present healing images of God so that the survivor can establish a healthy, personal relationship with God

In attempting to explain how these goals can be furthered through a collaboration of therapist and clergy, we will refer often in this chapter to our work with Teresa and her alters. We met with Lesley, Monica, and Brian (see Appendix A), but most of our work was with Mimic, the male alter who the others in the system felt was in most need of help. Steven spoke almost daily with Mimic for many months, discussing God and Jesus, attempting to heal Mimic's image of God. Perhaps, at this point, it is best to briefly review Mimic's story. (The identities of the other personalities can be reviewed in Appendix A.) Teresa's mother, using a variety of hypnotic and brainwashing techniques, as well as drugs, had apparently created Mimic. We are not aware whether the creation of this alter was actually intentional. Mimic believed himself to be a computer whose sole purpose was to carry out the Mother's commands. He would relentlessly punish the others inside as he carried out his "programming." It was through his relationship with us that Mimic slowly came to see himself as human, entitled to the love and forgiveness to which every human being is entitled. As he embraced his humanity, he was given a new name, Justin, in a naming ceremony at the church. In this chapter, as we explore the implementation of The Benevolence Model, Justin will occasionally explain how our work affected him personally and how he was transformed from Mimic, a computer programmed to punish, to Justin, a loving being, part of the human being called Teresa.

HEALING IMAGES OF GOD

Research has demonstrated that low self-esteem and negative self-image correspond to threatening and punitive images of God (Benson and Spilka, 1973). The relationship between self-image and images of God appears to be reciprocal—poor self-image contributing to negative views about God—"How could God love me? I am so terrible"—and negative images of God contributing to low self-esteem—"if God punished me like this, I must be very bad." As discussed in Chapter 2, our images of God are shaped by our experiences in life and our relationships with our parents. People who have been severely abused, especially by their parents, tend to hold extremely negative images of God—as angry, uncaring, judgmental, punitive, even vindictive. While many survivors struggle to experience a sense of close, personal relationship with God, in such cases, they strive for the impossible, since one cannot establish a loving relationship with a God who is hated and feared as vengeful. Furthermore, holding negative images of God makes it difficult, if not impossible, to experience God's unconditional love. As we discussed in the last chapter, God's grace is always available to us, but it is *we* who do not accept that grace so freely offered. People who have been abused cannot experience God's love, because they do not feel deserving of such love and forgiveness, or because their image of God as vengeful and punitive causes them to flee. Such people need help in transforming their images of God. As Brennan Manning has suggested, healing our image of God heals ourselves

(Manning, 1986). Working together, therapists and clergy can help bring about significant changes in the survivor's images and concepts about God.

> **Justin:** When that unconditional love was offered to me through Steven, Marion, and Susan, I was able to look at myself honestly. They did not judge me. Marion said to me, "I don't hold you responsible for what you did to the others inside. You were acting out of your programming. You didn't know any better." I then felt safe enough to tell Marion about my programming. Marion promised me that no harm would come to me. Isn't that what God promises? In the space of that unconditional love I was able to grow.

Justin's statement suggests that it is not only what a person is told which shapes a perception of God's nature, but also how that person is treated. M. Scott Peck in *The Road Less Traveled* gives a good illustration of the difference between words and actions in forming our understanding of God. He writes about a patient, Stewart, whose father was a fundamentalist preacher. Stewart could never understand why he had a view of God as vengeful. "My parents certainly believed in God," he explained. "They talked about it incessantly—but theirs was a God of Love. Jesus loves us. God loves us. We love God and Jesus. Love, love, love, that's all I ever heard" (Peck, 1978, p. 190). When Peck asked the man whether he had a happy childhood, Stewart replied, "no," that he had been physically abused by his parents: "I got the shit beaten out of me. Belts, boards, brooms, brushes, anything they could lay their hands on. There wasn't anything I could do that didn't merit a beating. A beating a day keeps the doctor away and makes a good little Christian out of you" (Peck, 1978, p. 190). Since people tend to form their images of God based on their experiences with their own parents, how could Stewart have had any positive images of the "Divine Loving Father?"

Survivors of severe abuse are likely to project many negative qualities onto God. This is especially true in Jewish and Christian traditions, where God is often described as a parent. Those who were raised in homes where the parenting was toxic and abusive would likely experience God as arbitrary, sadistic, and bent on punishment. In addition, because severely abused children often blame themselves for the way they were treated, they may feel they deserve punishment and project this need for punishment onto God. God may also be experienced as uncaring and unfeeling, and a survivor might understandably ask, "How could a loving God let this happen to me?"

Whether the survivor has formed an image of God as uncaring or as angry and punitive, both the therapist and the minister must help her tackle the most difficult questions of "how did God let this happen?" and "where was God in my suffering?" if any significant spiritual healing is to occur. At the very least the survivor may be helped to make sense out of what happened to her. At best, she will be able to ascribe meaning to her suffering as she emerges from this painful process of questioning.

Many have attempted to find answers to these questions. Most such attempts have seemed unsatisfactory or incomplete to us. There are those who postulate that bad things happen to people because they are receiving divine punishment for their sins or the sins of their parents or even of their ancestors. Such an explanation is not congruent with the spiritual model presented in this book of a loving, forgiving God. Similarly, we reject the idea that God does not care about the fate of human beings, and therefore does not intervene. Both therapist and minister must attempt to answer these questions for themselves before they can be of help to the survivor. The three of us spent many hours discussing our own thoughts, feelings, and questions about the issue of how a loving God could allow horrible things to happen to God's creations.

What follows is our own understanding (incomplete as it may be) of how to bridge the gap between the terrible things that happen to people and the existence a loving, caring God. Terrible things do happen to people—war, starvation, genocide, rape, devastating illness. Perhaps no explanation will really satisfy all who seek to understand why. Perhaps we limited human beings are not capable of comprehending the meaning of such occurrences. Joan Borysenko (1994) has referred to the universe as a sacred mystery.

Steven: It is not that God is uncaring or that we are receiving divine punishment for our "sins." As we discussed in the last chapter, God has given us free will to live in divine love—to extend love and forgiveness to others—or to choose not to live out of this love—to hurt one another, to cause pain for others. If we only chose good because God commanded it or because we expected to be rewarded or even to avoid God's punishment, then we have not freely chosen to do good. If we choose to be good, to extend love and forgiveness to others in our actions, then we have chosen the good because we know it to be God's way. We have demonstrated that we want to live in accordance with divine law and are being most God-like in our choice. While it is our task in life to find our way back to God—to live out of that love and extend it to others—most of us, at times, act in hurtful ways toward other people. As we have discussed, often we lash out at others out of our own pain. It is not that God abandoned us, it is we who have turned our backs on God and divine law.

Some people have strayed even further from God's love, and are capable of horrible acts of hatred toward their fellow human beings, such as the Nazis of the Holocaust. There are those, the perpetrators of severe, sadistic abuse, for example, who inflict terrible pain on innocent children. Yet God does not intervene, precisely because we have been given free will to choose our behaviors toward others. Since we must choose on our own to live in accordance with God's law, we must be allowed to make mistakes—to act out of fear and hatred—even if our actions hurt others.

While God does not intervene to prevent others from being hurt by our own poor choices, *God is always with us in our suffering.* This point cannot be overemphasized. God has not abandoned us, no matter how severe the abuse, no matter how intense our suffering. As Rabbi Wolpe (1990) has stated, if God is caring, then God cannot be indifferent to our suffering. Although we may never understand why we have suffered, and we may never assign any satisfactory meaning to it, we can be comforted by the knowledge that God has always been with us, and is always available to us in our healing. Robert F. Capon expressed this simply in his statement that "the only way God's love makes sense is when it is seen as personal (not mechanical). He doesn't start your stalled car for you, but he comes and sits with you in the snowbank" (Capon, in Draper, 1992, p. 258).

Menachem Rosensaft, founding chairman of the International Network of Children of Jewish Holocaust Survivors, in an interview reported in *The New York Times,* stated that God could be found within every Jew who told a story or a joke, or sang a song in the death camps to alleviate the suffering of a friend. The God he chose to pray to was present in Auschwitz, not in the manner in which the victims died, but in the manner in which they lived. In addition, Rosensaft suggested that Raoul Wallenberg, Oskar Schindler, and all those who helped the Jews escape the death camps also had within them a divine spark (Neibuhr, 1995).

This knowledge that God is with us always, even when we suffer, can provide much comfort to those who have been abused. Karen Hilgers (1992), who is both a clinical psychologist and a nun, has related the following enlightening story about one of her experiences working with the severely abused. She had been meeting with a client, a highly spiritual woman, who was describing some of the details of her childhood abuse. The woman told of being kept in a small box for a very long time. Dr. Hilgers asked the woman where God was during that time. The woman answered "God was in the box with me." Dr. Hilgers then asked her what God was doing, to which she replied "God was telling me that I could hold on, and God was weeping."

Justin (formerly Mimic) expresses similar sentiments:

> **Justin:** The question—where was God in all of this abuse— initially posed no difficulty for me since I had no concept of God. Coming to know God and his love for me has been a process, not a singular event. So my thinking on this issue has evolved over time. The God that I have come to know and love has been with me throughout my abuse and my healing. While I do not know the purpose of my suffering, in some ways I do not feel I need to know the answer to that question to live a happy and productive life. What I have come to know and believe is that God was there all the time. While God chose not to intervene to alter the Mother's abuse because that would

have taken away her free will, God provided for us until we could get away and find a place to heal. It is only through the grace of God that Teresa was able to become multiple. Her multiplicity is a gift, not a disorder. Teresa could have just as easily gone insane or killed herself.

God is not my personal bodyguard, there to fight those who would hurt me. I have come to believe that God was deeply saddened by the Mother's abuse and wept for us. While God did not come down from the mount riding a white horse as many of us would have liked, God did provide places and people at some well-chosen times in our lives so that Teresa would not go completely insane. God gave Teresa the strength to hold on until she could find a therapist who could help us. We had been in many therapies before but did not feel safe enough to come out and let someone know us. When Teresa first went to see Marion, we were very skeptical. There were many inside who assumed she would be just like all the others. Some of us inside watched and tested her for years before we sent Robot out to see how she would respond to him. She did not wish to harm him or deny his reality. So we see Marion as one of the greatest gifts that God could have given us. Out of knowing her, so many positive things have happened to us. I feel that I have been given a second chance at life and that my suffering can be used to help others heal. While I would have not chosen that for myself, I also realize that without having experienced this abuse I, Justin, would not exist today.

Steven: This concept of God being with us in our suffering is an important one. Many people want to grasp this idea, because they desperately want to know that God is there during those times of hurt, of suffering, of pain. The need for a feeling of God's presence is evident throughout our culture. People are yearning for knowledge that God walks with them, even in their darkest moment. The poem "Footprints" illustrates this point. Everywhere you go, you will find the poem—even in the homes of people who appear to be nonbelievers:

One night a man had a dream.
He dreamed he was walking along
the beach with the Lord. Across the
sky flashed scenes from his life.
For each scene he noticed two sets of
footprints in the sand: One belonged to
him and the other to the Lord.

When the last scene of his life flashed before
him, he looked back at the footprints in the
sand. He noticed that many times along the
path of his life there was only one set of footprints.
He also noticed that it happened at the very
lowest and saddest times in his life.
This really bothered him and he questioned
the Lord about it. "Lord, you said that once I
decided to follow you, you'd walk with me all
the way. But I have noticed that during the
most troublesome times in my life there is
only one set of footprints. I don't understand
why when I needed you the most you would leave me."

The Lord replied, "My precious, precious child,
I love you and I would never leave you during
your times of trial and suffering. When you see
only one set of footprints, it was then that I
carried you." (Author unknown)

The poem presents a God who walks with us throughout life. People need to experience this presence of God in their lives. Truly knowing that God walks with them gives them the courage, the hope, the endurance to go on. The concept is transforming. In Justin's case, the understanding of God's presence gave him the courage and the strength to go on. I explained to Justin that the Gospel of Matthew both begins and ends with the concept of God's presence in our lives. In the very first chapter it is announced by the angel that the coming one's name will be Immanuel, which means "God with us." The rest of the book talks about Jesus who comes to be *with* us. He's with the blind. He's with the lame. Not only did he heal them physically, but half the healing resulted from someone being with them in their pain. God came down to be *with* humanity, to live with them, to experience their grief and pain, to give them some hope, to give them the message that would release them from the situation they are in. Matthew ends with the promise that God will be with us always: "And surely I am with you always, to the end of the age." This is an incredible concept, and it is transforming.

Clearly, the survivor's images or internal representations of God can profoundly affect progress in therapy and the survivor's spiritual growth. How then can therapist and minister work together to address dysfunctional images of God so that deep psychological and spiritual healing can be fostered?

First, the minister and the therapist can undertake an assessment of the survivor's actual thoughts and feelings about God. The therapist can often assess the survivor's concept of God through direct questions about how she thinks of God. Such questioning will uncover primarily conscious images of God, but the therapist must be aware that despite a conscious belief in a loving, caring God, there may be a discrepancy between an intellectual understanding of God and unconscious images—projections onto God which result from abusive relationships with earthly parents (Rizzuto, 1979). Information on unconscious concepts of God can often be obtained indirectly through an examination of dream imagery. Leigh C. Bishop (1985) has suggested that God may be represented symbolically in dreams in a wide variety of images—people, animals, or objects. The presence of pastoral figures, biblical names, and biblical symbols such as crosses, doves, burning bushes, fishes, wine, or bread can be suggestive of God imagery. The therapist might want to consult with the minister if she is uncertain of the religious meaning of specific symbols.

Clinical impressions can be supplemented with some of the assessment instruments available in the literature—instruments that assess the survivor's God image as well as other religious and spiritual variables. For example, Bowman and colleagues (1987) have created a religious ideation interview. The Gorsuch Adjective

Checklist (Gorsuch, 1968) assesses God-image on nine dimensions. The Spiritual Well-Being Scale (Ellison and Smith, 1991; Paloutzian and Ellison, 1982) measures both religious and existential well-being. Daniel C. Batson's Quest Scales (Batson and Schoenrade, 1991) address existential questions in an open-ended way. The Quest is especially suited for survivors of severe childhood abuse, because this population often has religious and spiritual issues that are not easily addressed by conventional tests—issues such as the meaning and value of life, why bad things happen to good people, etc.

The minister can also gather information about how the survivor conceptualizes God through direct questioning of the survivor. Elizabeth Bowman and William E. Amos (1993) have suggested that the minister talk with the survivor about how she came to view God as she does. The minister might ask, "Who in your life acted as you believe God acts toward you?" and then discuss whether those images of God are supported in the Scriptures. A caution is in order here, though, since the images that the survivor describes may not correspond to those held by the therapist or the minister. In fact, the survivor may *never* develop an image of God that corresponds to our own. Each survivor has her own path to healing. We must be open to accepting many different images of God and help the survivor find one that is meaningful to *her*. We who want to help can follow along with her and provide support and even direction at times, but we cannot tell her where she should end up. It is not our job to change the survivor's images so that they agree with ours. It is our job to help survivors heal dysfunctional images of God that are contributing to their pain and confusion.

This might mean that rather than viewing God as a vengeful father, bent on punishing humanity for its sins, the survivor may finally adopt an image of God as a loving, nurturing mother or as the "Goddess." Those who are involved in a twelve-step program may adopt a term such as "Higher Power" to refer to the concept of God. The twelve-step tradition has adopted the concept of "Higher Power" because it is broader and more inclusive and does not alienate those who are put off by traditional divine imagery. Though such images of divinity might be unthinkable and even abhorrent to some members of the clergy—some Orthodox rabbis, conservative

Evangelicals, or Catholic priests, for example—to be truly helpful to the survivor, such images would have to be accepted and honored.

Although the minister might find great comfort and strength in an image of God he holds dear—such as God as loving father—most ministers will understand that such an image may not be helpful to all people, and that in the service of helping the survivor, new images can be explored. A statement by a survivor of severe abuse illustrates the need for clergy to search for many ways of imaging and conceptualizing God:

> I'm over 50 years old and I still visualize my father when I sing certain hymns about God. I'm starting to understand how this confusion has damaged my relationship with God. But it feels awkward trying to think of God as something other than a father. There's not much support for trying out other images. (Pellauer, Chester, and Boyajian, 1987, p. 178)

The challenge to the minister might be to stretch his thinking in the service of helping the survivor find her own image of a loving, forgiving God. Even if he were to reframe the "father" image—as "an ideal parent," for instance—the survivor may still have difficulty, asking why this ideal parent did not want to protect her from the abuse. The Bible is filled with a variety of divine images, as we discussed in Chapter 3, and it would be useful for any member of the clergy working with the severely abused to become well acquainted with alternative images of God. This does not mean that the minister cannot ever discuss his own views of God. In that sense the minister has greater freedom than the therapist, who must often restrict herself to helping the survivor find meaningful images of God without discussing her own beliefs.

The discussion of personal beliefs can facilitate healing in the survivor's thoughts and feelings about God. For instance, if the survivor is having difficulty with the concept of God as father, due to abuse by her own earthly father, keeping the above cautions in mind, the minister can explain how he personally sees God as differing from earthly parents. In his meetings with Mimic, Steven explained that God is represented in Jesus, and that everything Jesus does is a reflection of God. God had to become human to communicate who God is and what God is like. What then does the Bible teach us about Jesus? Steven pointed out that we never find Jesus abusing people in the Bible, quite the contrary. In the book of Luke, Jesus is depicted as reaching out to the poor, the outcasts, the wounded. To these people, his response is mercy and compassion.

As Mimic read the Bible on his own, he kept in mind Steven's description of Jesus as a reflection of God's true nature. Slowly, Mimic began to change his image of a hurtful God, and he was no longer *quite* as afraid of thinking of God as a divine father. However, despite this change in Mimic's thinking, Steven continued to focus more on images of God's love for us than on his personal images of God as a loving parent, because he knew that such imagery still held negative connotations for Mimic.

One way Steven taught Mimic about God's true nature was by referring to Jesus' parables. The parables were Jesus' message to all humanity about the nature of God's love. Brennan Manning has said that "the parables of Jesus reveal a God who is consistently overgenerous with His forgiveness and grace. He portrays God as a lender magnanimously canceling a debt, as a shepherd seeking a stray sheep, as judge hearing the prayer of the tax collector" (Manning, 1986, p. 17). Such images of God were much easier for Mimic to relate to than images of a divine father.

After an assessment is made of the survivor's images of God, the therapist and minister may want to meet to discuss what each has discovered. The therapist can, at that point, help the minister to understand the psychological issues underlying the God images, while the minister in turn can educate the therapist about the symbolic meanings and religious significance of the particular images uncovered. Both can use such a meeting to clarify their own understanding of God and how that understanding differs from that of the survivor.

Strategies about how to deal with dysfunctional images of God—as uncaring, punitive, vindictive—can also be discussed. For example, let us examine the case in which the survivor has formed an image of God as uncaring. When the survivor was being abused as a child, she may have lost faith in God, because when she reached out to God for help, no help was forthcoming. She might have felt abandoned by God, and experienced God as uncaring and cruel.

The job of the therapist might be to allow her to express her feelings—her disappointment, her anger at God, her fear that she has been and always will be all alone in the world. Then, having acknowledged the pain, the survivor might be ready to work on changing her image of God. The minister could help her heal her image of God as uncaring. The minister and the survivor could examine together those areas in her life where she *has* felt God's presence, when she *has* experienced God's grace. Although at first, she may have few, if any, incidents to explore, over time, with the help of the minister and perhaps the therapist, the survivor may begin to see that God had not abandoned her in her suffering. For example, the therapist might explore with her how the process of dissociation itself could be seen as a "gift" from God. The ability to "go somewhere else" in her mind during the abuse was a gift that allowed her to endure the horrific abuse without going insane. Even the lack of memories of some of the abuse can be seen as a "gift" which allowed her to continue functioning in the world to some degree. Similarly, there may have been people placed in her life—a grandparent, a teacher, a friend—who helped ease the pain and suffering in some way. Such insights, over time, help to counteract images of God as uncaring.

The therapist might help correct images of God as vengeful and angry by helping the survivor to see how she might be projecting images of her own parents onto God. The therapist might explain that people tend to project onto God characteristics of their parents and other significant others, and hopefully, the survivor might begin to see how she formed her image of God, the Father, based on her earthly experiences with rageful parents. The minister might then review the biblical images of God with the survivor, examining and evaluating the validity of the survivor's notion that God is an angry God bent on vengeance. Steven looked to images of God from Jesus' words.

Steven: Jesus spent much of his teaching challenging and re-framing people's image of God. Jesus called God his "Abba," daddy—an image of God who embraces us, cares for us, and nurtures us, a God of love, not of violence and wrath. Often the abused have only negative experiences and images of parents as abusive and violent. They fear those in authority and power. The last thing they need is a God of vengeance and power, who inconsistently controls their lives with his anger. In their broken condition they need to experience God as "daddy," the one who can transform their view of themselves as having worth and value, as dearly loved children.

A survivor's feelings of anger at God can also be examined in the therapy, since no true healing of dysfunctional images of God will take place without a healing of the anger. Some of her anger may stem from God's "refusal" to answer her prayers during the abuse. Rage at God for allowing the abuse to happen in the first place is not uncommon. There are often transference aspects of this anger too, as the survivor displaces unresolved angry feelings she has for her parents onto God (White, 1985). Often, the survivor will fear God's wrathful punishment for even having, much less expressing, such an unacceptable emotion. Such fears are too often reinforced by religious institutions. Many people have learned at home or at church or synagogue that it is sinful to feel anger toward God; though it is possible that some Jewish survivors may have *some-what* less difficulty expressing anger at God than some Christians, since open dialogue with God is an integral part of the Jewish tradition.

For some survivors, anger at God will be equated with evil. Fears of God's wrathful response may thus force some survivors to banish their anger into their subconscious, in an attempt to hide it from themselves, others, and especially God. Yet anger is most harmful when it is hidden from conscious awareness. Psychologist William Gaultiere has suggested that when this anger at God is hidden, it festers into a sore of resentment and bitterness that infects emotional and spiritual lives: "their emotions get clogged up inside and their relationship with God becomes sterile and void of intimacy" (Gaultiere, 1989, p. 38). Gaultiere further suggests that the best way for the therapist to help clients deal with their anger at God is to establish a therapeutic relationship in which the therapist serves as an ambassador or representative of God's love to the client. He has found that when clients see his empathy with their anger at God, they begin also to feel God's compassionate understanding of their anger: "Giving clients permission to be angry at God allows clients to go beyond repressing, internalizing or intellectualizing their anger to actually experiencing their anger and exploring its causes and consequences" (p. 44). We might add that the minister, who is clearly seen as a representative of God, also lends legitimacy to the anger by encouraging its free expression.

One particular problem encountered by survivors of severe parental abuse in dealing with anger at God is their fear of reprisal, based on their very real experiences with their earthly parents. Since expressions of anger, or even feelings *perceived* as anger by their abusive parents, often led to sadistic, horrible punishments, such survivors would expect similar treatment from the "Heavenly Father." The survivor must be helped to see that God does not reject us for our anger, nor are we punished. Examples of healthy parental reactions to their children's anger might be used to illustrate this point, since the survivor is unlikely to be able to discern normal, healthy parental behaviors on her own.

Marion: When attempting to explain about normal parents and how they react to anger in their children, I have often referred back to an experience I had many years ago. One of my first supervisors, Paul, had brought his six-year-old son to work one day. To amuse the child during the long day, Paul had brought along a portable tape recorder so his son could record his own voice and play the tape back, listening to what he had said. The child was delighted, and evidently wanting to make a message for his dad, he immediately set to work saying whatever first came to mind: "Hello, Daddy. I love you. I hate you. Goodbye." Paul smiled at his son, knowing that such ambivalence was normal, and that his son had found a healthy outlet for his anger at his father. When I tell this story to clients who are fearful of God's reaction to their anger, I ask, "Would you expect God to be any less understanding and accepting than my supervisor? How would you expect a loving God to react to our anger?" Based on the story, the only possible answer is that God would be at least as compassionate as Paul, if not more.

The therapist must also help the survivor deal with those aspects of her anger at God that represent hurt and pain from other relationships in her life. Important to the therapy is the attempt to distinguish between anger at God for allowing the abuse, and unresolved transference issues in which anger at the abuser is projected onto God. Needless to say, as this work progresses, the therapist has to be prepared to be the object of such transferred anger as well; just as people tend to project characteristics of their parents onto God, so they tend to do with their therapists.

Anger at members of the clergy can be a more complicated issue. First of all, as a "representative" of God, the minister is a likely target for the transference of angry feelings at God. However, sometimes the survivor has actually been abused by a member of the clergy. Such abuse does happen, though we tend to not want to believe it exists. Yet, when the abuse has been perpetrated by someone who represented spiritual or religious authority, such experiences have profound effects on the survivor's faith, on her image of God, and on her sense of trust in any member of the clergy. The minister must be mindful of these potential problems, but also of his great opportunity to promote healing of the survivor's images of clergy and of God.

Healing God imagery leads to the development or deepening of faith. For those who have been severely abused, faith in God may have been severely shaken, since despite passionate pleas for God's intervention on their behalf, the abuse continued. It would appear to a child that God had abandoned her, and that there really is no safety in the world. True safety, however, does not exist in the absence of danger, but is found in our sense that God has not abandoned us no matter what we have done, no matter what has happened to us. We cannot hide or run away from all the dangers of the world. Sometimes, bad things will happen, and we cannot look to God to prevent them. A true sense of safety in the world can only come when we no longer experience God as uncaring or vengeful and punitive, but as present with us.

Marion: I am reminded of a client of mine who had been raped by her father in her bedroom at night. Since her Catholic education had led her to view God as a father, she was terrified that God would hurt her, unexpectedly, especially when she was in bed at night. Although a grown woman, she feared God as violent and unpredictable, because her childhood experiences with her father had shaped her images of God. Nowhere in the world felt safe to her, because, at any moment, God might strike. She lived in a constant state of terror. It is not until she had healed her image of God through her work with me in therapy, and through many discussions with her priest, that she began to feel a sense of safety in the world.

Although we may never understand why bad things have happened to us, when we have healed our images of God, we can trust that ultimately, we will be okay. This sense that we will be "okay" no matter what happens relates to having "faith."

> **Steven:** When I think of faith, I always think of the image of the little boy who is in a burning house. The family has escaped, but the father notices that one child, a little boy, has been left behind. The house is blazing and the father cannot go back in to find him. All of a sudden, his son appears at a second story window, from which smoke is billowing. He yells, "Jump, Son. I'll catch you." The little boy cannot see a thing because of the smoke, and so he yells, "But Dad, I can't see you!" Dad implores: "Jump, Son!" The little boy replies again: "But Dad, I can't see you," to which the dad says "But *I* can see *you*." That whole image of having faith is like the child jumping out of the window when he does not really know for sure his father is going to be there to catch him—having faith, trusting that God is going to be there.

Reclaiming that sense of faith is important for survivors so that it can be used in the service of healing from the effects of the abuse. In sum, as the survivor's imagery of God is healed, she grows emotionally and spiritually, coming to feel a greater sense of security in the world. An unending cycle is at work here: healing images of God deepen faith, and the deepening faith leads to further emotional and spiritual growth, which in turn can lead to deepening and further development of faith. When the therapist and minister work together in helping to heal the survivor's conscious and unconscious images of God, the process of healing from the effects of abuse can be immeasurably enriched.

TRANSFORMING EXPERIENCE

God imagery is by no means the only area of the survivor's spiritual experience that has been damaged by the severe abuse. Often, there has been so much damage to her faith, her understanding of religion, and to her understanding of the Scriptures, that years of reparative work may be necessary. Once again, the collaboration between therapist and clergy can enhance the process, and they help the survivor transform dysfunctional thoughts, images, and behaviors that can result from the abuse. For instance, biblical language may take on different meanings for the survivor than for others who have not been abused, due to the circumstances associated with the abuse. The survivor may need help in changing her understanding of that language, help in ridding that language of its associations with the abuse, so that the true intention and meanings of the words can be appreciated.

Transformation of this order is accomplished using a therapeutic technique called "reframing." Paul Watzlawick, John Weakland, and Richard Fisch (1974) in their book on problem resolution, have explained reframing as a shift in one's conceptual and/or emotional viewpoint in relation to the situation that is being experienced, and then placing the situation into a framework which fits the facts of that situation even better. This shift in viewpoint changes the meaning of the situation entirely. The facts are not disputed, only the meaning attributed to the facts. Watzlawick, Weakland, and Fisch describe the process involved in reframing as follows:

1. Our experience of the world is based on the categorization of the objects of our perception into classes. These classes are mental constructs and therefore of a totally different order of reality than the objects themselves. Classes are formed not only on the basis of physical properties of objects, but especially on the strength of their meaning and value for us.
2. Once an object is conceptualized as the member of a given class, it is extremely difficult to see it as belonging also to another class.

3. What makes reframing such an effective tool of change is that
   once we do perceive the alternative class memberships we
   cannot so easily go back to the trap and anguish of the former
   "reality." (pp. 98-99)

This third point, in which reframing prevents a return to old
thinking patterns, is illustrated by the following example. Many of
us have had the experience in introductory psychology classes of
viewing an image in a text that can be perceived in two ways—
either as the profile of the face of an old witch, or as a profile of the
upper body of a young woman wearing a hat. Most of us will look at
the picture and see only one image—either the witch or the young
woman. Once the other way of looking at the picture has been
pointed out to us, we can no longer go back to seeing that picture
only the first way. We have forever changed our perception of the
picture to include both images. In a sense, showing us a second way
to view the picture is a "reframing" of our perception—the concrete
"facts" (represented by lines drawn on a page) remain the same, but
our interpretation of the "facts" has been forever altered.

In this sense, reframing can be an invaluable tool for both therapist
and minister in their attempts to transform dysfunctional thinking
patterns, behaviors, and images into mechanisms for healing. One
word of caution is in order, however. The purpose of reframing is to
find new, healthier, and more effective ways of looking at aspects of
the survivor's life which have been adversely affected by the abuse.
The aim is not to invalidate the survivor's *feelings*. We are not trying
to tell the survivor she should not feel the way she does. We are
merely helping her to change the meanings of certain images and
behaviors so that they will not cause her so much pain. Keeping this
in mind, let us now look at how the therapist and the minister can
help transform experience through the use of reframing.

For the survivor of severe childhood abuse, words that may pose
no problem for most of us have taken on very specific, terrifying
meanings. Reframing the meaning of those words and phrases is
essential to their transformation into less frightening language.

Susan: For instance, Mimic's programming had included the
following: "The Mother's love is pure. The Mother's love is
perfect. Nobody will love you like the Mother." Yet it was that

very mother who abused her child in sadistic, torturous ways. When Mimic heard in church that God's love is "perfect" and that no one could love him as much as God, alarms went off in his head. Based on his experience with the Mother, God's "perfect love" was something to be feared. In therapy, the concepts of "love" and "perfect" had to be explored and redefined to differentiate them from the words used by the Mother—words that had sounded the same but were meant to confuse and hurt, and which held such dark meanings.

A similar problem arose when Mimic heard about the "fear" of God in church. For someone who has been abused, to be taught that God is to be "feared" carries connotations that stand in the way of forming a healthy relationship with a loving God. The abuser was feared as someone who could for no apparent reason strike out and hurt, could lock you in a closet for the night, or worse. The abuser evoked fear and trembling in the child who was being abused. When a survivor reads about "fearing the Lord" in the Bible, she interprets this as literal fear, as she felt when confronted with the abuser. How then can one love or trust a God who must be "feared?" To continue to speak of the "fear" of God would be to create a barrier to accepting God's love for someone who has been severely abused. Clearly, the word "fear" had to redefined, reframed, so that Mimic could relate to God without shaking with terror at the thought of God's wrath.

Again, we must remember that the Bible we read today is a translation of a translation of a translation. Words often had very different meanings in the ancient languages, and such was the case with the word "fear." Evidently, stating that we should have fear and trembling when faced with God was, in the Hebrew Scriptures, a way of saying that we should approach God with awe, respect, and reverence. Members of the clergy with their extensive knowledge of the Scriptures and the cultures from which they arose are best able to reframe such concepts as "fear," putting them in their cultural contexts and redefining them when ministering to someone who has been abused.

Similarly, when people who have been abused go to church or synagogue and hear about a theology of submission and obedience to God, such admonitions echo the abuse they experienced as children. Children of abusive parents are told to be submissive to their parents, and yet nothing they do seems good enough; nothing they do seems to prevent further suffering and abuse. Submission to authority brings with it terror and unpredictability. For such people, church or synagogue, rather than being experienced as safe havens that could provide them with a sense of protection and peace, become a source of reinforcement of the original abuse.

Clearly, both minister and therapist must be sensitive to their use of language, aware of the possible effects of the words they choose. If the minister, for example, is a preacher who is accustomed to using the phrase "fire and brimstone," some adjustments will need to be made in the way he speaks to the survivor. Although the phrase "fire and brimstone" may match his style and belief system, those words will likely frighten the survivor of severe abuse. In the service of helping the survivor develop a loving, personal relationship with God, such phrases must be eliminated, or at the very least reframed, if any progress is to be made.

Since Scripture has often been cited and twisted by abusers to suit their ends, much work may have to be done in reinterpreting the meaning of specific scriptural passages. In many homes in which severe abuse is taking place, abusers are fond of quoting "Honor your father and your mother" (Exodus 20:12) and "Children, obey your parents" (Ephesians 6:1). Some victims of severe abuse have told of having Scripture read to them while they were being abused. Sometimes these abusers are active members of their synagogue or church, respected by many. One can only imagine the effect this type of abuse would have on a daughter's spiritual and religious growth—not to mention the harm to her emotional and psychological well-being. In cases such as these, clergy must be alert to the possible deleterious effects of quoting Scripture, and must be prepared to explain and reframe the meanings of the words.

The concept of sin, itself, may need to be reframed. It is important for both the therapist and the minister to take seriously feelings of guilt over perceived sinfulness by the survivor as she "participated" in her abuse. We must not talk glibly of God's grace and forgiveness, but need to gently reframe the concept of sin over time. We also can contribute to changing her self-condemnation through our continued acceptance of her *despite* her "sinful" behavior.

Just as we can work at reframing language for the survivor, therapists and clergy can further the process of healing from the effects of severe abuse by helping the survivor reframe the *meaning* of that abuse. Even though, as we have discussed, survivors of severe abuse may never be able to fully understand why bad things happened to them as children, they can be helped to find meaning from their horrible experiences, to learn from the abuse, and in some cases to use that learning to help others. Julian of Norwich has beautifully expressed her attempt to find meaning in humanity's pain and suffering:

> So we pray for the grace to discern the true meaning of our painful and frightening moments, and our times of trial and challenge. The storms do have a purpose and meaning. As we view them from a distance we do become more confident in a power beyond ourselves that strengthened and guided us through them. As time goes on we become more and more conscious of that same power within us in the present when we face another period of darkness and pain. (Julian of Norwich, 1978, p. 118)

As Julian of Norwich has pointed out, we can be strengthened by our struggle to find meaning in our pain. The survivor of severe childhood abuse may discover not only the presence of God in her life during the abuse, but also God's continued presence in her life now. Such a realization can only serve to strengthen her and bring her closer to healing.

We are by no means implying that people who are abused have on some level "chosen" their abuse, or that they are responsible for what has happened to them, as in some form of karmic experience of payment for past wrongdoing. We merely point out that no matter *why* the abuse has occurred, the problems and symptoms that have resulted from that experience of abuse can be viewed as opportunities for emotional and spiritual growth. Such a reframing of the abuse takes the survivor out of the victim mentality—moving beyond the blame, beyond the pain, beyond the guilt and shame, toward hope for the future.

In *Lion and Lamb,* Brennan Manning (1986) tells of a concentration camp survivor who left a note on the body of a dead child:

> O Lord, remember not only the men and women of good will, but also those of ill will. But do not remember the suffering they have inflicted on us; remember that we have borne, thanks to this suffering—our comradeship, our loyalty, our humility, our courage, our generosity, the greatness of heart, which has grown out of all of this, and when they come to judgment, let all the fruits we have borne be their forgiveness. (p. 78)

This short note conveys the sense that, at least to one person, the horrible suffering inflicted on the concentration camp victims had not been senseless—that some meaning could be found in that suffering and pain. This brutal treatment of innocent human beings had brought out the best in many of them, eliciting qualities that they may never have known they possessed. Rather than hating his oppressors, the anonymous writer of this note was able to find some good that resulted from their actions. He was able to transform the meaning of the abuse and killing into something other than terror, horror, and hatred. And in that transformation came a forgiveness of the oppressors. Such a transformation might be difficult for us to understand. How could he, having seen innocent people suffer and die at the hands of the Nazis, having suffered so greatly himself, find it in his heart to forgive, to even thank his oppressors for providing so many with the opportunity to grow? To fully understand such profound transformation of the meaning of the suffering and abuse, we must first look more deeply into the nature of "forgiveness."

The issue of forgiveness is an important and often delicate one for therapists and clergy involved in helping survivors heal from the effects of their abuse. When confronted with stories of forgiveness such as the victim forgiving his Nazi oppressors, myriad questions will arise for the survivor of the abuse, for the therapist, and perhaps even the minister—questions that must be addressed if any growth is to occur. The survivor might ask the therapist, "Does this mean I *have* to forgive my abuser in order to heal?" To the minister, she might ask, "Does this mean I *have* to forgive my abuser in order to be right with God?" The therapist might ask, "Is it my obligation to help this person reach the point of forgiveness?" The minister may ask himself whether forgiveness is necessary for spiritual healing.

The dictionary defines forgiveness as the giving up of resentment against or the desire to punish. The root meaning of the verb to forgive is "to let go" (Jampolsky, 1983). Clearly, forgiveness is an important theme in the Bible. *Salah,* a word we translate as "to forgive," occurs forty-six times in the Hebrew Scriptures and refers to God removing sin from humanity. Two other words also refer to forgiveness—*kapar* (to atone for wrongdoing) and *nasa* (to lift up a sin and carry it away). In the New Testament, the Greek word *aphiemi* is translated into English as "to forgive" and occurs twenty-two times (Vine, 1985). *Aphiemi* suggests sins that are sent away, divine punishment remitted, and harmony between God and the sinner restored (Holderread Heggen, 1993).

Forgiveness for a survivor involves letting go of the pain so that it does not keep her from being happy now. It does not mean letting the abuser off the hook, so that the abuser does not to have to accept responsibility for what was done. Nor does forgiving imply forgetting the abuse ever occurred; such a forgetting would constitute a further defense against the reality—tantamount to denial or repression. Religious people often have difficulty confronting the existence of sexual and physical abuse as perpetrated by other religious people, and so the tendency is to push the awareness out of consciousness. But, as Allender (1990) has suggested, forgiveness based on forgetting is a religious version of a frontal lobotomy. Carolyn Holderread Heggen (1993) has suggested that to forget personal history is to deny the very person the survivor has become. For the Jewish survivor, the act of remembering the abuse may have a particular meaning that should be honored. Jeffrey Jay (1994) has written that Judaism has raised the act of memory almost to the status of a commandment: "Thou shalt remember." Through ritual and community participation, the act of remembering trauma is integral to the Jewish religion.

Therapists and clergy working together can help the survivor deal with these complex issues related to forgiveness of the abuser. Caution must be exercised, however, in dealing with issues of forgiveness of the abuser. We cannot emphasize enough how delicately this issue must be approached, lest we risk engendering guilt, shame, and resentment in the survivor. Particularly in Christian homes and churches, great pressure is exerted on the survivor of the abuse to forgive and absolve her offender. But prematurely forgiving the abuser can bring no inner peace to the survivor. One survivor explained that she had been taught that blame was un-Christian and felt pushed by her family to forgive the abuser. Another survivor had been told that she must forgive her incestuous father so that God could forgive him. What an enormous burden this young woman must have suffered. Not only did she have to deal with the effects of the incest, but she was made to feel single-handedly responsible for her father's state in the afterlife. As Carolyn Holderread Heggen (1993) has suggested, "to put pressure on a victim to absolve her abuser is not only cruel and insensitive, it is also bad theology" (p. 127).

Forgiveness is a process that has its own timetable, its own course. We cannot force the survivor to forgive her abuser before she is ready. In fact, we must face the possibility that she may *never* be ready to forgive. No matter what the personal views of the minister or the therapist on the need for forgiveness, no amount of pressure or cajoling will bring the survivor any closer to feeling forgiveness for the offender. In fact, such efforts would lead to guilt at not being able to live up to the expectations of the therapist or minister; or a premature "false" forgiving in order to comply with the wishes of the therapist or minister; or, in some cases, anger at the therapist or minister for pressuring her to do something she was not ready or capable of doing—anger that could lead to premature termination of therapy or to leaving a church or synagogue.

Keeping these cautions in mind, the therapist and minister can help the survivor in the following ways:

1. *Discuss what forgiveness is and is not.* Often the survivor is unclear as to what constitutes forgiveness, and may believe that forgiving the abuser would involve forgetting the abuse or absolving the abuser. Therapists can discuss with the survivor that forgiveness is a process with its own timetable, which differs from person to person. The survivor can be assured that there is no rush to reach

the point of forgiveness. Clergy can discuss the meaning of forgiveness in the Scriptures and help the survivor with any questions she may have about forgiveness from a spiritual standpoint.

2. *Help the survivor differentiate between forgiveness and forgetting.* As we have discussed, from a psychological perspective forgetting the abuse is not helpful. The therapist can help the survivor honor the abuse and where it has led her in her life, while still working on freeing herself from the emotional and spiritual pain she carries around because of the abuse. Clergy can become involved in the process by helping the survivor keep the memory of the abuse alive while still forgiving her abuser. Ceremonies and rituals can be created which honor the memory of the trauma, and, in some cases where it is appropriate and desired by the survivor, they may include forgiveness of the person who perpetrated the abuse. Such ceremonies will be discussed in more depth in a later chapter.

Forgetting the abuse is hurtful to the survivor emotionally, and can have very real practical consequences. For instance, if the abuse is "forgotten" as part of the forgiving process, then the survivor may feel she can now trust the abuser. Such a trust would be misguided and even dangerous. For example, one survivor who felt that she had to "forget" the incestuous abuse of her father, left her young children in his care for a weekend—with disastrous results. Forgiving the offender could even mean cutting *all* ties with that person to avoid further abuse, since he or she continues to abuse the survivor. Survivors often have difficulty with this distinction. "How could I cut off ties with someone I have forgiven?" Therapists can help the survivor understand that forgiveness does not mean she must put herself in danger of further abuse if there is reason to believe that the offender will continue the abuse. Some of the literature on forgiveness emphasizes accepting the offender back in one's life as a final stage of the forgiving process. However, a distinction must be made between offenders who have perhaps been somewhat emotionally or verbally abusive in the past but who are of no danger in the present, and those who have demonstrated a capacity to inflict severe, sadistic, emotional and physical harm. Survivors of this kind of severe abuse may not be able to make peace with their abusers, nor may they be able to maintain contact with such people because the offenders are still capable of horrible abuse. In such a case, forgiveness of the offender would free the survivor from focusing on past hurt and pain, while still allowing her to cut off ties with a person who is still capable of abusing her.

3. *Help the survivor avoid premature forgiveness.* Often, especially in those from religious homes, pressure is exerted to forgive those who have hurt us; and while such a forgiveness can bring inner peace, for those who have been severely abused the process of forgiveness is a long one, and individual "timetables" must be respected. Any pressure to forgive before the person is ready will be detrimental to her healing from the abuse. In fact, coercing a survivor to forgive can be seen as a re-creation of abuse, because like the abuser, the therapist or minister would be attempting to bend her will, increasing her sense of shame.

Arlo Compaan (1985) has described the case of a woman, Grace, who felt that because she still held some anger at her abuser, she had really not forgiven and was not healed. She wanted to be without anger and wanted to achieve the ideal envisioned by the Christian community. In an attempt to rid herself of the anger, she had participated in two "healing of memory" experiences. The first experience was with a friend and involved prayer, Bible reading, and meditation. Not only was this experience of little help, it created problems in her relationship with her friend because she felt judged. The second experience was with a group of people in a church where healing had been practiced for some time. Grace found these people very supportive and caring, and when she left them, she felt much better toward her abuser. She no longer felt the anger, and finally thought she was healed. However, in therapy, she began to recall additional trauma from her childhood. She became aware of more anger at her abuser and at God.

Discouraged with her inability to heal from the anger and forgive, Grace experienced a crisis in faith. Grace's crisis in faith was precipitated by specific beliefs that were at best inaccurate. First, she was led to believe that she had to heal her anger and forgive her abuser to be a good Christian. Second, she believed that she must give up all her anger at the abuser and at God for true healing to take place. Finally, there was a related underlying belief that only the absence of anger would indicate a complete healing and forgiveness.

What Grace needed from a therapist was support as she worked her way through the ups and downs of the healing process. True healing does not follow a straight line of improvement; nor does forgiveness come instantaneously. The therapist would not only allow Grace her anger, but would explain the process of forgiving. This process can be seen as an unfolding—with layers of anger and hurt being worked through. At times the anger may abate, but as new traumas are remembered and worked through, temporary exacerbations of anger at the abuser may occur. These exacerbations are not indications that she is not truly forgiving, but represent levels or stages in the normal process of forgiving, and the survivor must be supported as she reaches each new level.

What the survivor needs from the therapist is support, assurance that she is normal, and the presence of a nonjudgmental atmosphere in which her feelings can be explored and expressed. What is needed from the minister is validation that she is still a good person, even though she still harbors anger and is not ready to forgive. The survivor may also need to know that she is not offending God even when she is not forgiving.

Chapter 5

Implementation of The Benevolence Model II: Healing Through Relationship

"It is the relationship that heals" is the single most important lesson that the psychotherapist must learn.

Irving Yalom

It has been theorized that women grow within the context of relationship. The work of Judith Jordan, Janet Surrey, and the others at the Stone Center in Massachusetts, as well as the writings of Carol Gilligan shed light on this approach to understanding women's development. According to this relational model, women construct their sense of self through psychological connection and mutuality in relationship (Jordan, 1991a; Gilligan, 1982). One would expect a woman who suffered severe and unrelenting abuse during childhood to have had significant disruptions in her primary relationships, adversely affecting her development. Therefore, a relational approach to treatment would be especially helpful for such women.

Relationship also has a meaning on a spiritual level as well. The Benevolence Model is based on a relational model. As we have seen, reframing experiences and language is an important component of challenging belief systems and in implementing The Benevolence Model, but is not enough in itself to replace the worldview of a survivor of severe abuse. In Teresa's case, the Mother had instilled a belief system based on hatred and lack of worth, based on terror in an unpredictable world. Through the collaboration of the minister

and the therapist, a new model based on love was presented to
Teresa both in her therapy and in the outside world. Through both
words and actions we presented Teresa with a radically different
worldview on which to build a new belief system about herself and
her place in the world.

In Steven's discussions with Mimic and, to some degree, in Marion's sessions with Teresa, we emphasized that:

1. God loves *all* people and that we are *all* lovable in God's eyes.
   God's love is not conditional on whether we are good or bad.
   God loves us, just because God is love. Therefore, Mimic is
   loved by God. A most important point was that Mimic was
   indeed human, and entitled to the same good things as any
   other human being.
2. All people have value and worth, therefore Mimic has value and
   worth. Steven would talk to Mimic about how Jesus reached out
   to the outcasts of society, those alienated from both society
   and themselves, bringing them back into relationship with
   others. Steven pointed to the many references, especially in
   the Gospel of Luke, of Jesus spending time with the lepers, the
   sick, and the lame (all outcasts of their societies), offering
   forgiveness and healing.
3. Since God made people to be in relationship, it is through
   relationship with others that Mimic could discover his worth.
   Steven and Marion would often point out specific instances in
   which Mimic and the others inside had been helpful, loving,
   and caring to members of the church congregation and to the
   people in the community through Teresa's work as a nurse.
   Steven would reinforce the concept that Mimic had worth because he had something to give others (Bilich and Carlson,
   1994).
4. Steven taught Mimic that God forgives us no matter what we
   do. In fact, God has given us the freedom to make mistakes,
   and it is through an examination of those mistakes that we can
   grow. In addition to discussing these ideas with Mimic, Steven
   had given him Brennan Manning's *The Ragamuffin Gospel*
   (1990), a book that Mimic found especially helpful. Two quotes
   had specific meaning to Mimic:

- To live by grace means to acknowledge my whole life story, light side and the dark. (p. 22)
- Grace strikes us when we are in great pain and restlessness. It strikes us when we walk through the valley of a meaningless and empty life. (p. 25)

These concepts contrasted sharply with the commands the Mother had instilled in Mimic and the others about punishment for the smallest infractions. Extending this new model of a loving God to Mimic not only served the purpose of replacing the old worldview instilled by the Mother, but perhaps more important, brought hope to Mimic and the others—hope that things could change, that there was love and forgiveness in the world. Hope is an essential component of the healing process. In addition, the new model of a loving God became the basis for a new personality structure within the system.

Despite the obvious value of these discussions and readings for Mimic and the others, words alone could not have counteracted the effects of the horrible abuse. Herein lies an advantage of the collaborative process. The Benevolence Model was not only presented but *demonstrated* through the actions of Marion, Steven, Michael, Susan, and the members of the congregation involved in the support group we had established—expanding the "therapy" to the world outside the therapist's office. It was the demonstration of this model that accounted for much spiritual and emotional healing. Teresa did not have an "aha" experience in which she came to know God's love for her. She came to know God's love slowly, through her relationships with several people who showed they truly loved her not only with words, but through very purposeful and loving interactions with her. Through those experiences she came to see that there is a God and that God could love her. For Teresa, healing came through *relationship.*

EXTENDING DIVINE LOVE INTO THE WORLD

We were created to be in relationship, and it is through relationship that God's love and grace enter the world. People come into our lives offering us what we need to heal. Even in the midst of the worst abuse, children often report that there were people who brought some measure of relief and comfort to them—a relative, a teacher, even a stranger. Teresa reported to us that her eighth grade teacher, who was able to see beyond the acting-out behavior of a troubled teenager, unknowingly gave her a sense of her own worth so that she was not totally crushed by the abuse. We each can bring God's love into the world through kind and loving acts toward our fellow human beings—psychotherapy based on love for the client, ministry based on love for the parishioner. These bring about deep healing from the effects of severe childhood abuse. Therefore, to implement The Benevolence Model it is critical that the minister and the therapist incarnate God's love.

> **Justin (formerly Mimic):** There are many paths to finding God and experiencing God's love for us. I did not take a traditional path. My journey began when I still considered myself to be a computer, a nonhuman. I knew nothing of a concept of God. When Michael Hardin, my pastor, first mentioned the word "God," it meant nothing to me. He might as well have used "chair" or "cat." The Mother had programmed me with a command that included the concept of "the Superior One," but she had defined it as a person, in the form of Dr. Bilich. As uncomfortable and distasteful as that was to Marion, she was "God" in my universe. And she was to be feared. In many ways, my first experience of God was one who was to be feared. I finally came to know who God really is through the loving efforts of Marion, Michael, Susan, and Steven. Michael told me that God is love, but at that point I did not have an experience of love, so all I had was an intellectual construct.
>
> Going to church helped on two levels. First, I was learning more about God and who Jesus was. This helped to replace my old programming from the Mother. Second, it also helped by giving me the experience of forming a different kind of family, a family of choice—the church family. My most direct and influential learning about the love of God came from the interactions with Marion, Michael, Steven, and Susan. Each interacted with me in very purposeful and powerful ways. Michael taught me how to function in the day-to-day world. He took

me to my first restaurant, and taught me how to interact with people. Susan took me on other outings—ball games, movies—and helped me learn social behaviors. Marion, Steven, and Susan loved and cared for me on so many different levels. Through their loving support and unconditional acceptance of me, I came to know God as a loving being, and I came to know that I was truly human and worthy of God's love.

I did not have to act any particular way to be acceptable to God. All I had to do was to be willing to receive his love. His love was there all along. While God waited patiently for me to learn who I was, he was not a passive God. He sent people into my life to teach me that I am worthy of love. Just like he sent Jesus as a model and teacher of love, he sent Marion, Steven, Michael, Susan, and so many others to show me how to love.

Although God's grace often enters our lives through serendipitous events and meetings with people, we chose willingly and deliberately to become vehicles through which God's healing love could enter Teresa's life. To that end, we needed a model on which to base our actions. Although the principles of The Benevolence Model guided us, we turned to Jesus as a concrete model for how to "live" those principles and how to implement them in our work with Teresa. In fact, the basic principles of The Benevolence Model that we eventually articulated grew in large part out of our understanding of Jesus' teachings. We focused on Jesus, because Teresa was Christian. With a Jewish patient, a different religious figure would have been chosen. Again, remember that even for those therapists and clergy who are not Christians, the teachings of Jesus Christ can serve as a *model* for how to extend God's love and forgiveness into the world. Jesus need not be seen as a religious figure to use him as a model for interactions with a Christian patient. However, if other models come to mind that one believes embody spiritual principles, they should be used as a guide; but for us, Jesus best exemplified the principles of The Benevolence Model as expressed in our work with Teresa.

Steven: Jesus was well acquainted with the difficult life. Born in a dirty barn, to a lower-class family, considered illegitimate, rejected and misunderstood, he was familiar with pain, humiliation, and suffering. He knew what it was like to be hungry, lonely, and abandoned by friends. He experienced grief at the loss of loved ones and wept bitterly. His life ended in brutality, violence, and shame, as he was beaten, kicked, whipped, and crucified on the cross. Clearly, Jesus was acquainted with abuse, the injustice of human evil, and the violence of humankind. Yet, despite the difficulties of Jesus' life, he acted in love and compassion, and forgiveness. He reached out to the lowly, the outcasts, those on the fringes of society, the sick, and those broken from living life.

Through his love, forgiveness, and healing he brought people back into society, back into relationship with family, and back into relationship with themselves. These persons experienced reconciliation with others, themselves, and God—all this centered in Jesus' self-giving love. In the brokenness of Jesus on the cross, we see God's love more clearly than ever before. On the cross, God's presence with us is realized in the words of love and compassion toward the ones who would kill Jesus, "Father, forgive them, for they know not what they do!" Such is the Jesus who has provided us with the model for how to live in love and how to extend that love to others.

Using the principles of The Benevolence Model we modeled the love we were trying to teach Teresa. Much of our work centered on Mimic, the self-proclaimed computer, who became Justin. Keep in mind that Mimic was initially created to carry out the Mother's commands to hurt the others inside and keep them in line. Despite his abusive behavior, we offered Mimic unconditional love through our words and behavior. Justin recalls the effect that extension of love had on his development:

Justin: When that unconditional love was offered to me through Steven and Marion, I was able to look at myself honestly. They did not judge me. Marion said to me, "I don't hold you responsible for what you did. You were acting out of your programming. You didn't know any better," and so I felt safe enough to tell about the programming. Marion promised no harm would come to me. Is that not what God promises? It felt like Marion was forgiving me. It was like when Jesus was on the cross and said, "Father, forgive them, for they know not what they do." I did not really know what I was doing, because that was what I was trained to do. But I was hurting people, and I did not know there was any other way to be.

Although Marion held me accountable for what I had done, she did not judge me or punish me. Every time I did something "bad," or in other words, acted out of my programming, she would say to me, "It's okay. You can tell me what you did. No harm will come to you." No harm came to me, and there was no withdrawal of her love or affection or care. Love was not used as a weapon. That was the unconditional love of Marion modeling the love of God. In the space of that unconditional love I was able to grow.

People who have been severely abused as children live in shame, convinced of their lack of worth. Taking in God's love helps to heal these negative feelings, but often the concept of God's love is too far from their experience, likely to be merely an intellectual concept. In addition, as we discussed in Chapter 4, survivors of severe childhood abuse tend to hold God images that are punitive and vengeful, not loving. Even a religious figure such as Jesus may seem too removed from their lives to allow them to take in this loving message. It is the real human relationship—such as with the minister and the therapist—that will provide the survivor with concrete proof of her own worthiness in the eyes of God.

Although Teresa could understand God's loving nature on an intellectual level through an examination of the words and deeds of Jesus, she found that Jesus was too pure and holy to serve as a model for her. She needed human examples. She could relate to a person who modeled that love. Steven modeled the love of Jesus in his every interaction with Teresa. Even simple acts, such as taking out Teresa's garbage or walking her dog, took on great significance in her life. Teresa had been taught that she was subhuman, not even worthy of taking out other people's garbage. When Steven helped her out one day by taking out *her* garbage, it was as though a crack suddenly formed in her belief system. She began to consider the possibility that, despite what she had been told by the Mother, she might be a worthy person nevertheless. Steven continued to emphasize that God loves *all* people, that we are *all* equal and lovable in God's eyes.

We are called to be compassionate, open to hearing the suffering of others. In our work with Teresa, this compassion often took the form of empathy for her pain and suffering. On a psychological level, this compassion constituted empathetic mirroring, which some psychologists have claimed is necessary to a child's healthy development. On a spiritual level, it was through our love and compassion for Teresa that she was brought back into the community of humanity.

Psychologist and theologian Carroll Saussy (1993) has distinguished between self-esteem that results from an infant's experience with good enough parenting and self-esteem that grows out of the process of socialization—in other words, *foundational self-esteem* and *secondary self-esteem*. Foundational self-esteem is always based on a true self, an authentic expression of feelings, sensations, and needs. The adult who has been severely abused in childhood is not likely to have good foundational self-esteem. However, secondary self-esteem can grow out of her experiences in loving, authentic relationships, where her feelings and needs are respected and validated. Therapist and minister, each in their own ways, can provide such relationships for the survivor, fostering both emotional and spiritual growth.

As the therapist and minister model God's love in the life of the survivor, she finally can begin to understand on an experiential level the *concept* of God's unfailing love. And, as she learns from her experiences and interactions with others, she may find that this loving stance can serve as a model for a loving way of treating *herself*. In the Bible, we are asked to treat ourselves with the same loving-kindness with which we were instructed to treat others. Keeping in mind that we are called to love God, our neighbor and *ourselves*, this model of healthy self-love provides a basis on which self-esteem can be established.

HOLY REGARD

As we discussed in Chapter 3 on The Benevolence Model, we are not only called to be in relationship, but to treat one another with holy regard—to seek out the presence of the divine in each individual we encounter in our lives and to respond to the holy within them. Through both their words and behavior, great religious figures have taught us how to treat one another with holy regard. All of humanity—not just those of the "right" religion, or those who were socially acceptable—were the recipients of Jesus' or Ghandi's caring, compassionate love. Every human being is valued and cherished. To truly promote healing, both the therapist and the minister must strive to treat the survivor with such holy regard. Brennan Manning has written that, "the gentleness of Jesus with sinners flowed from his ability to read their hearts and to detect the sincerity and goodness there. Behind men's grumpiest poses and most puzzling defense mechanisms, behind their arrogance and airs, behind their silence, sneers and curses, Jesus saw little children who hadn't been loved enough and who had ceased growing because someone had ceased believing in him" (Manning, 1992, p. 74).

It is not always an easy task to see the spark of God within another, to treat all human beings with a holy regard. We are all imperfect, all wounded, all like the little children who in some ways weren't "loved enough." Because of our personal issues—fears, prejudices, projected hatreds—we may be blinded to the goodness in another. Sometimes the therapist and the minister may need some help in getting past personal issues that may be blinding them to the divine spark, the holiness within the survivor. In this regard, they can help one another. For instance, the survivor may be engaging in behaviors that appear "sinful" to the minister. She may be prostituting herself, for example, and the minister might be having great difficulty in seeing beyond her promiscuous behavior to the goodness within. Such difficulty would hamper any efforts to treat her with holy regard. The survivor would immediately sense his disapproval and even rejection of her. In such a case, the therapist might help the minister to understand the psychodynamics of this promiscuous behavior—explaining that it is not uncommon for survivors of severe childhood sexual abuse to engage in "promiscuous" behavior, even to prostitute themselves. This behavior stems from low self-esteem, feelings of being unworthy of better treatment, and a vulnerability to further abuse which results from the childhood abuse. As the survivor's self-image improves, as she comes to see herself as worthy of being treated with respect and love, her sexual behavior tends to change as well. The therapist would remind the minister that if he begins to treat her with the respect she deserves, no matter how she behaves sexually, that she will in turn begin to grow and change. Conversely, the therapist might be judgmental of the survivor's acting-out and self-destructive behaviors—lying, stealing, prostituting herself—labeling her, and focusing on the "pathology." Traditionally, psychotherapists have been trained to look for pathology; however, more humanistic approaches contend that people grow most when the focus is on their strengths, their potential to solve life's problems, not on what is *wrong* with them. Psychologists such as Carl Rogers have built their therapies on the concept of emotional growth through "unconditional positive regard"—an unconditional, nonjudgmental acceptance of the client's feelings and thoughts. The minister could help the therapist who is being judgmental to move beyond a focus solely on pathology. He might suggest that the therapist think of the survivor as a wounded child who is reacting to her pain, reminding her as well to look past those surface behaviors—the acting out, the defenses—to the spark of God within.

> **Marion:** My orientation as a psychotherapist is closer to humanistic than psychodynamic; however, my earliest training in therapy was from a psychoanalytic stance. The emphasis was clearly on identifying pathology in the patient and effecting a cure through a talk therapy focused on insight into the past. Despite all the changes in my thinking, I sometimes fall back into thinking solely in terms of the patient's psychopathology, labeling her, focusing on what is wrong with her and how we can fix it. Sometimes I need to be reminded that true change can come from viewing the survivor as a wounded child of God and providing her with what she needs to grow into her potential. I find that talking to Steven about my work with the survivors sometimes serves to counteract these tendencies to fall back into old ways of thinking about therapy.

Another way in which the therapist or minister can attempt to see the spark of God within the survivor is to ask God's help in finding it. Sometimes that spark is so covered up with hurt, protective defenses, and hostility that neither the therapist nor the minister is able to find its presence, no matter how committed they are to the belief that it exists in every human being. Sometimes we need God's help to see beyond the "badness." God can always see beyond the hostile, angry exterior. So we may turn to the divine, in prayer and meditation, asking for the ability to see beneath the murky surface. Only when we see beneath the surface can we truly treat the survivor with the holy regard she deserves.

Holy regard, as psychologist Chris Schlauch has conceptualized it, is analogous to Carl Rogers' concept of "unconditional positive regard," but it is of a different order. Schlauch refers to holy regard, not as love, *per se,* but as a way of experiencing and relating to another as the God in her or him. That means

> an infinite respect and reverence, a devotion to the well-being of the other, a deep sense of humility of how to care for the other—and the most important, a way of experiencing and relating to another that is made possible precisely because of God's holy regard for us, through others. To speak about holy regard, then, keeps in the forefront our appreciation that I and another are mediating a presence greater and other than both of us, that is present in and through both of us. (Schlauch, 1993, p. 95)

Perhaps the act of treating the survivor with such a holy regard is the greatest gift the therapist and minister can ever offer the survivor. In doing so they become vehicles through which God's healing love is brought into the survivor's life.

Treating a person with holy regard also suggests seeing the *uniqueness* of each individual. We have each been created with our own gifts and talents. Each of us has intrinsic worth and is essential to the whole of humanity. We can find our worth and value by using our unique gifts to help others, by making our contribution to the world.

As helping professionals, we are thus called to find the uniqueness within the survivor with whom we are working. We must not stereotype the survivor or label her in a way that denies her potential gifts. Although the survivor may be acting self-destructively or may be engaging in activities of which we do not approve, we must look past the outward behavior. We must reach for the gifts and talents which lie within, for these people will be and will become only what we expect of them. Goethe has written that "if you treat a person as she appears to be, you make her worse than she is. But if you treat a person as if she already were what she potentially could be, you make her what she should be" (Goethe in Fox, 1983, p. 85).

Marion: Other than providing a safe environment in which her trauma could be examined, one of the most important things I could give Teresa was a *loving* environment. Seeing Teresa as a child of God, a child who was hurting and whose behaviors, destructive as they might be at times, were coming out of that hurt, was essential to her healing emotionally and spiritually. I tried to treat her with holy regard. This meant first seeing the goodness within her, viewing her as God would see her. That was not difficult for me. I could clearly see her gifts, what she would have been had she not been hampered by the severe abuse. She was extremely intelligent, caring, and had a way of using her own experience of abuse to understand other people's pain. Over time, as I conveyed to her how I saw her, Teresa's self-image and her behaviors slowly began to change. No longer was she hurting herself and engaging in self-destructive behaviors. She was becoming more the person she was meant to be.

TRANSFORMING POWER OF LOVE

As we extend God's love to the survivor through our interactions with her, and as we convey our sense of holy regard for her, she is changed forever. Whether that love comes in the form of a good psychotherapy relationship, the loving and caring ministrations of a member of the clergy, or from the support of members of her religious community, letting in God's love and grace will transform her life.

Brennan Manning has explored the powerful effect of being truly *liked* by another:

If you communicate to me that you like me . . . you open up to me the possibility of self-respect, self-esteem, and wholesome self-love. Your acceptance of me banishes my fears. My defense mechanisms—sarcasm, aloofness, name-dropping, self-righteousness, giving the appearance of having it all together—

start to fall. I drop my mask and stop disguising my voice. You instill self-confidence in me and allow me to smile at my weaknesses and absurdities. The look in your eyes gives me permission to make the journey into the interior of myself and make peace with that part of myself where I could never find peace before. I become more open, sincere, vulnerable, and affectionate. (Manning, 1986, p. 21)

Peace Pilgrim (a woman who dedicated her life to promoting world peace) once said that love is the greatest power on earth. It conquers all things. A person who is in harmony with God's law of love has more strength than an army, because one does not need to subdue an adversary; an adversary can be transformed (Peace Pilgrim, 1991). Our work with Mimic clearly illustrates this point. Among his many orders from the Mother was the command to inflict harm on any of the alters if they interacted with Dr. Bilich. This harm might take the form of making that alter eat dog food or stand out in the rain, cut herself with a knife, or to go to a bar and prostitute herself.

> **Susan:** When Mimic first began speaking with Marion in therapy, he proclaimed himself "the enemy." It would have been easy to engage Mimic in battle—a battle to save Teresa from the evil part of herself. But Marion refused to see Mimic as an enemy. She saw instead a troubled, wounded being, who was acting out what he had been taught by the Mother. She looked at him through the eyes of love. And, although she did not approve of Mimic's hurting the others, no matter what he did, she did not cease to love him. Steven, too, treated Mimic with love and respect, explaining that while he could not condone Mimic's hurtful behavior, that Mimic was still worthy of love.
>
> Over time, as Mimic began to see that he was truly loved, he began to question the Mother's "programming." He gradually replaced the orders to hurt the others inside with a command to protect them. In fact, he eventually became an important component of Teresa's healing, protecting the other alters from the Mother's hateful statements and hurtful behaviors. Mimic slowly found his humanity and, to reflect the changes, he took the

new name "Justin." As Justin, he began to reach out to people in the community. He became the alter who went to work each day, extending love and caring to the psychiatric patients with whom Teresa worked. He was clearly transformed by our love from an adversary into an ally.

Steven: I am reminded of the story of the prostitute Mary who poured expensive perfume on Jesus' feet. All the disciples were upset about what she had done, but Jesus saw that the woman was responding out of gratitude. Her life had been changed by this man who had shown her love and acceptance when no one else would. Jesus pointed to her as a model of faith, and said that "you who have been forgiven much will love much." When we realize God's great forgiveness, when we actually take it to heart, we are transformed by that love and, in turn, extend it to others. Justin did just that. There was so much guilt and shame in Justin, pounded and programmed into him for years when he was Mimic. To finally have someone come into his life and say, "None of that matters. It's not your fault. You had no control over that. You, in yourself, are a good and worthy person," transformed Justin into an incredibly loving and caring person because he realized the *magnitude* of that love and forgiveness. Those who have been forgiven much will also love much.

We are aware that in the treatment of dissociative disorders, transformation through the power of love is not always accepted practice. As we have seen, many who have been severely and sadistically abused in childhood, like Teresa, develop multiple personalities as a coping mechanism. Often one or more personalities or alters is violent and hurtful to the others inside. Such alters are called "persecutor personalities" or "internal persecutors." Psychiatrist Frank Putnam, in his book *Diagnosis and Treatment of Multiple Personality Disorder* (1989), has described persecutor personalities as alters who attempt to sabotage the patient's life and may inflict serious injury upon the body in attempts to harm or kill the host or other personalities. These alters, Putnam claims, may be responsible for episodes of self-mutilation or for "suicide" attempts that are actually "internal homicides" as persecutor personalities attempt to maim or kill the host. Mimic would therefore have been considered a persecutor personality. Putnam makes the important point that these internal persecutors, despite their history of hostile behavior toward the patient and their negative reactions to therapy, can be won over and enlisted in the patient's struggle to improve the quality of life: "In their anger, they contain much of the energy and strength that an MPD patient needs to survive and improve" (Putnam, 1989, p. 109).

A serious question arises when the inner persecutor is believed by the survivor, the therapist, or a Christian minister, to represent a demon who has taken possession of the survivor's body—a demon that must be exorcised. The most prominent proponent of this approach is psychologist James G. Friesen (1991). Although he does not recommend indiscriminate and frequent recourse to exorcism in working with survivors who have DID, he does believe some survivors are possessed by demons that cannot be dealt with solely by extending God's love and grace, but which must be expelled from the body through a ritual of exorcism. He claims to have had great success with such individuals.

This position has sparked great controversy in the field of the treatment of dissociative identity disorder. Psychiatrist George Fraser (1991) has reported on seven cases in which exorcism had extremely negative effects. While not rejecting the use of exorcism, psychologist Chris Rosik (1992) urged caution, suggesting that the host personality may want to reject the dissociative disorder diagnosis and may go along with an exorcism just to avoid facing the diagnosis. Survivors have written of the horror of the experience of exorcism and its negative effects on their lives.

A study conducted by psychiatrist Elizabeth Bowman (1993) of women with DID found that almost all involved in exorcism had negative experiences. Bowman reports that the exorcisms functioned as traumas, resulting in severely dysphoric feelings, symptoms of post-traumatic stress disorder (PTSD), and dissociative symptoms. New alters were sometimes created, and several women had to be hospitalized. Bowman concluded that spiritual sequelae were the most severe and led to a cessation or severe curtailment of religious participation for many.

Based on his experience with patients who have undergone exorcism, psychiatrist Colin Ross (1993) has found that attempted exorcisms are always countertherapeutic. Such rituals damage the treatment alliance and create more symptoms. Ultimately, they reduce the individual's overall level of functioning. Ross believes that these negative consequences are, quite understandably, the result of the person's anger at being defined as evil.

Ross treats "demons" as he would any other persecutor personality: by forming a treatment alliance, reframing the demon as positive, correcting the demon's cognitive errors, empathizing with the demon's pain, and working to bring the demon into therapy as a life-giving source of energy and self-assertion. This position is consistent with The Benevolence Model and parallels our work with Mimic—on a psychological level, integrating him into the therapy, and on a spiritual level, extending God's love and grace to him through relationship.

We do not condone exorcism, and if one is being considered, we ask that the following be kept in mind: Be aware of all the pitfalls and consequences of undertaking an exorcism ritual with anyone who exhibits signs of DID. First, consider whether an exorcism is actually necessary. Few members of the clergy have had the training and experience necessary to understand dissociative identity disorder and, without such training, a minister could easily mislabel a persecutor personality as a demon. Such a misunderstanding might result in "casting out" an important and potentially beneficial part of the survivor's personality system. To illustrate, we need only point to our experience with Mimic, the persecutor personality who eventually was transformed and emerged as central to Teresa's healing process. Another possible problem arises when a survivor is fleeing the diagnosis of a dissociative disorder. Sometimes, a host personality, unaware of the existence of the other alters (though aware of apparent losses of time), will reject the therapist's attempts to discuss the diagnosis, fearing that it means she is insane. She may run to a member of the clergy whom she believes will perform an exorcism of the unwanted parts. We are even aware of some *Jewish* women who, when given the diagnosis of dissociative disorder by their therapists, sought instead to enlist the services of a Catholic priest to exorcise the "demons" rather than accept the diagnosis. Such an exorcism at best would not lead to lasting inner peace, and at worst could be harmful to the survivor.

The potential for expulsion of alters important to the personality system speaks to the benefit of an ongoing collaboration between therapist and minister in working with someone who has been severely abused. The therapist can educate the minister about dissociation and the existence of alters or personalities within some survivors of severe childhood abuse. Then, together the therapist and the minister can determine the best course of action. Difficulties can arise, however, especially when the therapist and clergy come from different religious orientations. For instance, it is conceivable that a case might arise in which the therapist does not believe in the existence of demons but the minister is convinced that this survivor is possessed. As belief systems clash, the potential for power struggles and turf issues will increase. The therapist and the minister fighting over turf and spiritual beliefs would only serve to increase a survivor's sense of chaos and lack of safety in the world. Again, it should be stressed that in such cases both therapists and clergy should be mindful of the need to work *collaboratively* rather than at odds in the service of helping the survivor. What is best for the survivor is always the guiding principle.

If, despite our warnings, it is decided that an exorcism is to be undertaken, rather than performing a formal, traditional exorcism rite, perhaps the therapist and minister can devise a more personal, "symbolic exorcism." Both Judaism and Christianity are rich in healing and cleansing rituals, ceremonies and imagery that could be drawn upon. Such ceremonies and rituals are more consistent with a loving, gentle approach to healing from abuse. It would be helpful to tailor such a "symbolic exorcism" to the religious beliefs of the survivor.

Remember, it is through relationship that the survivor is able to heal. Clearly the transforming power of love is more powerful than any particular ceremony or ritual. As vehicles through which divine love enters the life of the survivor, therapist and minister have the potential to bring healing and wholeness into the life of one whose identity has been split because of childhood abuse. It is this love, this shared grace, which leads to healing for *all* who suffer.

Chapter 6

Working Together: Guidelines for Therapist/ Clergy Collaboration

And remember, we all stumble, every one of us. That's why it's a comfort to go hand in hand.

E. K. Brough

A young woman with a dissociative disorder asks, "When I told my pastor that I have MPD, she became very uncomfortable and changed the subject. I and my younger alters have a lot of questions about God and our abuse. What kind of help should I expect from my pastor?" (Anonymous, 1993, p. 4). Another woman says her therapist gets "glassy-eyed" when the subject of God is raised in therapy. Meylink and Gorsuch (1988) report that while 40 percent of all people seeking help approach a member of the clergy first, less than 2 percent are referred to mental health professionals. Similarly, psychologists rarely refer patients to clergy. This is a source of frustration for many survivors. People working to recover from the effects of severe abuse hunger to add a spiritual dimension to their work, but often ministers and therapists alike are unprepared to deal with their spiritually challenging questions. This is where collaboration between therapist and clergy can be of most use.

There is no one right way for therapists and clergy to work together. Collaboration can take many forms. At the very least, therapists and clergy can make referrals to each other. The therapist can act as a consultant to the minister, providing him with knowledge and practical suggestions about how to deal with survivors of severe abuse in his congregation. Similarly, the minister can act as a consultant, providing the therapist with information about the survivor's religious and spiritual traditions. In this chapter we will discuss in more detail the ways in which therapists and clergy can work together, providing guidelines and suggestions for successful interactions.

TYPES OF COLLABORATION

Minister As Consultant

When a therapist wants to add a spiritual dimension to her work with a religious survivor, but does not want to impose her own values or religious beliefs, she might want to consult with the survivor's minister on a one-time or regular basis. Such a consultation can provide guidelines and useful information to help the therapist better understand the survivor, and can be accomplished on the phone with minimal time constraints. In such cases, the minister is seen as an adjunct to therapy.

Therapist As Consultant

Although clergy generally have some training in psychology— some more than others—they receive little formal training in working with women who are suffering from the effects of severe childhood abuse. Few ministers have had experience dealing with abreactions and flashbacks, and fewer still know about working with dissociative identity disorders. Yet, sometimes, clergy are asked to minister to people in their congregations who are recovering from severe childhood abuse. In such cases, some ongoing contact with a therapist can provide the minister with much-needed information and suggestions on how to best serve the survivor's needs. Again, phone contact is often all that is needed, though at least one face-to-face meeting is suggested.

Referrals

In this model, the therapist and clergyman freely refer to each other. For example, if a minister is approached by a parishioner who tells him about her history of abuse, he can refer her to a therapist with whom he has worked and has built a base of trust and open communication. Similarly, a therapist may suggest to a survivor with whom she is working that she seek spiritual guidance from a particular minister with whom the therapist has already worked, knowing that this minister is easy to talk to and knowledgeable about such problems. Sometimes the spiritual and religious issues that arise are too complex and difficult to tackle for therapists who lack a strong theological background, such as anger at God for "letting" the abuse occur. For many survivors, resolving such issues is often necessary for a complete healing from the abuse. Referral to a minister whose religious and spiritual background is consistent with that of the survivor is invaluable in such cases.

Elizabeth Bowman and William E. Amos (1993) have provided a good clinical example of the value of referral. They describe a patient with dissociative identity disorder (DID) who had several religiously ignorant alters who questioned the religious practices of the host personality. These alters often pressed the therapist for her personal views on religion. The therapist declined to reveal her own views, and realized that basic religious education was needed. The therapist could not make the referral to the patient's own pastor, since at that point in the therapy, the patient could not tolerate contact with any males. Instead, a series of eight sessions was arranged with a female chaplain whom the patient knew from an inpatient treatment. These pastoral counseling sessions resolved several theological issues that were contributing to the patient's suicidality. In the psychotherapy sessions, reflection on the spiritual counseling allowed integration of spiritual and psychological growth. The eventual outcome was integration of the alters and the emergence of a vital faith in the survivor.

Limited Collaboration

In such cases the therapist sees the survivor for therapy, the minister sees her for spiritual guidance, and both therapist and clergy maintain regular contact. The difference between this type of collaboration and the first two discussed previously is the degree of mutual involvement of therapist and clergy in the survivor's recovery. With the full consent of the survivor, therapist and minister can share their experiences, perceptions, and ideas about the survivor's recovery process. Planning sessions between therapist and minister ensures a smooth blending of their work together.

Full Collaboration

In this final scenario, therapist and minister are copartners in the survivor's journey to healing. Richard Gorsuch and Willa Meylink (1988) have proposed a model of bidirectional, coprofessional interaction, a model which comes closest to the one we propose here. In a full collaboration, therapy and spiritual guidance are offered as an integrated whole. Therapist and clergy not only meet regularly to discuss their work together, but also meet with the survivor. Therapy sessions can sometimes include the minister. Religious functions can include the therapist (e.g., therapist attending services one day). In such a scenario, therapist and clergy form an equal partnership, working together to bring healing into the life of the survivor. The collaboration between Marion and Steven described earlier in this book is an example of a full involvement by both therapist and clergy. In our experience, full collaboration offers the richest experience for all involved. A synergistic effect is realized that far surpasses the results of therapist and minister working separately.

However, there is no one "best" type of collaboration for all circumstances. Before deciding on the degree of contact and collaboration, several factors must be considered. First, consider time constraints. Therapists working in agency settings may not have the luxury of spending large blocks of time consulting with a minister. Ministers may be too busy to spend time consulting with a therapist regularly just to help one individual out of hundreds to whom they must minister. The degree of participation of the minister or the therapist in a collaboration also depends in part on the willingness of the two to devote the energy and time to learning about each other's field. A full collaboration takes much time and energy, and unless both parties are willing and capable of making the commitment, other forms of collaboration should be considered. In our own work together, we were not encumbered by time restrictions, managed care requirements, or agency policy. However, we recognize that in many, if not most cases, such factors will need to be taken into consideration.

Finally, a determination of the degree of collaboration between therapist and clergy must include an examination of the needs of the survivor: What would be in the best interest of the survivor? What does *she* want? As with any interdisciplinary endeavor, the survivor must feel free to discuss any problems that arise due to the collaboration between therapist and clergy (personal communication, Meg Maginn). Since the therapist and the minister generally come from different orientations, their approaches can conflict, especially if they also come from different religious backgrounds. Different work styles between the two can also lead to conflict for the survivor. We suggest, therefore, that the therapist discuss this possibility with the survivor in the early stages of the collaboration and create an atmosphere in which open discussion of such problems is encouraged.

BENEFITS OF COLLABORATION

Collaboration Brings a Much-Needed Spiritual Dimension into the Therapy

Survivors of severe childhood abuse hunger for spiritual direction. Although the therapist can discuss spiritual issues in therapy, she is generally not able to provide the survivor with the spiritual *direction* she seeks. This is the province of the minister. Psychologist Karen Hilgers (1992) has explained that understandably many therapists tend to steer away from discussing spiritual issues in therapy for fear of imposing their own values on their patients and because they fear extending themselves into areas beyond their own competence. Similarly, ministers are generally not trained to handle the complex emotional and psychological issues that plague the survivor of severe childhood abuse. The therapist not only has the training to do so, but is also in a unique position to help the survivor *integrate* her psychological, emotional, and spiritual growth. Thus, a collaboration between therapist and minister is a good fit—each adding a special expertise in the service of a healing that will affect all levels of the survivor's being.

Collaboration Alleviates the Minister's Burden

Although some ministers may have backgrounds in psychology or pastoral counseling, most have little time or energy to serve as therapists. In fact, engaging in long-term pastoral counseling with any one parishioner puts the minister in danger of neglecting other pastoral duties (Underwood, 1985). One rabbi with whom we spoke had a PhD in clinical psychology and was a fully licensed therapist, yet he bemoaned the fact that so much of his time was taken up in his administrative duties in the synagogue that he had little time for pastoral counseling. He welcomed contact with therapists of all faiths who would be open to the spiritual and religious life of his congregants. However, like many other clergy with whom we spoke, he felt more comfortable with a therapist of the same religion as himself and the patient. Although we do not believe that therapists must share the same religious beliefs as the survivor to be helpful, we do recognize that many clergy would prefer a therapist whose own religious and spiritual beliefs are similar to those of their congregant.

Collaboration Can Broaden the Social Support Network of the Survivor

The inclusion of clergy in the survivor's therapy broadens her social support network, especially in times of crisis. Rather than the therapist remaining the sole source of support for the survivor, the minister becomes another important source of support. In addition, the minister can help bring the survivor back into community in a way the therapist cannot. The use of social support systems from within the religious community helps the survivor build trust in others and learn life-coping skills. (Chapter 7 will focus on the establishment of such social support groups.)

Collaboration Minimizes Some Problems Caused by Managed Care

Often, managed care insurance programs are inadequate to meet the needs of the survivor of severe childhood abuse. For those who experience a dissociative identity disorder or post-traumatic stress disorder, mandated short-term treatment is not enough. These individuals usually require long-term therapy, well beyond the fifteen or twenty sessions allotted to them each year. Collaboration alleviates the therapist's burden of providing *all* the care for the survivor.

Clergy may also address spiritual and religious issues, establishing support systems from within the religious community thus extending the treatment beyond the confines of the therapist's office.

Collaboration Helps Minimize Mishaps and Misunderstandings

When a religiously involved survivor is in therapy and neither her therapist nor minister have had contact with each other, serious mishaps and misunderstandings can occur. One therapist with whom we spoke shared a story that illustrates this point. His colleague was working with a patient, Sarah, a recovering alcoholic with DID who had been severely and sadistically abused by both her parents. She was very active in her church community; religion was an important part of her life. She was close with her minister and even spent considerable time with him outside the church. Although Sarah's therapist had suggested that she contact her minister so that they could coordinate their work, Sarah had initially refused. The subject was not pursued any further.

Apparently, many years ago Sarah had also been close to a nun who ran a spiritual retreat house for recovering alcoholics. Though Protestant, Sarah had been raised as a Catholic. She spent considerable time at this retreat house, as it was the only place she felt safe and cared for. The nun, Sister Mary, was kind and understanding. Knowing that Sarah could not afford long stays at the retreat house, she had offered Sarah free room and board many times. Sarah had never known anyone to extend such kindness. At that time, although she remembered some of the horrible abuse that she had undergone as a child and had told Sister Mary about her childhood experiences, Sarah did not realize that she had DID. Her dissociative disorder was not diagnosed until many years after she began therapy.

Sadly, Sarah's therapy for her dissociative disorder was long and difficult, involving several hospitalizations over a number of years. During that time, she had gradually lost contact with Sister Mary. In therapy, Sarah spoke about her fond memories of this loving woman and about how much she had learned from her. Sarah longed to reinitiate contact. After many years of therapy, feeling better and stronger, Sarah felt ready speak with Sister Mary again. She looked forward to coming back to the retreat house where she had felt so safe and cared for, but she was uncomfortable telling Sister Mary about her dissociative disorder.

One day, Sarah's pastor offered to accompany her on a visit to Sister Mary, although the therapist was not informed of this development. Sarah and her pastor went out to the retreat house, and the pastor told Sister Mary about Sarah's years of sadistic abuse and the development of a dissociative disorder. "Sarah has multiple personalities," he proclaimed. Sister Mary's response was not the loving, accepting one both Sarah and her pastor had expected. Sister Mary appeared highly agitated and upset as she told Sarah never to return to the retreat house. Sarah was devastated.

Apparently, despite her loving, accepting nature, Sister Mary was frightened by Sarah's multiplicity. One can only speculate about what it meant to her. Had the therapist been in contact with the minister, this incident may have had a different ending. The therapist could have prepared Sister Mary for Sarah's revelation, or at the least, assessed Sister Mary's ability to handle the disturbing news. Working together, therapist and minister could have gradually paved the way for Sarah to continue what had been a loving, supportive relationship.

Now that we have looked at some of the benefits of collaboration between therapist and minister, let us turn our attention to some guidelines to keep in mind when undertaking such collaborative efforts.

GUIDELINES FOR THERAPISTS

Seek Out Compatible Clergy in Your Area

Clergy members of a variety of religions near your office may be willing to participate in collaborative experiences. Remember, many clergy are rather busy with their various duties, and few have had any formal training in psychotherapy, so they might welcome your help.

Of course the easiest route is to seek out ministers of your own religion. For many this will be a good first step, since you are likely to feel more comfortable talking to someone of your own faith.

However, you will find that restricting contact to clergy of only one religion ultimately is too limiting, unless all your patients are also of that religion. Guidelines presented in this chapter will be of help in approaching clergy of other faiths.

> **Marion:** My initial contact with clergy was with a minister outside my own faith. I am Jewish, but Teresa was Protestant. Steven was a Protestant minister. Steven taught me a lot about Christianity, and I was better able to understand Teresa's spiritual and religious issues, though Steven remained her primary source of spiritual support.
>
> Once I had experienced the benefits of collaborating with clergy, I sought out rabbis in my area with whom I might also work. A large part of my practice was Jewish, and although at the time none of my Jewish patients had experienced the kind of severe abuse that might necessitate inclusion of clergy in the therapy, I realized that there were times I might want to consult with a rabbi. Even lesser forms of abuse bring up spiritual and religious challenges best understood by a member of the clergy.
>
> Next, I reached out to a number of priests and nuns in the area, since I had several Catholic patients as well. Again, they provided me with invaluable information and support in my work with Catholic women in my practice. When one of my Catholic patients revealed a history of childhood abuse, but was unwilling to talk to her priest, I already had relationships with a number of nuns to whom I could refer her.

Prepare Your Patient

When making a referral to a minister to discuss difficult religious issues (such as anger at God, or reconciling an image of a loving God with God's "allowance" of horrific abuse), it has been suggested that the therapist explain that resolving these issues is important to the survivor's healing. Furthermore, the therapist may add that she does not believe she is the best person to deal with these issues in depth (Bowman and Amos, 1993). If the survivor does not feel that she can talk with her own clergyperson, the therapist can help her find a suitable minister whose religious and spiritual beliefs are consistent with that of the survivor. The advantage of having made previous contact with a variety of clergy in the area is obvious.

As in any interdisciplinary endeavor, conflicts and misunderstandings may arise. As we have pointed out, the survivor must feel free to discuss any problems that may surface due to the collaboration between therapist and clergy. Since the therapist and minister come from different orientations, their approaches can conflict. We suggest, therefore, that the therapist discuss the possibility of such conflicts in the early stages of the collaboration and create an atmosphere in which open discussion of such problems is encouraged.

It should go without saying, but let us repeat it here: *Do not initiate any contact with the survivor's minister until the matter has been thoroughly discussed and she has agreed in writing to the contact.* We emphasize this step, because we have heard of nightmare situations in which the therapist has called a minister, apparently at the prompting of the survivor, only to be told later by the patient that she had given no such authorization.

The survivor must be made aware of all the possible benefits and risks involved in such contact in order to give an informed consent, and, in the case of a survivor with DID, *all* alters must be included to the extent possible.

Establish a Forum for Educating the Minister About Your Patient's Problem

If you are working with patients who suffered severe childhood abuse, you must ensure that any minister with whom you are working is knowledgeable about such phenomena as post-traumatic stress disorder, DID, abreaction, flashbacks, etc. Since few clergy have had formal training in psychotherapy, you will have the task of educating him in these matters. Make sure you set up a time when the two of you can talk, whether on the phone or (even better) in person. You might send a packet of articles and books about childhood abuse and post-traumatic stress disorder or DID. Bowman and Amos (1993) have suggested that sending such a literature packet serves many functions. It communicates your respect for clergy as professionals, dispelling any fears they might have about your attitude toward them. It also dispels any misconceptions they might have about these unusual psychological phenomena. Dissociative identity disorder, in particular, has received much press in the past few years, much of it inaccurate and misleading. If all the minister knows about dissociative disorders is what has been presented by the media, many misconceptions and misunderstandings are likely to occur.

Provide Emotional Support for Clergy Facing the Horrors of Childhood Abuse

Working with survivors of severe abuse can be very exhausting as well as rewarding. It is difficult to face the reality of how sadistically and horribly some children have been abused by their parents. It is one thing to read about flashbacks and abreactions. It is another to be in the room with someone actually "reliving" the memories of the sadistic abuse of their childhood. Many therapists who have chosen to specialize in working with survivors of severe abuse burn out quickly. Therefore, it is not surprising that many ministers also have difficulty hearing about the horrific abuse their parishioners suffered at the hands of their parents—parents who may perhaps be members of the minister's congregation. A minister's faith is sometimes tried, and he may suffer from secondary traumatization. This traumatization occurs when he has heard in detail about another's traumatic experience. It is *almost* as though he has actually suffered a trauma himself. Listening to the details of the abuse can trigger an "inner earthquake," a shaking up of one's most basic beliefs about the world and one's safety in it.

The therapist can thus provide the minister with emotional support as he attempts to cope with any emotional discomfort or cognitive disorientation resulting from his contacts with the survivor.

Help the Minister Set Limits

Psychiatrist James Chu (1988) has explained that part of the treatment of traumatized patients entails provision of a containing environment. This often involves setting appropriate limits on dysfunctional behaviors that the patients may exhibit. Although treatment of survivors involves a degree of flexibility, he suggests, "there is no need to endlessly gratify patients' demands" (p. 27). Not only would

this encourage potentially dangerous behaviors, but it sends the
wrong messages to the patient—i.e., that even excessive needs can
be met and that no change is necessary to meet the demands of
reality.

Like therapists, clergy tend to identify with and feel sympathy for
the survivor. They are invested in providing a corrective, loving
relationship to counteract the abuse of the parents. They do not
want the survivor to perceive them as withholding or abusive by
denying the survivor's desires. Survivors of severe childhood abuse
evoke very parental, protective feelings in those involved in their
healing. Their stories are riveting, like nothing one has heard before, and it is easy to get lost in the experience, wanting to do
anything to undo the damage the abuse has caused. These feelings,
however noble, can become a trap, drawing the minister into a relationship in which his own needs are increasingly neglected. Eventual
burnout and withdrawal are likely consequences. To avoid such an
occurrence, it is necessary to set limits on the survivor's intrusion
into the minister's life. This may be more difficult for the minister
to accomplish than one would expect. Fascination, guilt about saying "no," and a fervent desire to be of help often stand in the way.

Therapists often experience such problems in their own work
with survivors, but some differences make a minister's position
more difficult. Therapists presumably have had extensive training
in setting limits in psychotherapy and are well aware of the dangers
of not doing so. In addition, their contact with the survivor is limited to office visits and phone calls. The minister, however, sees the
survivor in the "outside world," with fewer time limits built into the
relationship.

The therapist can do several things to avoid problems. She can
educate the minister about the need for limits in therapy. Chu's
(1988) article "Ten Traps for Therapists in the Treatment of Trauma
Survivors" is a good resource for therapists and ministers. The
therapist can look for signs of overinvolvement, such as undue
fascination with the abuse or an increasing neglect of other pastoral
duties. Finally, she should create a warm, accepting atmosphere in
which the minister's reactions to the survivor can be openly discussed.

GUIDELINES FOR CLERGY

Seek Out Compatible Therapists

Just as therapists profit by seeking out clergy with whom they feel comfortable working, clergy should look for therapists in the community whose values and orientation are consistent with their own. The therapist need not be of the same faith, but they must be able to work with the clergy with a minimum of conflict. Often larger communities have seminars, workshops, or "bag lunch" discussion groups on topics of interest to both therapists and clergy. This might be a good beginning for meeting local therapists. Once you have contacted a number of therapists to whom you feel comfortable referring parishioners, you might try other types of collaboration. Try presenting a workshop on spirituality and psychology with one of the therapists, or offer to teach a therapist of another faith about your religion so that she will better understand the religious background of patients from your congregation.

Obtain Informed Consent

Just as therapists must inform the patient of benefits and potential risks involved in a collaboration, so should clergy when preparing a congregant for work with the therapist. The minister should ensure that the survivor feels free to discuss any problems or conflicts that may arise from the interdisciplinary collaboration.

It is essential to stress the confidentiality of the parishioner/minister relationship. The survivor needs to know that you are not going to gossip—that you will discuss information revealed to you with the therapist only. Furthermore, she needs to know that you will share information with the therapist *only* with her permission.

Establish a Forum for Therapist Education

If the therapist is of a different faith from the survivor, the minister can suggest books, articles, and Bible readings. The minister should also make himself available to answer any questions the therapist may have about the survivor's religious belief system.

Armed with such information, the therapist is better qualified to place the survivor's beliefs and behaviors in their religious context. Sometimes a therapist may want to know if a particular behavior or belief is normal for a person of a certain religion. For instance, one therapist with whom we spoke was working with a female survivor of childhood sexual abuse who often expressed fear of damnation for her participation in bizarre sexual acts during her childhood. The therapist was confused. He did not think that such a belief was customary for the religious group in which his patient was currently involved, but he needed to verify his perception with the survivor's minister. The minister was able to confirm that such a belief was not consistent with their religion, but that the particular religious sect in which the survivor's family of origin had participated had emphasized eternal damnation for one's sins. In cases such as this, the minister's participation is invaluable.

Explain How the Therapist Can Best Work
Within the Survivor's Religious System

The minister can provide the therapist, especially one of a different faith from the survivor, with helpful information. For example, most religions have special holidays and events that revolve around celebrations and rituals that may hold significant abusive memories for the survivor. By teaching the therapist about the true spiritual meaning of those holidays, the minister gives the therapist the information needed to reframe the holiday within a new religious and spiritual context. Together, the therapist and the survivor can create new associations with the holiday, thus restoring the holiday's spiritual significance.

> **Steven:** Christmas and Easter are two important events in the Christian tradition. For Teresa, these holidays were times in which she was subjected to abuse by other family members, most notably her uncle and cousin. The Christmas event of God's incarnation in order to identify with our suffering and pain, bringing us a message of salvation, became for Teresa a source of traumatic memories. Easter, a time of resurrection and the promise of a new life, became associated with destruction rather than hope. How important for the therapist to

understand and reinforce that Teresa had been wronged, and abuse was not what God intended! The therapist was then free to reframe the experience of those holidays apart from the abuse.

For the Jewish survivor, as well, holidays can have very different meanings from their original intent. For example, the holiday Yom Kippur, the Day of Atonement, can evoke guilt in the survivor of severe childhood abuse if she believes or has been told that she is sinful. Similarly, Passover, a holiday that celebrates God bringing freedom for an enslaved people, can be associated with memories of abuse. One survivor with whom Marion worked remembered being tied up and sadistically abused on such holidays. In cases such as these, a rabbi can be invaluable in teaching the therapist about the true meaning of these holidays and how their meaning can be reframed within the context of their spiritual significance for Judaism. Such information is especially helpful for the therapist who has no knowledge of the Jewish religion and culture.

The minister is in a position not only to educate the therapist, but to actively help her integrate the survivor's religious and spiritual beliefs into the psychotherapy. For example, in our own work with Teresa, Steven would often suggest ways in which Marion could introduce meaningful religious concepts to help Teresa heal from her abuse.

> **Marion:** Not surprisingly, after years of repeated sadistic verbal, physical, emotional, and sexual abuse, Teresa had low self-esteem. It was particularly distressing to me that she felt unlovable. While Steven spent much of his time with Teresa talking about Jesus' love for her, I, a secular therapist with a Jewish upbringing, had never thought to introduce those concepts into our psychotherapy. However, when I began to do as Steven suggested, remarkable things happened in the therapy. Steven suggested that I ask her sometimes when she was describing an incident of childhood abuse, "How do you think Jesus looked upon this little girl being abused?" Invariably she would answer, "Jesus would feel sad," or "Jesus would want to cry." Over time this questioning of how Jesus would view her, coupled with Steven's messages about God's love for her, greatly

helped to counteract the messages she had received from her abusive mother.

Be on the Lookout for Therapist Resistance

Due to her own negative experiences with religion or religious figures, the therapist may have some resistance to the inclusion of specific religious material in her work with the survivor. Even in cases in which the therapist has sought out your counsel, some residual effects of her earlier experiences may affect her interactions with you and/or the survivor. Therefore, in the early stages of your work together, it might be helpful to discuss with the therapist any negative experiences she may have had which might interfere with your work together or with her work with the survivor. This will keep the partnership focused on healing rather than on criticism.

OVERCOMING OBSTACLES TO COLLABORATION

Obstacles to Referral

Weaver, Koenig, and Ochberg (1996) have pointed out that "rabbis, priests, and pastors serve as front-line community mental health workers" (p. 848). In fact, a 1993 study found that clergy are just as likely as mental health specialists to have a severely mentally distressed person ask for help (Hohmann and Larson, 1993). Unfortunately, as we have already pointed out, few clergy have the time or the training to meet these people's needs. Many ministers have not had the training to assess emotional instability and suicide risk potential. Domino (1990) found that in his sample of 157 Protestant, Catholic, and Jewish clergy, the clergy had about the same knowledge level of the symptoms of emotional distress as a group of college undergraduates in an introduction to psychology class. In another study, clergy scored significantly lower than psychologists, psychiatrists, social workers, and marriage and family counselors in their ability to assess suicide risk (Domino, 1985).

As Weaver, Koenig, and Ochberg (1996) have stated, referral skills are, of course, closely related to evaluation skills since one's evaluation of a problem inevitably guides one's course of action. Therapists can be of help in this context, since they can teach clergy how to identify potential problems such as serious depression or high suicide risk and help them to make appropriate referrals. Naturally, this process will go more smoothly if the therapist and minister already have a good working relationship—another reason for therapists and clergy to seek out one another before the need occurs for collaboration about a specific survivor. Therapists might also consider presenting training workshops in identifying and assessing serious emotional psychological problems for clergy in their area. Such workshops would not only educate clergy about mental health issues, but could go a long way toward making them less wary of referral to mental health professionals.

Sometimes the reluctance to make a referral to a therapist is based on the minister's religious background (Lovinger, 1984). Fundamentalist Christian ministers are among the least likely to refer to secular therapists (O'Malley, Gearhart, and Becker, 1984), as are Jehovah's Witnesses and Christian Scientists. Lovinger (1984) suggests that seeing a patient from one of these denominations in one's own therapy practice is likely to signal the patient's own questions about her affiliation. Such patients may have been referred through a court order, or may have only entered treatment due to intense pressure from school authorities. Lovinger also points out that in Judaism, these kinds of concerns are less likely to be an issue for Conservative or Reform rabbis, but Orthodox and Hasidic rabbis are less likely to make any referrals for psychotherapy.

The therapist must keep in mind that conservative religious leaders may be wary of therapy because they view it as a threat to their religious value system. Again, Lovinger (1984) has asserted that the emphasis on self-actualization, liberation, and growth in some humanistically oriented therapies may appear to bring about an erosion of traditional Christian values of self-abnegation, obedience to God, and unconditional moral standards. It is important for therapists and clergy to keep open lines of communication, so that any real issues or any misconceptions can be dealt with promptly. Therapists need to reach out to such clergy, explaining why some individuals with severe depression, post-traumatic stress disorder, or DID might benefit from psychotherapy in addition to their religious involvement. The therapist could then explain specifically what she does in therapy, dispelling any myths and promising to consult with the clergy so as not to inadvertently trample on any religious values. Such an effort might make referral to therapists more likely.

Another approach to lessening clergy opposition to therapy is to address their concern in spiritual terms. One therapist with whom we spoke dealt with a minister's concerns about having a congregant in therapy by speaking to him about her view that all healing comes from God. "God is love," she said, "and as such, God is the agent of all emotional, psychological, and spiritual healing. Psychotherapy merely eliminates the blocks to spiritual growth, letting the natural healing process unfold."

Both minister and therapist have contributions to make in their own ways. Therapists have often neglected the spiritual dimensions of healing, while many ministers have been guilty of rejecting the importance of emotional issues as unnecessary to spiritual growth. Clergy and therapists must always remember that we are physical, emotional, and spiritual beings. *All* aspects of our being are essential to healing.

Turf Issues

Territorial and power issues endanger any effort at interdisciplinary collaboration. Counseling has been the province of the clergy since antiquity (Moss, 1978), and some ministers may resent being told they are not qualified to counsel their congregants. Similarly, some therapists resent the central role the minister and the religious community can take in the life of the survivor. We have found that the only way around such dilemmas is for each to acknowledge and respect the expertise of the other. In our own work together, we always tried to keep in mind the principles of The Benevolence Model, especially the principles concerning treating the other with holy regard. This allowed us to transcend many problems that interdisciplinary collaboration might have entailed.

The collaboration must be an equal partnership with each professional having his or her own area of expertise and specialization. Equally important in minimizing potential problems is that each recognizes the *limitations* of his or her expertise.

Another way to ensure that territorial and power issues are minimized is to discuss the possibility that they may rear their ugly heads early in the collaboration, and to establish ground rules about how they will be handled. First, both therapist and minister must be clear as to the other's area of expertise. For instance, in our own collaboration, Marion was clearly in charge of the therapy, but Steven was the acknowledged authority in all matters of a religious nature. So, if a question arose as to how to handle flashbacks and abreactions, Steven would defer to Marion. If the issue was about how the Church might handle a healing ritual designed to help Teresa's alters to be included in her religious life, Steven was in charge. Some issues are complex and might involve the expertise of both minister and therapist. For example, in assessing a survivor's God-image, the minister would clearly be the expert on how God is conceptualized within the context of his religion. However, the therapist might also have valuable insights about what degree the survivor's current God-image might represent an introjection of parental authority. Unhealthy God imagery may mimic parental authority and control, but many clergy are unaware of the degree to which a survivor's God-image is a reflection of her childhood abuse. In their ignorance of such issues, they may use words and images that further reinforce abusive imagery of God. Both therapist and minister thus have information helpful to the other. Together they can help the survivor heal her images of God in ways they could never accomplish alone.

When working in an interdisciplinary collaboration the issue of which code of ethics to follow must be addressed. Fortunately, a great deal of overlap occurs between most mental health workers' codes of ethics and that of clergy. Early in the collaboration, these ethical codes should be discussed, so that each will be somewhat familiar with that of the other profession. Then, if ethical questions do arise later, there will already be an open dialogue.

Problems with Time and Scheduling

Collaborative work can take time and effort, especially at the beginning. Phone contacts and face-to-face meetings require a time commitment by both therapist and minister, and busy professionals may find it difficult to adjust their schedules to accommodate the needs of the other. From the beginning both therapist and minister must make it clear to the other how much time will be made available for the collaboration and at what time he or she can be reached. In our own collaboration, we found that despite our busy schedules the work we were doing together was so exciting, and the rewards in terms of Teresa's progress were so great, that finding time to speak with each other was not a problem. Speaking to each other regularly was a *priority* for both of us.

Financial Considerations

Some therapists will engage in collaborations with no expectation of being reimbursed for their time; others will want to be paid for the considerable time and effort they put into this work. All such arrangements must be agreed upon at the beginning and must include the survivor's approval and acceptance. For some therapists and ministers collaborating on a case, telephone consultation can provide an inexpensive alternative to lengthy face-to-face meetings.

Agency Considerations

Therapists in private practice have the ability to determine with whom they want to collaborate and how much time they are willing to give to the work. They are free to do the work pro bono if they choose. Agency-affiliated therapists are not so free. Financial constraints are likely to hamper the work of therapists who want to spend agency time consulting or collaborating with members of the clergy. It is possible that money will not be made available to finance such endeavors. In addition, some agency policies may inhibit or even prohibit any efforts at collaborative work with clergy. For example, we were asked by one frustrated therapist, "What if your supervisor thinks it is a bad idea to work with a patient's minister?" Our response is that *before* you even propose the collaboration, that you create a well-thought-out plan, listing the benefits to this patient— how the collaborations will add a dimension to your work with her that would not be possible without the inclusion of her minister. The benefits listed in this book will provide you with some ideas. Back up your list with the inclusion of the extensive research that demonstrates the positive effects of religious commitment on mental health (Koenig, 1995). List some potential risks to this patient and how you plan to minimize them. Finally, explain some of the potential obstacles to collaboration and how you tend to address them.

Need for Patience

We cannot overemphasize the need for patience for all involved in the collaboration—minister, therapist, and survivor alike. As we have pointed out, interdisciplinary collaboration is fraught with potential obstacles, but the work to overcome them is well worth the effort. This kind of work, though valuable, is new to the professions, and few guidelines are available other than the ones presented in this chapter. Like us, you will probably make many mistakes along the way, and like us, you will learn from those mistakes.

In working with the survivor, patience is also necessary. Change comes slowly for survivors of severe childhood abuse, and each step, however small, must be celebrated as a triumph.

Remember the Overriding Principle: The Needs of the Survivor

The most important guideline we can offer is to always put the needs of the survivor first. No matter what the obstacle—be it a turf issue, a different value structure, a difference of opinion about how to handle a situation—all issues can be resolved as long as this principle is the guide. Even if there is a difference about what is in the best interest of the survivor, it is never in her best interest to be caught in the middle between her therapist and her minister. At the very least, come to some agreement, find some common ground for *her* benefit. Like two parents at odds over what would be best for their child, therapist and clergy must always keep the best interests of the survivor foremost in their minds.

Following this principle allowed us to work together harmoniously in our own collaboration. The potential for conflict was certainly present. Marion was a Jewish therapist working with Steven, a Christian minister. Yet, no matter what happened, we were able to keep in mind that the bottom line was Teresa's welfare, and thus we were able to transcend any religious differences or clashes in values that might have arisen.

Collaboration can be rewarding if both therapist and minister are well prepared for their work together. Interdisciplinary work can pose unique challenges, but our experience suggests that by following some simple guidelines, the rewards for all involved far outweigh any potential problems.

Chapter 7

Establishment of Support Groups

To love and be loved is to feel the sun from both sides.

David Viscott

Since we are all created to be in relationship, and since we extend divine love into the world through our interactions with others, all human relationships have the potential to teach us about love, and to foster healing from emotional stress. In M. Scott Peck's *The Road Less Traveled* (1978), love is proclaimed as the ultimate healing agent. Love is always therapeutic, Peck claims, whether as part of a psychotherapy or outside it. However, Peck points out, the therapist generally does not see the patient outside the office, especially not in social situations. Collaboration between therapist and clergy can to some degree extend the loving relationships outside the therapy room and into the world. In this chapter we will explore possibilities that lie well beyond the therapist's couch.

Psychiatrist Colin Ross has suggested that the use of social support systems can be an important part of the therapeutic process for survivors of severe abuse (Ross, 1989). Support groups can consist of friends and family of the survivor or of fellow members of a twelve-step or therapy group. This chapter will explore a specific type of support group, one that utilizes the unique benefits of a collaboration between therapist and clergy. We will discuss the establishment of support group systems within the religious community of the survivor.

Soon after Marion began her work with Michael, the pastor of Teresa's church, Michael called together a group of congregants from his church. Steven was an associate pastor at the church who had also become involved in Teresa's case as part of his internship. Susan was one of the congregants who attended this first meeting in Michael's living room. Since she was a social worker by profession, she was to become an integral part of the support system network.

Michael had called together a group of people he felt would be "authentic models" for Teresa. He had spoken to each person individually, suggesting they might want to become involved in helping another congregant who had been severely abused in childhood. Marion and Michael met with this group initially to discuss the concept of multiplicity (what it is, why and how people adopt multiple identities, etc.), and to introduce them to some of Teresa's alters. Many mistakes were made that night—mistakes that will be discussed later in this chapter. However, this meeting formed the basis for a support group that was to become an integral part of Teresa's healing. The people in the support group established that evening became involved in Teresa's life in an intimate way. They spent time with the child alters—going to the zoo, the movies, or out to eat. They spent time with her more adult alters, engaging in conversation, helping with chores, going shopping with her, or to the movies. They provided her with an opportunity to comfortably be "all her selves," never labeling her sick or bizarre. She was no longer in hiding from the world. Marion and Michael continued to meet informally with individual support group members to discuss concerns and issues that arose out of their interactions with Teresa's alters.

The benefits of such a support system in helping a survivor heal from the effects of her abuse cannot be understated. But the benefits extended well beyond the survivor, bringing emotional and spiritual growth to all involved. Let us first turn to a detailed examination of the needs fulfilled by such a support group and the benefits for the survivor.

BENEFITS OF THE SUPPORT GROUP

The research literature is filled with studies attesting to the benefits of social support systems in healing from trauma. Numerous studies have demonstrated a positive correlation between social support and mental health and negative correlation between support and physical illness and mortality. In several studies of people in crisis, social support systems have been shown to be associated with better recovery from physical illness, decreased stress following crises (such as job loss or loss of spouse), and better emotional adjustment to crises of all types (Dunkel-Schetter, 1984; Silver and Wortman, 1980). Clinicians have attempted to describe support systems in terms of function to better understand the various benefits. Psychologists Sheldon Cohen and Thomas Wills propose four aspects of social support based on types of resources offered (Cohen and Wills, 1985). Let us look at each type, focusing on how they relate to support systems for survivors, especially those described in this chapter.

Esteem Support

Support people provide the survivor with feedback about her worth and value, adding to her sense of self-esteem. Survivors of severe childhood abuse often have very low self-esteem, and the abuser has likely made them feel worthless and unwanted. In Teresa's case, the Mother had told her she was "subhuman," not entitled even to interact with normal human beings. The messages she received from the members of the support group, assuring her that she was valued and loved, greatly contributed to a change in her self-perception. The group reinforced that it was not just a rare individual who found her acceptable, but that she was cared about by many people of various genders, ages, and ethnicities.

Instrumental Support

This type of support involves the provision of financial assistance and material resources. In Teresa's case, the church support group provided her with emergency money when she was having trouble one month making ends meet. They helped her with chores she could not have accomplished otherwise—moving furniture, painting rooms, etc. They did for her the things the therapist is *unable* to do (due to constraints of the therapy relationship) and the things the minister does not have *time* to do. In providing this instrumental support they greatly added to her experience of being cared for.

Informational Support

Informational support refers to the ability of group members to provide information that helps the survivor cope with problems by offering information or advice. Survivors often have poor problem-solving skills and impaired judgment. Support group members can provide them with much-needed guidance in problem solving in their everyday lives.

Social Championship

This aspect of group support refers to the availability of others as companions for social and leisure activities. Survivors of severe childhood abuse are often socially isolated. Social support systems can help compensate for this isolation. Members of Teresa's support group spent time with her—going out to eat, going to movies, inviting her to parties and important social events.

Although social support systems aid in healing from abuse, survivors are often wary of reaching out, having learned to distrust others. In addition, Bowman and Amos (1993) state that while most psychiatric patients tend to turn to their families for support, treatment of survivors of severe childhood abuse often leads to a severing of ties with the abusive families of origin. Unfortunately, this social isolation cuts survivors off from the very source of support they need for healing. It is important to keep in mind that before a congregational support group or *any* support system is created, the survivor should have already formed a trusting relationship with the therapist. The support group can then provide her with an opportunity to extend that trust to a larger, though still somewhat structured and controlled environment. This is a step in the process of learning to reach out to others on her own. In a sense, one could say that support groups can help bring the survivor back into community.

> **Justin:** Bringing someone back into community is probably one of the most important functions of the support group. I do not think people can really understand the depths to which a survivor can become isolated and withdrawn. It becomes very lonely to walk around in the world—and you look at all the people, and you see that they seem to be having a life . . . and

you're not sure that you are having a life. You're living a shell of a life—a little private hell that nobody knows about. When you can have a group of people and then talk to those people about what happened to you, and those people hug you or just sit and listen to you, then you do not feel as desperate and alone.

Marion: The support group provided a significant resocialization experience for Teresa. Severe physical, sexual, and emotional abuse had seriously impaired Teresa's abilities to interact with people on a social basis. Trips to the zoo, the ballpark, computer stores, and the movies with members of the group were helpful in teaching Teresa about what people do together in a "normal" course of life.

Support groups can also serve as a laboratory, a safe place to learn about boundaries and relationships in the "real world."

Justin: In a support group you learn about different levels of friendship and caring. Before the group you have unrealistic expectations about how to be in relationship, and not everybody is going to fulfill those expectations. For example, Tommy was never reliable when it came to time, but I learned that he loves me anyway—even if he could not be there when he told me he would. I learned that Tommy's inconsistencies did not have anything to do with how he felt about me. He was an inconsistent individual about time, but not in his friendship toward me. I learned that there were other people who would be there fairly consistently for me—and that there were others who would want to just check in periodically, or who might just want to have a periodic dinner with me. But I learned that is what happens when you make real friends. You have friends you go out to dinner with, and some people you just go to the theater with, and then you might have friends you see all the time.

Marion: Actually, Justin's learning about the nature of friendship and the different kinds of friends one can have in the world did come through the interactions with support group members, but those realizations did not come easily. It was very disheartening at first, and sometimes even infuriating to Justin when Tommy was inconsistent about time, when Tommy would show up two hours late. However, what was particularly helpful was Tommy's ability to discuss this with Justin and claim it as his own problem—pointing out that the inconsistency in time did not mean inconsistency in all areas of their relationship. Justin's experiences with group members allowed him to examine relationship issues that arose outside the therapy room in a somewhat "structured" environment.

The support group can become a place in which the survivor can "break the silence," telling her story to others who listen with interest and love. The support group also can become a sort of "extended family" for the survivor. According to Robert Kluft, a leading psychiatrist in the field of dissociative disorders, traumatized families may openly reject the patient when they learn that the patient is revealing long-hidden family secrets in therapy (Kluft, 1984b). Psychotherapist Yvonne Dolan has pointed out that if the family members of a survivor are not willing to be supportive of her, she may have to separate from them to end her victimization. Dolan explains further that this separation can be a painful and demanding process, and that at times the survivor may doubt herself. She adds that the risk of suicide is especially great during this transition. Adequate support at such a time is essential. Dolan suggests that when the survivor can establish a nurturing and healthy circle of significant others with whom to celebrate traditional holidays, this is a significant "healing sign" for the adult survivor of incest. "A major turning point in the survivor's life occurs," she suggests, "when she is able to realize that breaking ties with her family of origin doesn't have to mean being alone or unloved. In fact, given the inherent dysfunction of most incestuous families, the converse is probably true" (Dolan, 1991, p. 82). Bowman and Amos (1993) state that the church or synagogue and the member of the clergy can serve as a transferential family. In this regard a congregational support group can serve as a new, healthy "family"—providing the survivor with companionship on holidays, and other forms of support generally associated with families.

Marion: On one occasion, for example, a crisis was precipitated on Thanksgiving when Teresa's mother told her at the last moment that she would not be welcomed at the family dinner. There were members of her support group who were happy to welcome Teresa to share the holiday with them.

On another occasion, when I was out of town, Mimic drank a bottle of wine and then brought out Teresa. The persecuting personality then commanded Teresa to go out driving in her car. Devastated because she believed she had broken her sobriety, Teresa was thrown into a panic. She was able, however, to phone Susan, who stayed with her for several hours, making sure that she would not leave the house and drive in an inebriated state.

Steven: Once, Dennis, a thirteen-year-old male alter "came out" at a church concert. He blurted out, rather loudly, "Hey Rev, how about buying me a *Playboy?*"

This scenario could have been a disaster, but those around us, members of the support group, understood. They were informed and handled the experience with humor, understanding, and delightful guidance instead of criticism.

Another great advantage of the use of support groups from within the congregation is that it can lead to decreased dependence on the therapist. Chu (1988) has asserted that the potential always exists for profound dependency and neediness in patients who have been severely abused. Establishing a network of people who are available for support makes it less likely that the therapist will be viewed as the sole person who can be depended on to nurture and care for the survivor.

Now that we have looked at some benefits of a support group, let us turn to an examination of how such groups can be put together.

GUIDELINES FOR ESTABLISHING SUPPORT GROUPS

The following steps provide a framework for therapists and clergy who wish to establish support groups for the survivors using the resources of a synagogue or church. The assumption here is that both the therapist and minister have agreed to work together with the consent of the survivor. If a minister is interested in putting together a support group for a congregant, but is not currently working collaboratively with the therapist, arrangements should be made for some kind of clinical supervision of group members—unless the minister has extensive training and experience working with women who have been severely abused and has the time to devote to the support group.

Step 1: Assessment of Current Social Support Network

Before establishing a support group from within the survivor's faith community, it is important to conduct a preliminary assessment of the network of support people currently in her life. Her environment may already contain people who can support her in her healing. There may be family members, friends, support groups such as twelve-step programs. If such support systems are already in place there may be no need to develop others. However, since many survivors are socially isolated, it is likely that very few social resources will be found. The existing current network should be examined toward determining which of the survivor's needs are not being met, i.e., needs for companionship, needs for emotional support, etc. The therapist will do most of the assessing in this area, but ideas from the minister are usually welcomed.

Step 2: Assessment of Congregation

This level of assessment requires both the expertise of the minister and the therapist. The minister needs to assess the various members of the congregation to determine who would be suitable for a support group, i.e., level of spiritual development, openness to new ideas about spirit and consciousness. The therapist acts as consultant, providing information and guidance to the minister in choosing suitable members. For example, the therapist might suggest certain qualities to look for in prospective support group members—responsibility, flexibility, open-mindedness, empathy, compassion, etc. Once the minister has narrowed down the list of potential group members, each should be met with individually to further assess their suitability and/or willingness to participate. Basic information about the nature and purpose of the support group would be provided, carefully protecting the anonymity of the survivor at this point. In addition, if the survivor is dissociative, further assessment may be necessary. The therapist or the minister might want to ask about the prospective group member's beliefs about or experiences with multiple personality disorder.

> **Marion:** One of the first mistakes we made was not consulting with one another when group members were being screened. Michael and I should have spent more time discussing the qualities he should be looking for in a group member, and I should have been involved in the initial talks with the potential individuals. I also could have relied on Susan's opinion, since she had clinical training. Some people chosen for the initial group were not prepared for the degree of commitment and level of consistency needed to be of help to Teresa. Had I been a part of the screening process, perhaps better choices could have been made.

Step 3: Establishing Educational and Information Sharing Sessions

A series of preliminary meetings should be arranged during which the group members meet with the therapist, member of the clergy, and the survivor. The purpose of the group is explained in detail—with emphasis on the kinds of activities and tasks that constitute support for the survivor. In addition, the group members could be taught how to be supportive friends and listeners to the survivor. Information about severe abuse of children and its consequences for the survivor could be included. If the survivor is dissociative, especially if she has multiple personalities like Teresa, information on dissociative disorders is necessary. Chris Rosik, a psychologist in California, has stated that often people in a religious congregation are likely to have obtained their knowledge of dissociative disorders from an unrepresentative sample of patients found on talk shows, in autobiographical novels, and in films (Rosik, 1992). This lack of information or, in some cases, misinformation, can be harmful to the survivor, since the congregation members will possibly view the survivor as dangerous or psychotic. Such misinformation must be addressed and reevaluated early in the process. If the survivor is experiencing flashbacks and abreactions, these phenomena can be explained to the group members, with descriptions of what they are, what they "look like," and how to deal with them if they occur while spending time with the survivor. If possible, the survivor should attend this first meeting, and speak for herself as much as possible.

Step 4: Establishing a Mechanism for "Supervision"

In *The Road Less Traveled,* M. Scott Peck proclaimed that "laymen can practice successful psychotherapy without great training as long as they are genuinely loving human beings" (Peck, 1978, p. 179). Credentials are not as important as the ability to bring love into the life of the survivor. Once the group members have been screened and given rudimentary education about trauma and its effects on the individual, they are now free to interact with the survivor in loving ways that will foster healing from the abuse. However, some sort of supervision should be continued throughout the course of the support group's life, focusing on continued education, examination of difficulties that arise, and examination of the meaning of participation in the healing of the survivor in the group member's life. Both individual and group meetings should be scheduled—the frequency being determined by the needs of the support group members as well as the time constraints and availability of the therapist and the minister. The group members should be encouraged to discuss their own frustrations, mistakes, fears, and misunderstandings. Creating an atmosphere in which such issues can be freely discussed not only provides the support group members with a forum to discuss their own problematical emotional reactions, but it also allows them to learn helpful, practical ways to relate to the survivor.

GUIDELINES FOR SUPPORT GROUP MEMBERS

From our experience and from the words of women who have been severely abused in childhood, we have compiled the following list. It consists of helpful information for all group members:

1. *Education about trauma and its effects on children.* If necessary, dissociative disorders should also be explained and demystified.
2. *Emphasis on honesty and the need to avoid secrets.* Survivors of severe abuse are extremely sensitive to their surroundings. They can often sense when someone is being dishonest with them, and any dishonesty will further increase their natural distrust. One woman with dissociative identity disorder explained, "If you care about a person who has MPD, be honest as you can in the relationship, especially about feelings. We can feel when something is up but when that awareness is denied it makes us feel more crazy" (Diana, cited in Cohen, Giller, and Lynn W., 1991, p. 201).
3. *Importance of keeping promises.* Although promises are often broken in life, the survivor's level of trust tends to be so low that any unkept promises provoke anxiety and anger and lead to greater social distance. Although such experiences can be dealt with in the therapy should they arise, generally group members are to be cautioned not to make promises unless they are certain that they can be kept (Rosik, personal communication).
4. *Importance of consistency.* Since the world of the abused child is frightening and unpredictable, survivors of severe childhood abuse often have enormous fears of the unknown and of inconsistency. Inconsistency mimics their abuse, as they cannot prepare themselves for whatever is to come. One survivor of abuse described her need this way: "It is really important to me that friends be consistent, supportive, and honest. Because of MPD, I'm never sure I did a thing well, or offended somebody. The more friends understand my vast insecurity and confusion about ordinary life matters which they can take for granted, the better off we'll be" (Caitlin, cited in Cohen, Giller, and Lynn W., 1991, p. 184).
5. *Importance of asking questions.* Another survivor has written that "people who know someone with MPD should feel free to talk about it, or ask questions, and be interested. The worst things are being afraid to mention it and pretending it doesn't exist" (Cindy, cited in Cohen, Giller, and Lynn W., 1991, p. 196).

For more in-depth understanding of what survivors need, we suggest reading a wonderful book written by survivors titled *Multiple Personality Disorder from the Inside Out* (Cohen, Giller, and Lynn W., 1991). In fact, each group member could be given a copy of the book.

PITFALLS TO AVOID

Our experience suggests that establishing a support group for the survivor can be an important part of the survivor's healing from her abuse. However, such groups are fraught with potential pitfalls and issues to be kept in mind. For example, although ideally each member wanted to offer a loving, caring relationship to Teresa, some of them, having grown up in abusive homes themselves, were unable to provide the consistently loving and nonjudgmental relationships Teresa needed. In such cases, ongoing supervision of group members' contacts with the survivor is essential. Such "supervision" does not have to be in depth, but the therapist and minister should make themselves available on a regular basis for discussion of progress and problems. In addition, provisions should be made for emergency contacts with the therapist if the need arises. For those who have had no experience in dealing with a person who has been severely abused, a forum should be scheduled in which the intense feelings evoked by interactions with the survivor can be explored. Kluft has cautioned that with people who have multiple personalities "the activities of the personalities may compromise the patient's access to support systems. Their inconsistent and disruptive behaviors, their memory problems and switching, can make them appear to be unreliable or even liars. Concerned others may withdraw" (Kluft, 1984a, p. 52). While Teresa's personalities were neither unreliable nor untruthful, their activities and feelings were at times overwhelming to the members of the support group, leading to confusion, anger, and sometimes, withdrawal.

Second, as we learned from our experience, the survivor should be included in every phase of group development if possible. One of the greatest mistakes we made was asking Teresa to leave during the first meeting so that group members would feel free to ask questions they might have been uncomfortable asking in Teresa's presence. This approach angered and frightened Teresa, and certainly did not help her establish a sense of trust in the group. Group members are advised to avoid defining the survivor solely by her disorder— another common mistake.

Finally, although not a pitfall, the need for mutuality is an important component of a successful experience often overlooked when establishing a support group of this type. At times the support group felt artificial to Teresa, because everyone was there to help *her*. No avenue for mutual support existed. To some degree, Teresa found that mutuality in her relationship with Steven. It was through this relationship that much of Mimic's growth occurred. (You will remember that Mimic was the name of the alter who believed himself to be a computer, and who eventually became Justin, a major personality in the system.)

However, not enough attention was paid to developing this kind of mutuality within the support group itself. If the support group is to serve as a source of resocialization as well as support in the survivor's life, then the relationships established cannot be based solely on the group members taking care of the survivor. Although the members of the group must at times of crisis attend to the survivor's needs, focusing solely on the caretaking functions is limiting. The establishment of mutually supportive friendships, on the other hand, teaches the survivor about healthy relationships, and also contributes to the development of a sense of self-worth.

Lest we end this chapter on a negative note, focused on pitfalls and problems that can occur, let us turn our attention to the tremendous impact such support group systems can have on all involved. Obviously, for the survivor such support systems offer innumerable benefits. We explored some of those earlier in the chapter. However, everyone involved in the process—therapist, minister, support group member—can grow as well. One member of the support group we established for Teresa, Jim Smollon, has described his experience as having taught him a lot about his own inner psyche. His experiences with Teresa and learning about her multiplicity made him begin to look at his own different "selves." He came to understand that Teresa differed from most other people in terms of the degree to which she had separate parts within her, and, through his experiences with her, he became more open to exploring those different parts within himself. Jim has since obtained degrees in both theology and social work, and clearly his clinical work will forever be influenced by what he learned from Teresa.

The establishment of support groups within a congregation can also open the door for others who are suffering to come forth. Once *one* person has revealed her struggles with mental health issues, and the minister and congregation have responded positively, that person will serve as a beacon. As social worker Frances Allen has suggested, "that person will eventually tell someone else in the congregation. They will spread the word, just like they will spread gossip. They'll spread the good news. It allows other people to say, 'Well, I'm welcome'" (Shifrin, 1995, p. 1).

From our experience, the support group can have a spiritual significance in the lives of all involved. The members of Teresa's support group attempted to model the love and benevolence that formed the basis of their religious beliefs, extending community to someone who was wounded. They attempted to manifest God's love in Teresa's life through their relationships with her. Simple acts by the group members—taking out the garbage, painting her apartment, walking her dog—were transformed into meaningful acts of love for Teresa who had been taught by her mother that she was not even worthy of taking out other people's garbage. For Teresa, the support group formed one component of her healing process. For some of the members of the support group, this experience constituted a once-in-a-lifetime chance to actively participate in another's healing and growth, an opportunity to put their spiritual beliefs into practice. For others this experience became the foundation on which future professional, spiritual, and social lives would be based.

Chapter 8

Healing Interventions

A picture is worth a thousand words.

Anonymous

What makes a therapy spiritual depends more on what is in the therapist's heart than which techniques are employed in sessions. Psychologist Joyce Vesper has pointed out that in working with those who have been severely abused, talk therapy and abreactive work is not enough to move them to wholeness: "Such instances require the therapist to move beyond the usual practices of techniques of therapy and to create alternative methods that will bring the client emotional relief. These procedures may involve any number of the adjunctive therapies as well as the use of ceremony to complete the release and resolution of the memory" (Vesper, 1991, p. 109). In our own experience in working with survivors of severe abuse, we have found that particular interventions as used by both therapist and minister can promote healing on a deep spiritual and emotional level. These interventions reach a deeper level of being, as they go beyond mere words.

We will describe a wide variety of healing interventions. Some can be used exclusively by the therapist during sessions, others may be more helpful to the minister, while others, such as rituals and ceremonies, can be used by therapist and minister together. However, all the interventions described in this chapter have three things in common, in that each:

1. bypasses the logical, rational mind, tapping a deeper level of consciousness, and effecting change at a subconscious level;

2. bridges the gap between therapy and spirituality; and
3. leads to creative solutions, strategies, and insights into the survivor's situation, often without conscious effort by the survivor.

Let us first look at metaphors, since all the other techniques
involve the concept of metaphor in some way.

METAPHORS

Simply put, metaphor means something that stands for something else. We are constantly thinking in metaphor, though we are
often unaware we are doing so. As psychologist Richard Kopp put
it, "You could be knee-deep in metaphors and not realize it" (Kopp,
1995, p. xiii). In therapy, metaphoric communication can come in
the form of pure metaphor "My life is a nightmare," or as a simile,
"I'm like a chicken without a head." Metaphor can be generated by
the client, as in the above examples, or the therapist can suggest a
metaphor that appears to sum up a client's state of mind, "It sounds
like you are a doormat." In either case, the intentional use of metaphoric language can greatly enhance the therapeutic process.

In her book, *Healing the Incest Wound,* psychologist Christine
Courtois (1988) has suggested that metaphor can promote relaxation, contribute to the breakdown of defenses, allow memories to
emerge, and enable clients to gain or maintain control. For some
survivors, she explains, metaphoric language may provide the only
vehicle through which they can speak, at least initially. She gives
examples of common metaphors used by survivors—the image of
oneself being well defended behind a wall or under a bed or in a
closet, or of having memories safely locked away in dusty attics or
in strongboxes tied securely with heavy chains and locks. A skillful
therapist can work with such metaphoric language, helping the
survivor to explore the metaphor in depth, reframe it as something
creative and adaptive in its own way, and possibly transform it into
something more positive.

Religious language is rich in metaphor. Since such language is an
attempt to explain the Divine—a concept that is beyond human
understanding and language—metaphor is used to convey meaning
that is otherwise ineffable. Raymond Stovich, in his article on meta-

phor and religious imagery in therapy, explains that the word metaphor derives from the Greek words *meta,* a prefix that implies a passing over, a going from one place to another, and *phorein,* which means to move or carry. In other words, a metaphor is something that carries us from one place to another. Furthermore, Stovich has suggested "religious language, when properly functioning, serves to move the psyche, drawing it out of its narrow ego confines toward a larger, transpersonal realm, a realm that exists as another dimension in our lives. In this process religious language serves to facilitate movement across inner boundaries and stuck places within the psyche" (Stovich, 1985, p. 117).

Now, having laid a brief foundation for the understanding of metaphor, let us turn to the use of imagery, a form of metaphor, in working with survivors.

IMAGERY

What is imagery? Most simply, it is the mind thinking in pictures. Before we had words, we had images. Babies do not have words to describe their experiences, but they have feelings and images that go with those sensations. Take, for instance, the image of "mother." Such an image evokes a wide variety of pictures and feelings. When babies think about "mother" they think of an image, a picture, but that image is alive with sensation. We can imagine the baby hearing his or her mother's voice, smelling her perfume, or feeling her hugs. We can imagine the baby feeling love, or anger, or frustration associated with that image. Imagery is thus clearly more than the mind thinking in pictures. It is so much more than "seeing." It is the mind thinking in pictures with a sensory quality—sight, smell, sound, texture, taste, movement, and most important for our purposes here, *feeling.*

Emotions for adults as well are intimately connected to imagery. Every emotion can be visualized as an image. For example, if each reader were to now conjure up an image of "happiness" we would have as many different images as we have readers. Each of us has our own unique image and each image will tell us something about the inner workings of our mind.

Although we have learned to think in words, we often still think in images, supplying the words afterward. In fact, we are constantly generating imagery, consciously and unconsciously—images that affect us in very profound ways psychologically, emotionally, and physically. Most important, we can learn to utilize this tendency to think in images to bring about positive changes in our lives. We can learn from those images, and we can harness their power. And, as therapists and clergy, we can use them to facilitate this process in survivors of abuse.

Imagery has certain properties that we can utilize in our work with survivors:

1. Imagery underlies our thinking processes, preceding verbal thought, and so taps a deeper level of consciousness. It allows us to peer into the unconscious.
2. Images capture more than words can ever express. Hence the expression "a picture is worth a thousand words."
3. Images help us express and release emotions for which we may be unable to find words.
4. Goal-directed behavior is image oriented. We can help others reach their goals by utilizing goal-directed imagery. For example, we can suggest that a survivor picture herself as healed.

The uses of imagery in therapy are so vast and far-reaching that we will barely scratch the surface, but we hope to give you a good introduction to the use of imagery techniques in a spiritual therapy for survivors. Like metaphor, on which it is based, imagery can come in many forms. In this chapter we will be looking at two types of imagery—survivor-generated images, and therapist- or minister-generated images—and how they can be utilized in healing.

Survivor-generated imagery refers to images that arise spontaneously during therapy sessions or conversations with the survivor. Clients in therapy often speak in terms of images, whether they are describing their dreams, or presenting a metaphoric image that represents their current state. A good example of how powerful this form of imagery can be in promoting healing was described in a paper about the therapy of a Christian woman. The therapist reports that early in treatment, a powerful experience initiated a healing process in the way she perceived herself. At the beginning of the fifth session, the woman reported that she felt trapped and out of control. A period of relaxation was followed by her visualization of the images surrounding her trapped feelings. She described in detail being trapped in a clear, flexible, plastic cube from which there was no exit, yet she could see through the transparent material. She felt as if her back was encased in an iron, viselike apparatus that allowed her to take only shallow breaths. She then saw an image of Christ opening a door in the cube and beckoning to her. As she stepped out she heard the iron brace fall to the floor and Christ saying these words to her, "You are okay; you are loved." Following this visual encounter, she started to weep, saying she felt like a little bird released from its cage. This experience laid the groundwork for the realization that she could explore and integrate the painful events of the past with the comfort and support of Christ within her; that she was not alone (Bruun, 1985).

> **Marion:** This example not only speaks to the power of survivor-generated religious imagery in effecting change, but also to the importance of the therapist being open to the religious language of the patient, even if those images are unfamiliar to the therapist. In fact, when the therapist is of a different faith from the patient, the therapist may have to actively encourage the patient to speak of her own religious images. Many survivors with whom I worked who were Protestant or Catholic had to be encouraged, at least initially, to talk openly about their religious beliefs with a Jewish therapist. However, once it was established that I was open to hearing and learning more about their religious convictions, they began to share more and more. It then became easier for them to spontaneously generate the religious images important to their healing. So, it would not be unusual for a survivor working with me in therapy to talk about images of Christ, since I had made it clear that I was comfortable working with such material.

Ministers may notice survivors using religious imagery in their conversations with them. A survivor might talk about no longer feeling God's presence, or may picture an angry God looking down upon her. Both minister and therapist can help the survivor to explore such God images, and to transform them into more positive ones. In such cases, collaboration between therapist and clergy is most helpful. Through their discussions together, each can contribute to an understanding of the religious image, how it is meaningful to the survivor, and when it might be helpful to attempt to change the image into something more positive.

For example, a survivor might reveal in therapy that she has a feeling Jesus is watching her and shaking his head in disapproval at her behavior. A Jewish therapist who has little exposure to ideas about Jesus might *suspect* that such an image is somewhat dysfunctional. It might appear that the survivor is projecting aspects of a judgmental parent onto God. Yet, not wanting to interfere with the survivor's religious beliefs, the therapist might not know how to handle this material. In a collaborative effort, the therapist could discuss with the minister the meaning and significance of Jesus in the context of the survivor's religion. The minister might explain to the therapist that Jesus is not viewed as a judgmental religious figure in Christianity. Together therapist and clergy might discuss how the survivor came to view Jesus this way, and what could be done to shift this dysfunctional imagery to an image more consistent with current religious thinking, which would be more conducive to promoting healing. Armed with this knowledge, the therapist could then explore that image of a judgmental Jesus more thoroughly with the survivor, comfortably challenging the image as inaccurate and exploring the origins and functions of this painful image. Concurrently, the minister could work with the survivor, examining the real meaning of Jesus in the life of a religious person of their faith, perhaps suggesting new ways Jesus could be imaged.

When working with survivor-generated imagery, the therapist will generally want to ask questions about the image to help the survivor explore it in depth, such as: Can you describe what you are seeing/ feeling/sensing/hearing/smelling? (bringing the image into awareness of all the senses) What is happening now? Is anyone else with you in this image?

Once the image has been fully explored, the therapist might then ask questions about the meaning of the image (e.g., What is this object/person trying to tell you?) and help the survivor transform the image into a more positive internal force (e.g., What do you need to bring into this image that will make it easier to deal with?

What do you need to change to make this image less scary?) In this way, dysfunctional, frightening images can be transformed into vital, health-promoting vehicles through which healing can occur.

Survivor-generated imagery is generally simple and arises spontaneously from the survivor herself. However, therapist-generated imagery can consist of elaborate guided visualizations or meditations written by the therapist herself, or read from a book. It can also consist of spontaneous images that pop into the mind of the therapist while the survivor is talking. For example: "As you were speaking, I got the image of a fly trapped in flypaper. Does that image describe what you're feeling?"

Spontaneous therapist-generated imagery can be worked with in much the same manner as the survivor-generated imagery described above, as long as the survivor agrees that the image is an accurate representation of her thoughts and feelings. Sometimes the survivor will reject the therapist's image as inaccurate, and in other cases slight modifications to the image will need to be made to best fit the survivor's current thinking.

Guided imagery, also known as guided fantasy or guided meditation, is another form of therapist-generated imagery that can be used in therapy with survivors. Such imagery exercises, whether they are taken directly from a book, or created by the therapist herself, tend to share certain common characteristics. First, since guided imagery calls for a switch in consciousness to a deeper level in which imagery is the natural language of thought, it is helpful to be as relaxed as possible. Imaging is a right-brain activity and relaxation counters left-brain logical thinking and negativity. There are many types of relaxation, and when working with a survivor, it is important to tailor the type of relaxation experience to *her* needs, rather than relying on the therapist's pet relaxation exercise. Environment plays a part in the relaxation experience, so often lights are dimmed and eyes are closed (unless the survivor is frightened by such activities). Music can sometimes be helpful. Once relaxation has been achieved, the survivor is led on a guided "trip" inside her mind, in which the therapist describes a scenario for the patient, trying to make the experience as vivid as possible, taking in as many sense modalities as possible (location, sight, smell, sound, touch). The therapist acts as a guide, allowing the survivor to set the pace as much as possible and encouraging the survivor to "let go" into the experience as much as possible.

Marion: It is important to emphasize that there is no one right way to do these imageries—and no wrong way either. Each survivor must find her own way to relax and to image. For example, I tell all the women with whom I work that they can image themselves actually *in* the fantasy, feeling everything as though it were really happening to them, or they can image themselves somewhat detached, as though watching a movie on a screen. Either way is okay.

Some women believe that they cannot do imagery. I assure them that everyone can. It's a part of our human heritage. I expand the concept of imagery for them to include more than just visual images, but also sensations, feelings, smells, and sounds. I explain that one can have a very successful imagery experience without ever "seeing" anything. I also point out that people get better at doing imagery work with practice.

In doing this work, it is also important to allow for the different needs of each survivor. Some survivors do not feel safe or comfortable with their eyes closed, for example, and the therapist must be flexible and sensitive enough to accommodate such situations. The therapist must be ever alert to the effect of the imagery on the survivor. For example, some imagery that might appear innocuous to the therapist may hold very different connotations for the survivor. I once worked with a woman who had been raped repeatedly in a meadow, and when I unknowingly began a guided fantasy with a relaxation exercise that took place in a meadow, she was thrown immediately into a panic.

Keep in mind that whenever you introduce any healing intervention into the therapy, be it guided visualizations, rituals, or ceremonies, you must proceed slowly. Survivors are particularly vulnerable to adverse reactions. No intervention should be undertaken casually.

Many good books are available on guided imagery, several of which deal specifically with religious or spiritual imagery. A few are described in "Appendix F: Resources for Guided Imagery." We have included a few guided meditations which Marion has written and used in her work to demonstrate the power inherent in this type of work.

This first guided meditation aims at helping the survivor create a safe place internally—a place she can turn to when she is feeling especially anxious or when life is feeling out of control. This fantasy has many variations, as many people have written and published similar types of guided meditations.

Creating an Inner Sanctuary

(Begin after a relaxation exercise tailored to the needs of the individual.) . . . Now, I would like you to imagine yourself to be in a peaceful, comfortable place—it could be a natural environment or it could be a room in a house . . . just make sure that you choose a place in which you feel safe and peaceful. Be aware of your surroundings . . . the sounds . . . the colors . . . the smells . . . the sights around you.

Now, do anything you like to make this place even more comfortable and safe for you. You might create some shelter or an altar, or you might want to surround the whole area with a golden white light of protection, peace, and love. . . . You can be alone, or you can have someone join you here. This is your inner sanctuary, a place you can go whenever you need to relax or whenever you need to feel protected from the outside world. No one can hurt you here. No one can disturb you here . . . . You are free to do whatever you wish, to think whatever you wish, to *be* whatever you wish. . . . It is a place that holds a special power for you.

Take a few minutes to experience the joy and the peacefulness of this wonderful place. (pause for a few minutes) . . . Now, when you feel ready, prepare to say good-bye to this place for now, knowing that you can return any time you wish . . . . And finally, come back to your normal existence and open your eyes.

This guided meditation is a particularly powerful one for survivors of severe abuse, since often they feel that no place in the world is safe. Besides providing a safe relationship in the therapy, the most important thing a therapist can do is help the survivor find some safety within her own mind. Guided meditations such as these are a step in the creation of an internal safe place. Even if the therapist does not want to work with guided fantasies in the therapy, religious imagery can be useful in creating an internal safe place for the survivor. The therapist can begin by asking the survivor about any positive religious images or memories. The images may differ widely based on the particular orientation of the survivor, or they may be essentially similar, since some symbols appear to be universal. One woman, a Jehovah's Witness, focused on the image of Jehovah's cleansing waters flowing over her. Similarly, a Jewish survivor also focused on the cleansing properties of water.

The next guided imagery exercise is a particularly powerful one in which the survivor meets an "inner spiritual guide." This exercise can be used both diagnostically—to assess the survivor's concepts of God—and in helping the survivor learn to take a less judgmental, more accepting attitude toward herself. The imagery can be adapted to the needs of the survivor. In the version of the fantasy presented here, the spiritual guide will be referred to as a female, but keep in mind that in this work, adjustment must be made to the gender and identity of the guide based on the wishes of the person with whom one is working. When working with a survivor for whom Jesus has a great meaning, the fantasy can be designed with Jesus as the central figure. For a Jewish survivor, images of angels or other religious figures representative of God's love can be used. For others, one might want to talk about a loving being, clothed in brilliant white light.

Meeting a Spiritual Guide

> Close your eyes and relax. . . . Imagine yourself in a meadow at the edge of a forest. . . . You are standing next to a stream with cool, clear running water. . . . It is a beautiful, warm, sunny spring day. . . . Above you see the clear blue sky with little puffy white clouds. . . . All around you is the deep green, luxurious grass of the meadow. No pollen, nothing to disturb you . . . just a beautiful meadow on a beautiful day. . . . Feel the gentle breeze on your face. . . . Breathe in the fresh, clean air. . . . Feel the sun shining on your face. . . . You can hear the birds chirping. . . . Out in the meadow, there are many wildflowers of many colors and shapes

with butterflies flitting from one to another. . . . There is nothing to worry about, and nothing to do, so take some time to enjoy yourself in this meadow.

Now, walk toward the stream. Watch the clear mountain water as it flows over the rocks and downstream. . . . Bend down and touch the water . . . feel its coolness, a contrast to the warmth of the sunny day. Now as you stand up, you notice that across the bank a figure is coming toward you. . . . You can't see this being clearly yet, but you know that this is your spiritual guide. She steps in the stream, washing her face and hands in the cool, clear water. Then she begins to walk toward you on your side of the stream. . . . As she approaches you begin to see her more clearly. . . . Look at her feet. . . . What is she wearing on her feet? . . . Look at her legs. . . . Notice the skin tones. . . . What is she wearing? . . . Notice the color, the textures of the clothes. . . . See her hair. . . . What is its color and texture? . . . Now look at her face. Notice the color and texture of the skin. . . . As you look at her face you notice that she is smiling at you, and in her eyes is a look of great love for you. . . . Her whole face radiates a joy at meeting you here today. . . . How do you feel when you see her great joy at meeting you? . . . She is looking at you lovingly, and humbly. . . . How do you feel as you see her looking at you humbly and with great love? . . . As she reaches the bank of your side of the stream, she extends her hand and says something to you. . . . What is she saying?

Prepare to say goodbye to your guide for now. . . . Remember, you can come back to see her any time you wish. . . . She turns and walks back across the water to the other side of the stream. How do you feel as you watch her leave? . . . Walk back into the meadow, and take some time to absorb this experience.

Marion: This guided meditation can provide the survivor with a very powerful experience of God's love. One woman with whom I worked stated that "the guided imagery really made me *feel* for the first time in my life that I am loved by God." She had been able, over the years, to maintain at least an intellectual understanding of the concept that she is loved by God, but had never before experienced a feeling of that love.

Most of the Christian survivors with whom I have worked
have used the image of Jesus in this fantasy. The reactions
were varied and interesting. One woman was unable to even
visualize Jesus looking at her with love and compassion. Discussion of her reaction led to many months of examination of
her internal representation of God and a gradual transformation of her God imagery into a more positive force in her life.
Another woman with whom I did this meditation was so
touched by the idea that Jesus could love her so deeply that she
began doing this fantasy on her own each morning. She would
sometimes talk to Jesus, asking questions. Using this guided
meditation allowed her to feel safe and loved as she began
each day during her continuing recovery from abuse.

A Jewish survivor, Sarah, pictured an angel coming to talk
with her. This angel was a beautiful, warm, nurturing woman,
dressed in a white, flowing, gossamer gown. This angel gazed
at Sarah with a look of deep love and compassion greater than
Sarah had ever known. It has been many years since Sarah did
this mediation, but she tells me she has never forgotten how
wonderful it felt.

Again, literally hundreds of already written guided meditations
are available, designed for various functions. Some aim at self-
discovery, some at goal setting, some at guidance for life's problems. Some of the books described in Appendix F contain instructions on how to bring this work into your practice, and even explain
how to construct original guided meditations. For those new to
using guided imagery in work, we offer several pointers:

1. These guided meditations are not Scripture. They can be
changed to suit the needs of the survivor.

2. Since creating and working with imagery is primarily a right-
brain activity, an intuitive process, it is necessary to temporarily let
go of the logical, analytical mind-set and trust intuition. When working with an image, a thought might come that makes no logical
sense (e.g., "See if you can fold up this scene and put it in your
pocket."). It is not necessary to have a theoretical reason to use what
arises from one's unconscious—just trust it.

3. When using the word "visualize" with survivors, be clear that this does not just mean "seeing" an image. Some people may get a clear image, but others may get just a vague impression. Others may see colors or sense feelings or thoughts. Others may even report just *thinking* about the fantasy. It is important to validate that however the visualizer works is okay.

> **Susan:** Visualization does not come easy for me. I envy those who can create lush pastoral scenes in their minds. I, however, do not create "pictures" in my head. Mostly, I think in media headlines: "Film crew at eleven!" I also hear pieces of songs that have meaning. I have learned that this is a form of visualization. We tend to think of visualization as involving our eyes, but there are many ways people visualize. I prefer to use the term *visceralizations,* since this term better describes the experience. I use the concept of visceralization in my work at the Clubhouse (a program for the chronically mentally ill).
>
> Once, in one of the groups in my program, I was working with a woman, Madeline, who was an incessant talker. She could not stop talking, and she would interject herself in a loud and intrusive manner. This was especially disruptive to others in her group. We had been talking about this problem for a while, but nothing seemed to help her change her behavior. Finally, I gave her the "image" of what was going on in my head. I said to her, "When I think of you, a song keeps coming into my head—Simon and Garfunkel's '59th Street Bridge.'" And then I sang, "Slow down, you move too fast. You got to make the mornin' last." She laughed, as did the others in the group, and everyone yelled, "Yeah!" Weeks later, I overheard one of my staff trying again to deal with Madeline's disruptive behavior by saying, "What was that song that Susan sang to you?" Madeline, stopped what she was doing, laughed, and sang the lyrics. She added, "I have been trying to sing that every time I have a problem."
>
> I call this the "Ally McBeal" school of therapy, where everyone has a theme song.
>
> **Marion:** As one who is easily able to create lush pastoral scenes in my mind, I have always envied those, like Susan,

who are able to use humor in their "visceralizations." Susan does make a point. We each have our own way of "visceraliz-ing," and as therapists, we must be open to other ways of working. We must also be careful not to create a mind-set that visualizers must *see* the images.

4. Pacing is important too. Allow plenty of time between utter-ances. The therapist's sense of time may be different from that of the person doing the fantasy. One way to ensure that the pace is slow enough is to practice beforehand. Tape the fantasy and try it out, or try it out on friends or colleagues and get their feedback. Finally, when introducing the concept of guided meditation to the survivor, work out a way for her to signal if the pace is too fast.

5. The tone of voice should be gentle and soothing. Again, prac-ticing with tapes and other people will help to alleviate problems with sound of voice, etc.

STORIES AND PARABLES

The power of the parable is well known in both Western and Eastern cultures: "These parables of the storyteller do not shine, they burn. They force us to rethink our faith, get in touch with God of our own interiority, and reexamine our attitudes toward others," exclaims theologian Brennan Manning (1982, p. 61). Similarly, John Jacob Raub proclaims that parables are riddles intended to "blow" our judgmental minds—and thus our worlds—apart (Raub, 1992). Just as the images and symbols described above, stories and parables aim at a deeper level of consciousness, bypassing the ratio-nal, critical mind. They literally have to the power to shake up the psyche in a way no rational argument ever could. However, the process of listening to a parable is not a passive one, as Matthew Fox has pointed out. In his discussion of Jesus' parables, Fox sug-gests that Jesus' stories are not merely moral lessons or elaborate allegories. They require the listener's participation just as does a koan between a Buddhist guru and a disciple (Fox, 1988).

In Christianity, the parable is most associated with Jesus. Several of his parables can have meaning in our work with Christian survi-vors. The "Barren Fig Tree" parable speaks to the extent of God's love for us, as the "Good Samaritan" illustrates the limitlessness of that love. The "Prodigal Son" speaks to God's forgiveness, and has special meaning to survivors who feel they have been "bad" people, too bad to deserve divine love.

In Jewish culture, stories and parables also have an important place. Many rabbis teach in the form of story. In their book, *Everyday Miracles: The Healing Wisdom of Hasidic Stories,* Howard Polsky and Yaella Wozner (1989) give hundreds of examples of such stories, many of which are in keeping with The Benevolence Model, which formed the basis of our spiritual work with Teresa. Polsky and Wozner suggest that parables and stories shake us up, because they do not follow the logical path we expect. The following Hasidic story from their book illustrates this point:

> A man once confessed a sin to the Rabbi of Apt and told him with tears how he had atoned for it. The *tzaddik* [holy man] laughed. The man went on to tell what more he intended doing to atone for his sin; the rabbi went on laughing. The man wanted to speak on, but the laughter robbed him of his speech. He stared at the *tzaddik* in horror. And then his very soul held its breath and he heard that which is spoken deep within. He realized how trivial all his fuss about atoning had been, and he turned to God. (Polsky and Wozner, 1989, p. 222)

Rituals are an important part of religious life as we will discuss in the following section, but sometimes rituals become lifeless, dry, behavioral repetitions stripped of meaning. As Polsky and Wozner state, "powerful circuits need strong circuit-breakers" (Polsky and Wozner, 1989, p. 222). The confessor in the above story is expecting acceptance of his atonement from the rabbi, a confirmation that in expressing his plan to atone for the sin, he is doing the right thing. The confessor is trapped by such a ritual. His atonement lacks heart. He is pious only in that he is conforming to the letter of the law, i.e., "atoning for his sin." Yet, the wise rabbi does not point this out to him directly. Instead, he laughs. This laughter shocks the confessor to the point where something "snaps," and he stops all attempts to explain his story. Then, the miracle occurs. He begins to listen to his own heart and let in God. How many of us, as we read this story, become aware of instances of our own mindless adherence to ritual?

The unexpected response is what astounds the listener in the parable told by Jesus in "The Vineyard Laborers." In this story workers are paid the same wage, despite the number of hours they work. The wage was based on a full day's workload and was meted out to all. The workers who had worked all day complained to the landowner about the injustice of his policy: "These last worked only one hour, and you have made them equal to us who have borne the burden of the day and the scorching heat." The owner replied, "Friend, I am doing you no wrong; did you not agree with me for the usual daily wage? Take what belongs to you and go; I choose to give to this last the same as I give to you. . . . Are you envious because I am generous?" This parable eloquently speaks to God's love for us—a love that does not follow human rules. It tells us that no matter what we do, no matter how much we accomplish or dedicate ourselves, we are all equally loved by God. God's love is distributed evenly; it does not have to be earned.

Some stories teach through humor, as in following story of the Hasid and the German Jew:

Once, not long ago, a Hasidic Jew and an athletic, strong German Jew were playing golf together. The Hasid played superbly—finishing with a score well below par. The athletic German Jew, struggled through the course, missing very easy shots, and finally finished with a score of 100 above par.

The German Jew complained, "I don't understand why I did so poorly. Over the years I have taken lessons from some of the best pros in the business and I can't hit a shot or sink a putt. You, on the other hand, played fantastically. I wonder, where did *you* take lessons?"

"I never did," the Hasidic Jew replied, "but I do pray to God every morning when I go to *shul* . . . "

"That's it? That's all you do?" asked the German Jew, incredulously.

"That's it," the Hasidic Jew replied. "I pray an hour each and every morning."

The following week, the two played the same course again. The Hasidic Jew continued to play marvelously, finishing with a score even lower than before. The German Jew again came in well over par.

Exasperated, the German Jew complained to the Hasid, "I don't understand. I did exactly what you said. I went to *shul* every morning this last week and prayed for at least an hour each time."

"Where did you go?" asked the Hasid.

"Temple Beth Israel, on Grove Street."

"That's the problem!" cried the Hasid. "That temple is for *tennis*."

This amusing tale illustrates quite nicely the silliness of believing that God watches over us and will fulfill all our wishes, *if only we do the right thing*.

> **Marion:** One of my patients told me that story several years ago. I have used this story of the Hasid and the German Jew in my work with survivors, both Jewish and Christian, who talk about God granting wishes like Santa Claus, exclaiming that they must have done something wrong, because God has never granted them their wishes. Without telling them they are *wrong* to feel this way, I am able to get the point across humorously that notions about God fulfilling our desires if we do the right thing or say the right words is a magical fantasy.

RITUALS AND CEREMONIES

Recent studies of artifacts from the Ice Age have suggested that humans may have been performing rituals for over 30,000 years. Ceremonies and rituals are important to religious life, and have meaning to many abuse survivors. In this chapter we are speaking only of those ceremonies that are used in a healthy, growth-producing way. We are aware that some survivors were abused in a ceremonial or ritualistic manner. We are also aware that some survivors of severe abuse are involved in self-inflicted destructive rituals, such as cutting themselves, binge drinking, and self-deprecatory behaviors. However, in this chapter we are addressing only the creation of new, healthy rituals and practices, aimed at promoting wholeness and growth.

Health-promoting rituals can be as simple as developing habits of self-nurturing. In her book, *Resolving Sexual Abuse,* psychotherapist Yvonne Dolan (1991) writes about such self-nurturing rituals that the therapist can encourage the survivor to develop. Examples include buying oneself fresh flowers each week, writing regularly in a journal, cooking a special meal for oneself once a week, laying clothes out the night before and preparing to make mornings more serene, and taking weekly dance classes. Dolan suggests that these self-nurturing ritual tasks be repeated for a few weeks like a homework assignment and then discussed in sessions. The repetition within the therapy context allows it to become familiar enough for the survivor to continue it when it is no longer assigned.

Other ceremonies and rituals may be more elaborate and may be performed only once, but they can provide a powerful experience of change or closure for the survivor. Combs and Freedman (1990) have pointed out that although ceremonies can take a wide variety of forms, at the most general level they perform two functions—to validate an occurrence and to promote change. We have used rituals and ceremonies sparingly in our own work with Teresa; however, the ceremonies we did perform incorporated aspects of both validation and change.

A most significant and moving ceremony involved Teresa's alter Mimic. The ceremony took place at the point when Mimic had finally realized that he was indeed human. Members of the support group, including Susan, the pastor Michael Hardin, Steven, and Marion gathered in the church to take part in a ceremony in which Mimic was given a human name. The name "Justin" had been suggested by Michael who had explained to Mimic that the Latin root for the name was the word *justice*. Steven began the ceremony with an explanation of the importance of names in the Bible—from the naming of the animals in Genesis to the giving of the name Paul to Saul as he entered a new covenant with God. This was followed by a candlelighting ceremony in which Marion lit candles representing the old and new names. This portion of the ceremony made concrete the transformation of Mimic into Justin. Each person present was then given an opportunity to express feelings about Justin and about the significance of the naming ceremony to him or her. Thus, the ceremony marked both a change in Mimic's identity, as he became human, Justin, and served as a public validation of Justin's meaning and worth to people with whom he had become close.

Ceremonies and celebrations marking Teresa's birthday and her graduation from her nursing program also contributed to her growing sense of self-worth and importance to others. The celebration of a birthday can be an affirmation of joy over one's birth. Teresa had never had such celebrations, and sharing this joy with a group of people who had come to care about her and her other "personalities" was a significant step in her healing.

Many types of rituals and ceremonies can be useful to the survivor. Yvonne Dolan describes a ceremony she labels "An Imaginary Funeral for Lost Family of Origin," (Dolan, 1991, pp. 132-133) in which the survivor imagines holding a funeral service for the family members she lost because of her abuse. In preparation, she is told to collect and discard pictures or objects that symbolize her past connection to them. Burning the pictures, Dolan explains, has a special significance for some women. The survivor can then invite understanding and supportive others and hold a wake in which she speaks about her feelings toward each person she is "laying to rest." Or the survivor may want to hold the funeral alone, or in the presence of the therapist. At the conclusion, the survivor is to bury something that symbolizes the person for whom she is holding the funeral. Dolan reports that survivors of severe sexual abuse who have devised their own version of this ritual have described powerful feelings of closure and relief.

> **Susan:** Several years ago, I worked at the Clubhouse with a woman, Dorothy, who had been severely abused, and who had been diagnosed with DID. She had become pregnant by her boyfriend. In her eighth month, during a routine prenatal checkup, the doctor discovered that the baby had been strangled by the cord and had died. Unfortunately, she would have to carry the baby to term. Her therapist and I worked with her on this issue, as she was deeply distressed. When she finally went into labor, both her therapist and I went to the hospital to be with her.

Dorothy wanted to have a funeral for her baby, but she had no money, no church affiliation, and no particularly strong religious beliefs. Yet, she did not want to bury the child "in Potter's Field." So, I spoke with Michael Hardin, the pastor of my own church. He was deeply touched by the story, and he offered Dorothy an opportunity to have the funeral at our church. As a result of his contacts with funeral directors, he was able to obtain a donated casket and burial plot. While I was aware that there could be boundary issues by having the funeral at my church, I realized that she had no place else to go. Furthermore, although I was working with her in my capacity as a mental health professional, I was not her therapist.

The funeral was held at the church, and all the helping professionals involved with Dorothy attended, as did her mother, her father, and the baby's father. Michael had created a special service that was designed to meet Dorothy at her level of understanding. He spoke to all Dorothy's alters at all levels of her psyche. He even wrote music for the ceremony. Michael created a service that touched Dorothy on many levels. Dorothy felt loved, cared for, and supported, and she felt she was not alone in her suffering. There was not a dry eye in the church. He touched all of us in a meaningful way.

After the ceremony, a small reception was held in the church basement. Coffee and cake were served. This reception was designed to provide Dorothy with an experience of "normalcy"—to learn about how many families deal with death. This funeral enabled Dorothy to deal with grief in a normal way. Without the inclusion of clergy, Dorothy would not have had this kind of opportunity. It was a profoundly moving experience for all involved.

When working with a survivor with dissociative identity disorder such as Teresa, it is important that the preparation for the ceremony include all the alters. If any alters do not understand the reason for the ceremony, problems in the implementation may result. For example, frightened child alters may disrupt the ceremony, while hostile alters may seek to sabotage it. The preparation process, therefore, should include the participation of involved alters. Some alters may decide not to participate, but may agree not to disrupt the proceedings. Other alters may want to be a part of the planning process from beginning to end.

Rituals and ceremonies are appropriate even for those survivors who have been ritually abused, provided the therapist and minister remain aware of potential problems. Carolyn Holderread Heggen (1993) has suggested that the very symbols that may have been used during the ritual abuse—candles, boxes, or certain garments—may be included as part of the new healing ceremony, as the survivor reclaims the power of those objects for good. We might add that ministers must be sensitive to the sinister meaning that seemingly innocuous religious symbols can have for the survivor of ritual abuse. Similarly, if the survivor is to include some of the symbols formerly associated with the abuse in a healing ceremony, the therapist must spend much time in therapy preparing the survivor for their usage. Both therapist and minister can help the survivor transform those symbols into positive forces beforehand. The ceremony then becomes the final stage in the transformation of those symbols.

Psychologist Joyce Vesper concurs. She points out that because ceremonies are used to heal and bring closure to highly painful memories, they can be used with individuals who have suffered ritualistic abuse: "The use of a healthy, planned, behavioral activity and a meaningful written script teaches the ritualistic abuse survivor the possibilities of positive gain from prescribed actions and predetermined words. By enlarging the survivor's knowledge of the healing benefits of ceremony, the ritualistic abuse patient discovers him/herself enriched, enhanced, and supported by a previously dreaded and, perhaps, hated exercise" (Vesper, 1991, p. 111). Vesper suggests that before initiating a ceremony procedure with survivors of ritual abuse, the therapist should explore all possible fears and thoughts. Helpful questions to consider include: Are there certain phrases or sounds that might trigger a flashback or picture which the survivor cannot handle? Are there locations or environmental reminders that might provoke an abreaction?

The creation of such healthy ceremonies and rituals is an excellent opportunity for therapist, minister, and survivor to collaborate. As Combs and Freedman (1990) point out, for the survivor, preparing for, thinking about, and remembering it afterward, all contribute to the meaning and power of that ceremony. In fact, for some people preparation or thinking about a ceremony can serve the same purpose as actually conducting it. The therapist and the minister serve as consultants to the survivor in this process—the minister helping her to find meaningful symbols and activities, the therapist helping ensure that the process feels safe and authentic.

As we have seen in this chapter, many opportunities exist for therapists and ministers to work together in bringing a spiritual dimension into the therapy, whether through the use of religious imagery aimed at the unconscious, or in the telling of stories with a spiritual message, or in adjunctive activities such as the creation of healthy ceremonies and rituals. The collaborative effort can only bring a deeper, more meaningful dimension into the survivor's life.

Chapter 9

Therapists and Clergy
Growing Together

In scattering the seed, scattering your "charity," your kind deeds, you are giving away in one form or another, part of your personality, and taking into yourself part of another. He who received them from you will hand them to another. And how can you tell what part you may have in the future determination of the destinies of humanity?

Fyodor Dostoyevski

Grace is only truly appreciated and expressed in the actual, immediate experience of real life situations. Finally, it can only be "lived into."

Gerald May

STEVEN

As a new dad watching my daughter grow, I am amazed at how quickly she comprehends and learns. Everything is new, exciting, challenging, and sometimes overwhelming. She watches my wife and me, imitates our actions, learns from our modeling, and certainly makes her needs known to us. Each day brings a new opportunity to understand this new world around her. When she toddles into the room, gives me a big smile and says, "Hello, Daddy," my heart melts. It is an experience of *shared grace* as we as parents both give and receive from our child.

This give and take of parenthood, in a way, reflects my experience with Marion and Susan, helping Teresa move toward healing and wholeness. For me, the learning curve was steep, and the challenge sometimes overwhelming. I was stretched as I tried to understand the therapeutic process at a deep level, and I was challenged to apply these newly discovered counseling techniques to my work. Yet, through this time, I grew in my understanding of the wonderful complexity of human beings, a complexity that allows individuals to continue functioning even under conditions of extreme hardship. The experience of shared grace, working together as clergy and therapist, has truly ministered to *me* as well as Teresa.

On an educational level, I grew in my knowledge of clinical psychology and psychotherapy. My knowledge of therapy had been limited to basic psychology courses in college and my training in pastoral counseling at seminary. Before meeting Teresa and Marion (Dr. Bilich), I had a somewhat skewed understanding of DID—a Hollywood version of Sybil. I was not even sure that multiple personalities really existed. At first it appeared that Teresa was just a good actor, making up the different personalities, and pretending to be different people. I quickly came to experience the consistency of actions and behaviors of each alter, a consistency that could not possibly have been rehearsed or acted out. By working with Marion, I learned about the kinds of experiences that lead a child to this condition. Marion taught me what to look for when Teresa dissociated. I learned how and why symptoms manifest themselves and about the various treatment options. I also learned how to deal with flashbacks and the violent memories that plague survivors of severe childhood abuse. I was given a vocabulary that brought clarity as I tried to describe to Teresa or to others what was happening to her.

Marion was able to answer the questions I had about how I could spend my time with Teresa without creating more fear or misconceptions. The therapy sessions in which I participated gave me a new insight into a model of professional care that was not only applied to my work with Teresa, but to my work with others over the years. I came to have high regard for therapy and the need for people to have an opportunity to work through issues and pain from the past before healing can take place. Working with a psychologist clearly gave me the opportunity to be educated and trained at a new level.

Our shared experience has also helped me to take my understanding of God—my theology—and apply it to my pastoral care, to bring healing and wholeness into the lives of my parishioners. I have a greater belief in the power of God's love and the healing presence in and at work through people. I received direct confirmation of the power of our collaboration as I witnessed and experienced a real transformation in Teresa's alters. As we worked together, emotional and spiritual healing took place. The truth of a benevolent God who loves, forgives, and redeems was evident in Teresa's experience. With the realization of this truth came hope—hope for a way of life apart from the dissociation. For me, there has been a recognition that human beings are complex and wonderful, and that wholeness comes as people experience healing spiritually, emotionally, and physically.

I know that I have been better able to deal with other people under my pastoral care because of the broader understanding of psychological disorders that our work together has brought me. In the years since our collaboration began, there have been many occasions in which my newfound understanding has been helpful to others. One parishioner had a panic attack during a youth event she was chaperoning. From my work with Marion, I had the knowledge to immediately identify the panic attack and was able to reassure her and calm her down. I have since worked with teens who are self-mutilating and have been able to counsel them, identifying issues from their past that were contributing to their hurtful behavior.

I now have an understanding of eating disorders and have talked with young women to encourage them to seek counseling. I ministered to a young man with a borderline personality who was unable to function in the social or work world. I was able to identify his need for appropriate boundaries and counsel him in basic life skills and social behaviors that moved him forward. Because of my knowledge and experience with dissociative disorders, I have been able to educate my peers. Once, a pastor called me for counsel on how to best minister to someone in his congregation who had identified himself as having multiple personalities.

In my youth ministry, Teresa's story has been especially helpful, both as an example of the transforming power of extending love to others, and as a way of teaching teens about people who are different. Teresa's dramatic story demonstrates to teenagers that we never know what a person has been through in life just by looking at her, that we should not judge people by their outward appearances and behaviors. I also use the example of our work with Teresa to communicate another important message—that modeling God's love is a way of extending grace to all people.

As a result of my collaboration with Marion and Susan and my increasing understanding of psychology, I am also more aware of the importance of establishing healthy boundaries between minister and parishioner. In so many ways my ability to minister to and help people has deepened and grown. Certainly, my ministry was changed forever.

The experience of *shared grace* has also ministered to me personally. I have come to understand myself better through our experience of working together. To some degree, I was able to share some of my own struggles and hurts, thus giving Teresa a chance to give back, to experience her own ability to extend love and care to another. This experience helped her develop a sense of her own worth.

God revealed himself to me through Teresa. I saw his grace at work in a person who had been so terribly abused. God loved Teresa, had compassion for her. She had done nothing to deserve what had happened to her. She needed only to allow God to love her, accept her, transform her. I saw a bit of myself in Teresa, certainly not in the horrific abuse she had suffered, but in another way, I, much like Teresa, had been robbed of my own belovedness. I know that God loves me, accepts me just as I am. In allowing that love in my own brokenness, I, too, can find healing. I was also blessed by working with Marion, who was a mentor and friend. Her openness to hearing my concerns and heart from a spiritual perspective gave our relationship depth. Because of this experience, my eyes were opened to my *own* need to pursue therapy. I have learned that any time you are ministering to others, your own issues can get in the way. Therapy is a way to work through issues and at least become aware of where those personal issues may create difficulties in your work with other people. I thank God for allowing me to enter this experience of shared grace, and pray that others will find our experience an inspiration and opportunity to realize the same.

SUSAN

Marion, Steven, and I were three people with very different backgrounds, people whose paths in life otherwise may never have crossed. We were joined together to help another human being heal. It was a remarkable set of circumstances, and many gifts resulted from it.

The Benevolence Model was nothing short of extraordinary. We had started out with only vague notions of how to integrate spirituality into our work. The model evolved from our work with Teresa, in that as we worked with her we realized that we were creating a framework that reflected our spiritual beliefs, and out of which we could live our lives.

I had always loved to read spiritually oriented books. I wanted to use Jesus as a model, but had never found a way to integrate His teachings into my life consistently. There were moments of consistency, *just moments*. I did not want to be the kind of person who would think about God in church on Sundays, and on the way home, run my neighbor down in the parking lot fighting for a spot. It is not that I walk around being holy—I am far from that—but what I am striving for is an internal consistency in the way I live my life. The Benevolence Model allowed me to integrate my intellectual understanding of Jesus and my *experience* of Jesus. The principles of The Benevolence Model permeate all that I do.

If one were to reject The Benevolence Model as a merely a Christian model, one would be missing the point. We used the model in a Christian context with an emphasis on Jesus because Teresa was Christian. The spiritual underpinnings of this model transcend any specific religious beliefs. The Benevolence Model could easily be adapted to different belief systems depending on the needs of the survivor. Whatever spiritual framework used, it is important that the work be done with heart, with intention. Clearly, this collaboration was done with intention. It was evident from watching Marion and Steven work with Teresa that they were deeply committed to her.

We can speak of "a strong therapeutic alliance" or about "good engagement skills," but no matter how it is expressed, we are discussing healing through relationship. Collaboration brings relationship to a deeper level. Marion trusted that Teresa knew what she needed to heal from her childhood abuse, and she provided a "holding environment" in which Teresa could heal. Steven mirrored the love of Jesus, which gave Teresa the experience of God's love. The support group provided Teresa with a "laboratory" in which she could learn about mutuality in relationships. All those experiences allowed Teresa to feel loved. Those experiences were very powerful, more powerful than any one relationship could be.

Our collaboration became a rich experience for *all* involved. It did not start out that way. We came together with the intention of helping Teresa heal. We did not intend to develop the deep friendships which evolved from our work together. I came to love Marion and Steven deeply, and I am thankful for their presence in my life.

Healing through relationship. Collaboration with heart. These are the experiences of *shared grace*. We all become vehicles through which God's grace comes into our lives.

MARION

"I try to listen to what God wants. The path I'm walking is so difficult, and I feel so alone at times. I know on some level that it is the right path, but I don't know anyone else on this path. It's so hard and lonely." Those words, spoken by a young woman client, touched me deeply. Kathy was a freshman in college. The daughter of a minister from the rural South, she had moved to New York City to study art. Kathy was following a religious path, so far removed from the lives of her friends at school that at times she felt totally alienated. Her pain brought tears to my eyes. I replied, "Think about Jesus and about what God asked of him. His path was going to lead him to great physical suffering and the death of his body, but he kept on that path."

Kathy brightened as she heard those words. "That's why God came to us in human form," she continued, "so that he, as Jesus, could experience the struggles and pain we do." As Kathy spoke a sense of peace came over her. She was visibly relieved.

A small, seemingly insignificant snippet of conversation from a therapy session—yet contained within this short interchange are hints of the profound changes in the way I work and live as a result of my experiences with Steven, Susan, and Teresa.

First, this conversation reflects my increased awareness of both the importance of dealing with religious and spiritual issues in therapy and my newfound knowledge of other people's religious beliefs. Steven and Susan taught me about Christianity, and more specifically, about Jesus. I, in turn, have been able to use that knowledge to help my Christian patients. Without this background in Christianity, I would not have been able to help Kathy understand the meaning of her difficult path. So, one might say that using the learning obtained during the collaboration, I was able to bring a moment of grace into the life of still another person.

This conversation with Kathy also reflects a trust I have developed in my own inner wisdom. The practice of psychotherapy is as much an art as it is a science. Despite numerous studies about what is effective in therapy, we still often do not know what makes one intervention successful and another fall flat. Although still mindful of the scientific aspects of my work (research findings, ethical issues, proper procedure, etc.), I am also more in touch with an inner wisdom that guides my work with patients. Through Steven I learned that we are all instruments of God, vehicles through which God's love comes into the lives of others. When I talked to Kathy about Jesus' path, I did not know *why* I chose to say what I did. It was certainly not an intellectual decision, but the impetus came from a deep level of my being. In this case, I allowed myself to be open to an inner guidance, and in doing so, I became a vehicle through which grace came into her life.

That is what *shared grace* is all about. We each can become vehicles through which love and grace come into other people's lives. So many people have benefited from our work together. When Teresa asked me to speak to her minister, little did I know what she had set in motion, nor did I realize how profoundly this experience would change my life and the lives of all involved. It was my job to help Teresa heal, but God's grace came into *my* life as I worked with her. I grew and learned from my contacts with Teresa and all those she brought into my life. From Teresa I learned a bit more about how people heal from pain. She taught me how she could *heal herself* if I provided her with a loving, secure relationship. She taught me about the importance of love and spirituality in therapy. I have brought these invaluable lessons into my work with others. Through my work with Teresa I also met Steven, Susan, and Jim Smollon (another member of the support group). All three became close friends whom I love dearly. I know that I brought as much into their lives as they have brought into mine. In giving to Teresa, we all received tenfold. It was truly an experience of *shared grace*.

It is our hope that this book has inspired you, too, to join in collaboration with others. In doing so, who knows what you might set in motion. . . .

Appendix A
Teresa's Personality Structure

Teresa	Robot
The Host Personality: Thirty-five-year-old divorced woman who works as a nurse in a community hospital. She is a recovering alcoholic, co-caine addict, and bulimic.	*The Executive Alter:* Robot is responsible for organizing all of the others inside. He believes himself to be devoid of feeling.

Terry	Monica
The Professional: The alter who went to work and nursing school. She was the "adult" who did what had to be done.	*The Keeper of the Rage:* Nineteen-year-old angry alter who covers up a soft, caring interior. Initially she was self-destructive and harmed the others inside.

Brian	Sarah and Sandy
The Protector: An eighteen-year-old with a love of music. He is shy and sensitive, and he is protective and loving of the child alters.	*The Keepers of Innocence:* Two child alters, ages five and six respectively, who crave love and attention.

Lesley	Dennis
The Internal Self-Helper (who does not like the term): She provides wise counsel to the therapist about how to help the alters.	*The Teenager with Raging Hormones:* He is a thirteen-year-old with an intense curosity about sex.

Mimic	Justin
The Internal Representation of the Mother: Originally perceived himself as a computer. Mimic's belief system was based on the concepts of malevolence and hatred. After the naming ceremony, he became Justin (see box at right).	*The Pivotal Alter:* He became the major alter who was most affected by The Benevolence Model. As his belief system changed, he operated out of the belief that "benevolence and love are better than malevolence and hate." He is fond of saying "we can all integrate as long as we all become Justin."

Appendix B

Resources for Therapists

ORGANIZATIONS

International Society for the Study of Dissociation (ISSD), 60 Revere Drive, Suite 500, Northbrook, IL 60062. Phone: (847) 480-0899. When working with survivors of severe childhood abuse, therapists are likely to encounter those who are suffering from dissociative disorders. Working with such individuals requires specialized training and/or supervision. The ISSD is a professional organization which provides professional and public education about dissociative disorders and promotes the development of local groups for study, education, and referral.

American Association of Pastoral Counselors, 9504-A Lee Highway, Fairfax, VA 22031-2303. This is a nonsectarian organization that sets professional standards for pastoral counselors and counseling centers throughout North America. They are committed to respecting the religious beliefs of those who seek help without imposing the counselor's own beliefs onto the client.

BOOKS AND ARTICLES

(We wish to thank Elizabeth Bowman, MD, for her help in compiling this list.)

Bloch, James (1991). *Assessment and treatment of multiple personality and dissociative disorders.* Sarasota, FL: Professional Resource Press. This is an excellent and short (100 pages) reference, suitable for learning the basics.

Bowman, Elizabeth and William E. Amos (1993). Utilizing clergy in the treatment of multiple personality disorder. *Dissociation* 6(1):47-53. This paper does not focus on a true collaboration between therapist and clergy, but does discuss in detail many ways in which therapist and minister can consult and refer to each other. Specific treatment interventions that involve religious content are also discussed. Each section is illustrated with case examples.

Chu, James (1988). Ten traps for therapists in the treatment of trauma survivors. *Dissociation* 1(4):24-32. This article is a must for all therapists involved in working with survivors of severe childhood abuse. Chu makes the point that such survivors tend to be among the most difficult patients with whom one can work. Their testing of limits and deep issues of dependency often create traps for the therapist. Included in the article are suggestions on how to deal with issues of trust, idealization, distance, boundaries, and the setting of limits.

Chu, James (1998). *Rebuilding shattered lives: The responsible treatment of complex post-traumatic and dissociative disorders.* New York: John Wiley & Sons. This excellent book provides the clinician with a detailed explanation of dissociative theory, and through the use of clinical vignettes, also provides the reader with valuable techniques for treatment.

Figley, Charles (Ed.) (1995). *Compassion fatigue: Coping with secondary traumatic stress disorder in those who treat the traumatized.* New York: Brunner/Mazel. Those of us who provide care for traumatized individuals can find ourselves subject to a secondary traumatic reaction or even disorder, a kind of "compassion fatigue." This book, compiled by a number of mental health and health professionals, helps the reader identify the signs of such secondary traumatization. Prevention and treatment are discussed.

Holcomb, Wayne (1987). Promoting collaborative aftercare: Tapping support within the religious community for both mental health clients and agencies. *Psychosocial Rehabilitation Journal* 10(3):63-75. This article discusses the advantages for mental health agencies to develop relationships with churches and synagogues to facilitate greater patient access to community resources. It also provides guidelines for mental health agencies and religious organizations endeavoring to develop programs together.

Lovinger, Robert (1984). *Working with religious issues in therapy.* New York: Aronson. According to the book jacket, this book "shows the therapist how to understand and respond to the problems religious patients present in psychotherapy and the problems religions present to therapists." The book will be useful to all therapists, but is especially useful for those therapists who are cautious about bringing religious or spiritual issues into therapy. Two chapters are particularly helpful for therapists working with individuals of religions other than their own: "Selected Specific Religious Terms and Issues," and "Religious Denominations and Some Implications for Personality." Also included in the book are sections on how to deal with religious differences, and working with clergy and families.

Meylink, Willa (1988). Impact on referral training of psychologists on the clergy: Psychologist-professional interaction. *Journal of Psychology and Christianity* 7(3):55-64. This article suggests that referral training seminars can facilitate collaboration between therapist and clergy.

Pargament, Kenneth (1997). *The psychology of religion and coping: Theory, research, practice.* New York: Guilford Press. An in-depth examination of the role of spirituality and religion in the coping process based on current research findings. Pargament's examination of which religious beliefs are helpful and which are harmful is especially important for the clinician. He also provides ample information on integrating religious material into psychotherapy sessions.

Putnam, Frank (1989). *Diagnosis and treatment of multiple personality disorder.* New York: Guilford Press. This comprehensive guide to the diagnosis and treatment of dissociative disorders is almost a classic in the field. Contains many clinical examples.

Ross, Colin (1996). *Dissociative identity disorder: Diagnosis, clinical features, and treatment of multiple personality* (Second edition). New York: John Wiley and Sons. Another classic that details the diagnosis and treatment of dissociative disorders. This second edition contains new chapters on epidemiology, skepticism of DID, and a discussion of the false memory controversy.

Spiegel, David (Ed.) (1996). *Dissociative disorders: A clinical review.* Lutherville, MD: Sidran Press. (Sidran Press is located at 2328 W. Joppa Road, Suite 15, Lutherville, MD 21093. Phone: 410-825-8888.) This book contains excellent comprehensive overviews of dissociative phenomena—including DID, depersonalization, and the connections between dissociation and conversion, somatization, and trauma.

Weaver, Andrew, Harold Koenig, and Frank Ochberg (1996). Posttraumatic stress, mental health professionals, and the clergy: A need for collaboration, training, and research. *Journal of Traumatic Stress* 9(4):847-856. Relying on clinical experience and research studies, this paper builds a strong case for collaborative efforts between therapists and clergy.

WEB SITES

<www.issd.org>—The Web site for the International Society for the Study of Dissociation, this site offers information on education for those mental health professionals new to work with survivors of severe childhood abuse. A section on "guidelines for treatment" focuses on diagnostic procedures, treatment planning, and boundary management, among other issues. Books and annual conferences on trauma and dissociation are suggested for further education. An online membership form is provided.

<www.idealist.com/wounded_healer/>—This Web site is intended for psychotherapists who have themselves survived traumatic experiences, including childhood abuse. It offers a chat room, and a bookstore of trauma-related publications. Even those who have not suffered from abuse may learn from reading some of the topics included on the site: "What it is like to live with multiple personality disorder," and "Living with post-traumatic stress disorder."

<www.mentalhelp.net>—The "Professional Resources" area of this Web site offers chat groups on such topics as: DID case discussion, trauma intervention, and post-traumatic stress disorder.

Appendix C

Resources for Clergy

ORGANIZATIONS

Association of Mental Health Clergy, 1701 East Woodfield Road, Suite 311, Schaumburg, IL 60173. This organization publishes a quarterly newsletter.

Pathways to Promise, 5400 Arsenal Street, St. Louis MO, 63139. Phone: (314) 644-8400. This organization was founded by fourteen faith groups and mental health organizations to help the faith community's response to mental illness and their families. **Pathways** provides technical assistance and serves as a resource center for clergy. They publish a wide variety of informational booklets, worship resources, manuals, curricula resources, pamphlets, bulletin inserts, and videotapes. Some of the material is written specifically for Roman Catholic, Protestant, and Jewish clergy and congregations.

BOOKS AND ARTICLES

Adahan, Miriam (1992). *It's all a gift (though it may not seem like it at first glance)*. New York: Feldheim. Written from a Jewish perspective, this book focuses on dealing with life's struggles by drawing on the wisdom of Torah and maintaining a sense of closeness with God in the midst of the distress. Adahan claims that through our life struggles we grow spiritually, and it is through finding the hidden meaning and goodness within those struggles that we discover our own inner Godliness. Despite its Jewish orientation, *It's all a gift* is a gem that will appeal to ministers of all faiths.

Chu, James (1988). Ten traps for therapists in the treatment of trauma survivors. *Dissociation* 1(4):24-32. Although intended for psychotherapists, this article is invaluable in avoiding common pitfalls we all encounter when dealing with individuals who have suffered from severe childhood abuse. Among other concerns, Chu discusses how to deal with boundary issues and how to set limits.

Ensley, Eddie (1988). *Prayer that heals our emotions.* San Francisco, CA: Harper/San Francisco. A guide to prayer and meditation written from a Christian perspective. It offers concrete suggestions on how to bring God into our deepest unconscious to heal our emotional hurt.

Pargament, Kenneth (1997). *The psychology of religion and coping: Theory, research, practice.* New York: Guilford Press. This extremely scholarly book examines in depth the role of spirituality and religion in the process of recovering from trauma and illness. Specific religious coping methods are presented, including spiritual support, religious explanations of suffering, religious rituals associated with death and forgiveness. This book, aimed at both mental health practitioners and religious professionals, will be especially useful to clergy who want a strong psychological base to their religious interventions.

Rosik, Christopher (1995). The misdiagnosis of multiple personality disorder by Christian counselors. *Journal of Psychology and Christianity.* 11(3):263-268. This paper, although intended for Christian counselors, is applicable to clergy of all faiths. Rosik examines the reasons religious counselors are vulnerable to misdiagnosing a dissociative disorder, and provides help in making distinctions between DID and other psychiatric disorders. He also discusses a number of instruments and strategies for assessing the individual with a dissociative disorder.

Roukema, Richard, R. (1997). *The soul in distress: What every pastoral counselor should know about emotional and mental illness.* Binghamton, NY: The Haworth Press. This book is an excellent primer for ministers who want to learn more about psychiatric problems. It summarizes the major emotional disorders and provides information about ethics and referrals. Case histories make the material interesting and highly readable.

Shifrin, Jennifer (1995). *Pathways to understanding: A manual on ministry and mental illness.* This book is invaluable for clergy interested in working with mental health issues. It focuses on the importance of fostering a faith connection in people with mental illness and their families. Included are chapters on the nature and description of various mental illnesses, how to counsel and when to refer, and how to differentiate between true spiritual and religious crises and pathology masquerading as spiritual and religious issues. We especially appreciate the emphasis on viewing the person with mental illness not only as an individual separate from the disorder, but as a child of God.

Shifrin, Jennifer (1997). *Pathways to partnership: An awareness and resource guide on mental illness;* Shifrin, Jennifer (1991). *Pathways to partnership: An awareness and resource guide on mental illness for the Jewish community.* These two booklets, one a Christian version, the other intended for Jewish clergy and congregations, contain information about mental illness and serve as practical guides for responding to the needs of those with mental health problems within the congregation. They provide suggestions for specific congregational activities aimed at reaching out to the mentally ill and their families. They are also designed to be used as a springboard for discussions within the congregation on mental health issues. Study and action guides will be particularly helpful to clergy wishing to develop mental illness awareness within their congregations.

The previous three resources can be ordered through the **Pathways to Promise** (5400 Arsenal Street, St. Louis, Missouri, 63139. Phone: (314) 644-8400.

Weaver, Andrew (1993). Psychological trauma: What clergy need to know. *Pastoral Psychology* 41(6):385-408. This helpful paper provides concrete guidelines for clergy who are dealing with survivors of severe trauma and who are suffering from post-traumatic stress disorder.

Whitaker, Howard (1994). *A pastoral commentary on dissociative disorders: A primer for pastoral care.* Clinical Pastoral Services, 744 McCallie Avenue, Suite 516, Chattanooga, TN 37403. This book is an excellent introduction to dissociative disorders for clergy, especially since Whitaker discusses theological issues associated with these disorders. He presents useful information about assessing the survivor's God-image, and a chapter is included on using Scripture as a resource in work with survivors.

WEB SITES

<www.aapc.org>—The Web site of the American Association of Pastoral Counselors. It includes a code of ethics.

<www.mentalhealth.com>—Describes the fifty-two most common mental disorders.

<www.nimh.nih.gov>—This is the Web site of the National Institute of Mental Health in Washington, DC. It also offers information on mental disorders.

<www.psych.org/public_info/>—This is the Web site of the American Psychiatric Association. It also has information on mental health awareness, medication, and community resources. They publish a mental illness awareness guide for clergy, which you can order for free on the Internet. This guide not only has a glossary of mental illnesses, but also provides information on how to reach out to someone who has a mental illness.

Appendix D

Resources for Support Group Members

BOOKS

Cohen, Barry, Esther Giller, and Lynn W. (Eds.) (1991). *Multiple personality disorder from the inside out.* Baltimore, MD: Sidran Press. If you read only one book on dissociative disorders, let it be this one. The book is a compilation of stories, each told by an individual with DID. It is the best book we know adresses what it *feels like* to have multiple identities.

Davies, Laura (1990). *Allies in healing.* New York: HarperCollins. This is a support book for partners of survivors of childhood sexual abuse. Although it is aimed at *partners* of survivors, it provides information useful to members of a support group for the survivor.

Gil, Eliana (1988). *Outgrowing the pain: A book for and about adults abused as children.* New York: Dell Publishing. This is a wonderful little book which explains dissociative disorders in a simple, straightforward way.

Gil, Eliana (1992). *Outgrowing the pain together: A book for spouses and partners of adults abused as children.* New York: Dell Publishing. Again, although this book is meant for the *partners* of survivors of abuse, it is a good book for anyone involved in helping survivors heal. Eliana Gil writes in a simple, straightforward manner that makes her books a delight to read.

WEB SITES

<www.movingforward.org> The Web site of the organization **Moving Forward** is aimed at helping those who are experiencing emotional trauma and loss. The organization publishes a news journal for survivors of childhood abuse.

Appendix E

Resources for Survivors

ORGANIZATIONS AND NEWSLETTERS

The Healing Woman Foundation, P.O. Box 2840-W, San Jose, CA 95159. Phone: (408) 246-1788. E-mail address: HealingW@healingwoman.org. Web site: **<www.healingwoman.org>—Healing Woman** is a nonprofit organization which provides recovery resources for survivors of childhood abuse. They publish a bimonthly newsletter on all aspects of recovery. The newsletter includes advice from mental health specialists as well as contributions by survivors.

Many Voices, P.O. Box 2639, Cincinnati, OH 45201. This newsletter is written by and for people with DID. It is a very interesting publication, and as in the Healing Woman newsletter, has a column by a mental health professional in each issue.

Voices in Action, P.O. Box 148309 Chicago, IL 60614. Web site: **<www.voices-action.org>**—Voices is an international organization meant for survivors, support people, and professionals involved in treatment. It publishes a newsletter, *The Chorus,* a sample of which can be viewed online. There are also special interest groups, among them, groups for survivors with DID, survivors interested in women's spirituality, and survivors who are Christian.

BOOKS

Gil, Eliana (1988). *Outgrowing the pain: A book for and about adults abused as children.* New York: Dell Publishing. This is one of the easiest, most delightful books about survivors of abuse. Many survivors have told us how much they loved this book, and that it feels as if the book was written about them.

Muller, Wayne (1987). *Legacy of the heart: The spiritual advantages of a painful childhood.* New York: Simon & Schuster. This book may help survivors find meaning in their suffering.

Appendix F

Resources for Guided Imagery

GENERAL BOOKS ON IMAGERY

Fezler, William (1989). *Creative imagery: How to visualize in all five senses.* New York: Simon & Schuster. This book helps the therapist teach imagery to the patient step-by-step, and extends the concept of imagery to include all the sense modalities.

Fezler, William (1990). *Imagery for healing, knowledge, and power.* New York: Simon & Schuster. The chapters titled "Facts About Imagery," "Profound Relaxation," and "How to Create Your Own Imagery" are especially helpful for therapists or clergy new to imagery work.

Gawain, Shakti (1978). *Creative visualization.* New York: Bantam. This is a good introduction to imagery work. The book includes chapters on the basics of visualization, how to connect to one's Higher Self through visual imagery, and goal setting.

Shorr, Joseph E. (1983). *Imagery: Theoretical and clinical applications.* New York: Plenum Publishing. A good academic text on imagery work.

Smucker, Mervin R., Edna B. Foa, and Constance V. Danc (1999). *Cognitive-behavioral treatment for adult survivors of childhood trauma: Imagery, rescripting, and reprocessing.* New York: Jason Aronson. This book is ready-made for work with survivors.

Stewart, William (1998). *Imagery and symbolism in counseling.* Philadelphia, PA: Taylor & Francis. This book is a comprehensive exploration of spontaneous imagery, myth, and legend. It is a guide to the use of imagery and symbolism to enhance healing, and aims at bridging the gap between theory and practice.

BOOKS FOCUSING ON JEWISH IMAGERY

Cooper, David A. (1997). *God is a verb.* New York: Riverhead Books. This wonderful book on Jewish mysticism has many guided visualizations of interest. One particularly striking one is the "Archangel Meditation," based on the Jewish prayer: "May Michael be at my right, Gabriel at my left, Uriel in front of me, Raphael behind me, and above my head, the *Shekkina*—the Divine Presence." This visualization is one of the best for creating a sense of comfort, safety, and healing.

Davis, Avram (Ed.) (1997). *Meditation from the heart of Judaism.* Woodstock, VT: Jewish Lights Publishing. One chapter by clinical psychologist Edward Hoffman is particularly interesting. He presents the reader with three beginning guided imageries aimed at fostering a connection with the divine within.

Elkins, Dov Peretz (1996). *Jewish guided imagery: A how-to book for rabbis, educators, and group leaders.* Growth Associates. Although intended for rabbis, this book is helpful for therapists working with Jewish survivors.

Kaplan, Aryeh (1995). *Jewish meditation: A practical guide.* New York: Schocken Books. Among topics discussed are mantra meditation, contemplation, and visualization from a Jewish perspective. Few books on spiritual and religious meditation are written from a Jewish perspective, which makes this book, written by an Orthodox rabbi, all the more important.

BOOKS FOCUSING ON CHRISTIAN IMAGERY

Bohler, Carolyn Stahl (1996). *Opening to God: Guided imagery on Scripture.* Upper Room Books. The fifty meditations in this book focus on experiencing God through Scripture.

de Mello, Anthony (1978). *Sadhanda: A way to God: Christian exercises in Eastern form.* New York: Image Books. Each of the forty-seven guided imageries in this book endeavors to bring the reader closer to feeling God's presence. His exercise "Seeing him looking at you," in which the reader imagines Jesus looking at oneself, is deceptively simple and extremely powerful in its effect.

de Mello, Anthony (1995). *The way to love: The last meditations of Anthony de Mello.* New York: Image Books. The thirty-one imagery exercises in this book are designed to dissolve the illusions that stand in the way of our experiencing love. Each exercise is preceded by a Gospel quotation. De Mello's basic premise is that "love springs from awareness," and to that end, he guides the reader on a journey of "seeing" oneself and others without illusions.

Powers, Isaias (1995). *Quiet places with Jesus.* Mystic, CT: Twenty-Third Publications. Each exercise in this guided-imagery primer begins with a quote from Scripture. Topics include discouragement, anger, and others' opinions of us.

Powers, Isaias (1995). *Quiet Places with Mary.* Mystic, CT: Twenty-Third Publications. This book, similar to his book on Jesus, will be of special interest to many Catholics with its emphasis on Mary.

References

Allender, Dan B. (1990). *The Wounded Heart: Hope for Adult Victims of Childhood Sexual Abuse.* Colorado Springs, CO: Navpress.

American Psychiatric Association (1994). *Diagnostic and Statistical Manual of Mental Disorders,* Fourth Edition (DSM-IV). Washington, DC: APA.

Anonymous (1993). Bowman, Elizabeth (Ed.). *Multiple Voices Newsletter,* December.

Batson, Daniel C. and Patricia A. Schoenrade (1991). Measuring Religion As a Quest 1: Validity Concerns. *Journal for the Scientific Study of Religion* 30(4): 416-429.

Benson, Peter L. and Bernard Spilka (1973). God Image As a Function of Self-Esteem and Locus of Control. *Journal for the Scientific Study of Religion* 12(3): 297-310.

Bilich, Marion and Steven Carlson (1994). Therapists and Clergy Working Together: Linking the Psychological with the Spiritual in the Treatment of MPD. *The Journal of Christian Healing* 16(1):3-11.

Bishop, Leigh C. (1985). The Dream Magician: A Case of Paratixic Distortion. *The Journal of Psychology and Christianity* 4(2):12-14.

Bliss, Eugene (1984). Spontaneous Self-Hypnosis in Multiple Personality Disorder. *Psychiatric Clinics of North America* 7(1):135-148.

Borg, Marcus J. (1987). *Jesus: A New Vision.* San Francisco: Harper/San Francisco.

Borysenko, Joan (1990). *Guilt Is the Teacher, Love Is the Lesson.* New York: Time Warner.

Borysenko, Joan (1994). *Fire in the Soul: A New Psychology of Spiritual Optimism.* New York: Warner Books.

Bowman, Elizabeth (1993). Clinical and Spiritual Effects of Exorcism on Fifteen Patients with Multiple Personality Disorder. *Dissociation* 6(4):222-238.

Bowman, Elizabeth and William E. Amos (1993). Utilizing Clergy in the Treatment of Multiple Personality Disorder. *Dissociation* 6(1):47-53.

Bowman, Elizabeth, Philip Coons, Stanley Jones, and Mark Oldstrom (1987). Religious Psychodynamics in Multiple Personalities: Suggestions for Treatment. *American Journal of Psychotherapy* 41(4):542-554.

Bradley, Ann Kathleen (1999). Seeking Forgiveness in the World's Spiritual Traditions. *Spirituality and Health* 2(1):29-30.

Bruun, Christine V. (1985). A Combined Treatment Approach. *Journal of Psychology and Christianity* 4(2):9-11.

Campaan, Arlo (1985). Anger, Denial, and the Healing of Memories. *Journal of Psychology and Christianity* 4(2):83-85.

Casarjian, Robin (1992). *Forgiveness: A Bold Choice for a Peaceful Heart.* New York: Bantam.

Chu, James A. (1988). Ten Traps for Therapists in the Treatment of Trauma Survivors. *Dissociation* 1(4):24-32.

Clay, Rebecca A. (1996). Psychologists' Faith in Religion Begins to Grow. *The APA Monitor* 27(8): P. 16.

Cohen, Barry, Esther Giller, and Lynn W. (Eds.) (1991). *Multiple Personality Disorder from the Inside Out.* Baltimore, MD: Sidran Press.

Cohen, Sheldon, and Thomas Wills (1985). Stress, Social Support, and the Buffering Hypothesis. *Psychological Bulletin* 98(2):310-357.

Combs, Gene and Jill Freedman (1990). *Symbol, Story and Ceremony.* New York: Norton Books.

Courtois, Christine (1988). *Healing the Incest Wound: Adult Survivors in Therapy.* New York: W.W. Norton & Co.

Dolan, Yvonne (1991). *Resolving Sexual Abuse.* New York: Norton Books.

Domino, George (1985). Clergy's Attitudes Toward Suicide and Recognition of Suicide Lethality. *Death Studies* 9(3/4):187-199.

Domino, George (1990). Clergy's Knowledge of Psychopathology, *Journal of Psychology and Theology* 18(1):32-39.

Draper, Edythe (Ed.) (1992). *Draper's Book of Quotations for the Christian World.* Wheaton, IL: Tyndale House Publishers.

Dunkel-Schetter, Camille (1984). Social Support and Cancer: Findings Based on Patient Interviews and Their Implications. *Journal of Social Issues* 40:77-80.

Ellison, Craig and Joel Smith (1991). Toward an Integrative Measure of Health and Well-Being. *Journal of Psychology and Theology* 11(1):330-340.

Erikson, Erik (1968). *Identity: Youth and Crisis.* New York: Norton Books.

Fox, Matthew (1983). *Original Blessing.* Santa Fe, NM: Bear & Co.

Fox, Matthew (1988). *The Coming of the Cosmic Christ.* San Francisco, CA: Harper.

Fraser, G.A. (1991). Exorcism: Clinical Effects on Multiple Personality Exposed to Exorcism Rites. *Proceedings of the Eighth International Conference on Multiple Personality/Dissociative States.* Chicago, IL.

Friedman, Maurice (1992). *Religion and Psychology: A Dialogical Approach.* New York: Paragon House.

Friesen, James G. (1991). *Uncovering the Mystery of MPD.* San Bernadino, CA: Here's Life Publishers.

Gaultiere, William J. (1989). A Biblical Perspective on Therapeutic Treatment of Client Anger at God. *Journal of Psychology and Christianity* 8(3):38-46.

Gil, Eliana (1988). *Outgrowing the Pain: A Book for and About Adults Abused As Children.* New York: Dell Publishing.

Gilligan, Carol (1982). *In a Different Voice: Psychological Theory and Women's Development.* Cambridge, MA: Harvard University Press.

Gorsuch, Richard (1968). The Conceptualization of God As Seen in Adjective Ratings. *Journal for the Scientific Study of Religion* 7(1):56-64.

Gorsuch, Richard and Willa Meylink (1988). Toward a Co-Professional Model of Clergy-Psychologist Referral. *Journal of Psychology and Christianity* 7(3): 22-31.

Guntrip, Harry (1975). My Experience of Analysis with Fairbairn and Winnicott. *International Review of Psycho-analysis* 2(2):145-156.

Hardin, Michael (1991). "The Role of the Church in Healing MPD." Presented to the Christian Association for Psychological Studies, Maryland.

Hilgers, Karen (1992). Deliver Us from Evil: Recovery from the Spiritual Wounds of Traumagenic Abuse. *Proceedings of the Ninth International Conference on Multiple Personality/Dissociative States,* Chicago, IL.

Hohmann, Ann and David Larson (1993). Psychiatric Factors Predicting the Use of Clergy. In Worthington Jr., Edward (Ed.), *Psychotherapy and Religious Values* (pp. 71-84). Grand Rapids, MI: Baker Book House.

Holderread Heggen, Carolyn (1993). *Sexual Abuse in Christian Homes and Churches.* Scottsdale, PA: Herald Press.

Jampolsky, Gerald G. (1983). *Teach Only Love: The Seven Principles of Attitudinal Healing.* New York: Bantam Books.

Janoff-Bulman, Ronnie (1992). *Shattered Assumptions: Towards a New Psychology of Trauma.* New York: Free Press.

Jay, Jeffrey (1994). Walls for Wailing. *Common Boundary* 12(3):30-35.

Jordan, Judith (1991a). Empathy, Mutuality, and Therapeutic Change. In Jordan, Judith, Alexandra Kaplan, Jean Baker Miller, Irene Stiver, and Janet Surrey (Eds.), *Women's Growth in Connection* (pp. 288-289). New York: Guilford Books.

Jordan, Judith (1991b). The Meaning of Mutuality. In Jordan, Judith, Alexandra Kaplan, Jean Baker Miller, Irene Stiver, and Janet Surrey (Eds.), *Women's Growth in Connection* (pp. 81-96). New York: Guilford Books.

Julian of Norwich (1978). *Showings.* Translated by Edmund Colledge and James Walsh. New York: Paulist Press.

Kinsler, Philip (1992). The Centrality of Relationship: What's *Not* Being Said. *Dissociation* 5(3):166-170.

Kluft, Robert (1984a). Aspects of Treatment of MPD. *Psychiatric Annals* 14(1): 51-55.

Kluft, Robert (1984b). Treatment of Multiple Personality Disorder. *Psychiatric Clinics of North America* 7(1):29-79.

Kluft, Robert (1993a). The Initial Stages of Psychotherapy in the Treatment of Multiple Personality Disorder Patients. *Dissociation* 6(2/3):145-161.

Kluft, Robert (1993b). The Treatment of Dissociative Patients: An Overview of Discoveries, Successes, and Failures. *Dissociation* 6(2/3):88-106.

Koenig, Harold G. (1995). *Research on Religion and Aging.* Westport, CT: Greenwood Press.

Kopp, Richard R. (1995). *Metaphor Therapy.* New York: Brunner/Mazel.

Linn, Matthew, Sheila Fabricant, and Dennis Linn (1988). *Healing the Eight Stages of Life.* Mahwah, NJ: Paulist Press.

Lovinger, Robert J. (1984). *Working with Religious Issues in Therapy.* New York: Aronson.

Lowenstein, Richard and D.R. Ross (1992). Multiple Personality and Psychoanalysis: An Introduction. *Psychoanalytic Inquiry* 12(1):3-48.

Manning, Brennan (1982). *A Stranger to Self-Hatred.* Denville, NJ: Dimension Books.

Manning, Brennan (1986). *Lion and Lamb.* Grand Rapids, MI: Fleming H. Revell/ Baker Books.

Manning, Brennan (1990). *The Ragamuffin Gospel.* Portland, OR: Multnomah Press.

Manning, Brennan (1992). *The Signature of Jesus.* Portland, OR: Multnomah Press.

McCullough, Michael, E., Everett Worthington, and Steven Sondage (1997). *To Forgive Is Human: How to Put Your Past in the Past.* Madison, WI: Intervarsity Press.

Meylink, Willa D. and Richard L. Gorsuch (1988). Relationship Between Clergy and Psychologists. *Journal of Psychology and Christianity* 7(1):56-72.

Miller, Patricia (1983). *Theories of Developmental Psychology.* San Francisco: Wh. Freedman.

Mitchell, Stephen (1991). *The Gospel According to Jesus.* New York: Harper/Collins.

Moss, David M. (1978). "Priestcraft and Psychoanalytic Therapy: Contradiction or Concordance?" Paper read at the American Psychological Association Convention, 86th Annual Convention, Toronto, Canada, September 1.

Neibuhr, Gustav (1995). Looking for God in the Lives, Not the Deaths, of the Holocaust's Death Camps. *The New York Times,* Saturday, February 11, p. A11.

O'Malley, Michael N., Robert Gearhart, and Lee A. Becker (1984). On Cooperation Between Psychology and Religion: An Attitudinal Survey of Therapists and Clergy. *Counseling and Values* 28(3):117-121.

Olson, Jean (1992). "The Centrality of Relationship: What's *Not* Being Said": Response. *Dissociation* 5(3):174-175.

Paloutzian, Raymond and Craig Ellison (1982). Loneliness, Spiritual Well-Being and Quality of Life. In Letitia Anne Peplau and Daniel Perlman (Eds.), *Loneliness: A Sourcebook for Current Therapy.* New York: Wiley-Interscience.

Peace Pilgrim (1991). *Peace Pilgrim: Her Life and Works in Her Own Words.* Santa Fe, NM: Ocean Tree Books.

Peck, M. Scott (1978). *The Road Less Traveled.* New York: Simon & Schuster.

Peck, M. Scott (1983). *People of the Lie.* New York: Touchtone Books.

Pellauer, Mary D., Barbara Chester, and Jane Boyajian (1987). *Sexual Abuse in Christian Homes: A Handbook for Clergy and Religious Professionals.* San Francisco: Harper/San Francisco.

Polsky, Howard W. and Yaella Wozner (1989). *Everyday Miracles: The Healing Wisdom of Hasidic Stories.* Northvale, NJ: Jason Aronson.

Putnam, Frank (1989). *Diagnosis and Treatment of Multiple Personality Disorder.* New York: Guilford Press.

Raub, John Jacob (1992). *Who Told You That You Were Naked? Freedom from Judgment.* New York: Crossroad Books.

Rizzuto, Ana-Maria (1979). *The Birth of the Living God.* Chicago: Chicago University Press.

Rosik, Christopher (1992). On Introducing Multiple Personality Disorder to the Church. *Journal of Psychology and Christianity* 11(3):263-268.

Ross, Colin (1989). *MPD: Diagnosis, Clinical Features and Treatment.* New York: Wiley.

Ross, Colin (1993). Critical Issues Committee Report: Exorcism in the Treatment of Patients with MPD. *International Society for the Study of Multiple Personality and Dissociation* 11(2):4.

Saussy, Carroll (1993). Pastoral Care and Counseling and Issues of Self-Esteem. In Wicks, Robert and Richard D. Parsons (Eds.), *Clinical Handbook of Pastoral Counseling* (Vol. 2) (pp. 363-389). New York: Integration Books.

Schlauch, Chris (1993). Revisioning Pastoral Diagnosis. In Wicks, Robert and Richard D. Parsons (Eds.), *Clinical Handbook of Pastoral Counseling* (Vol. 2) (pp. 51-101). Mahwah, NJ: Integration Books.

Shafranske, H.P. and Malony, H.N. (1990). Clinical Psychologists' Religious Orientation and Their Practice of Psychotherapy. *Psychotherapy* 27(2):72-78.

Shifrin, Jennifer (1995). *Pathways to Understanding: A Manual on Ministry and Mental Illness.* St. Louis, MO: Pathways to Promise.

Silver, Roxanne, and Camille Wortman (1980). Coping with Undesirable Life Events. In Garber, Judy, and Martin Seligman (Eds.), *Human Helplessness: Theory and Application* (pp. 77-80). New York: Academic Press.

Smedes, Lewis B. (1994). *Shame and Grace.* San Francisco: Harper/San Francisco.

Stiver, Irene (1991). The Meaning of Care: Reframing Treatment Models. In Jordan, Judith, Alexandra Kaplan, Jean Baker Miller, Irene Stiver, and Janet Surrey (Eds.), *Women's Growth in Connection* (pp. 250-267). New York: Guilford Press.

Stovich, Raymond (1985). Metaphor and Therapy: Theory, Techniques, and Practice in the Use of Religious Imagery in Therapy. *The Psychotherapy Patient* 3(1):117-122.

Tillich, Paul (1948). *The Shaking of the Foundations.* New York: Charles Scribner's and Sons.

Torem, Moshe (1993). President's Message. *ISSMPD News:* 11(2) 1.

Underwood, Ralph (1985). Pastoral Counseling in the Parish Setting. In Wicks, Robert, Richard D. Parsons, and Donald Capps (Eds.), *Clinical Handbook of Pastoral Counseling* (Vol. 1) (pp. 332-348). Mahwah, NJ: Paulist Press.

Vesper, Joyce H. (1991). The Use of Healing Ceremonies in the Treatment of Multiple Personality Disorder. *Dissociation* 4(2):109-144.

Vine, W.E. (1985). *An Expository Dictionary of Biblical Words.* Nashville, TN: Thomas Nelson.

Watzlawick, Paul, John Weakland, and Richard Fisch (1974). *Change: Principles of Problem Formation and Problem Resolution.* New York: Norton Books.

Weaver, Andrew J., Harold G. Koenig, and Frank M. Ochberg (1996). Posttraumatic Stress, Mental Health Professionals, and the Clergy: A Need for Collaboration, Training, and Research. *Journal of Traumatic Stress* 9(4):847-856.

White, Francis J. (1985). Earthly Father/Heavenly Father. *Journal of Psychology and Christianity* 4(2):76-85.

Wiederkehr, Macrina (1988). *A Tree Full of Angels.* San Francisco: Harper/San Francisco.

Wise, Carroll (1983). *Pastoral Psychotherapy.* New York: Jason Aronson.

Wolpe, David J. (1990). *The Healer of Shattered Hearts: A Jewish View of God.* New York: Penguin Books.

Wolpe, David J. (1992). Quoted in Article "Talking to God," *Newsweek,* January 6.

Worthington, Everett Jr. (1999). The Forgiveness Teacher's Toughest Test. *Spirituality and Health* 2(1):30-31.

Index

Order Your Own Copy of
This Important Book for Your Personal Library!

SHARED GRACE
Therapists and Clergy Working Together

_____ in hardbound at $49.95 (ISBN: 0-7890-0878-5)

_____ in softbound at $24.95 (ISBN: 0-7890-1110-7)

COST OF BOOKS_____

OUTSIDE USA/CANADA/
MEXICO: ADD 20%_____

POSTAGE & HANDLING_____
*(US: $3.00 for first book & $1.25
for each additional book)*
*Outside US: $4.75 for first book
& $1.75 for each additional book)*

SUBTOTAL_____

IN CANADA: ADD 7% GST_____

STATE TAX_____
*(NY, OH & MN residents, please
add appropriate local sales tax)*

FINAL TOTAL_____
*(If paying in Canadian funds,
convert using the current
exchange rate. UNESCO
coupons welcome.)*

☐ **BILL ME LATER:** ($5 service charge will be added)
(Bill-me option is good on US/Canada/Mexico orders only;
not good to jobbers, wholesalers, or subscription agencies.)

☐ Check here if billing address is different from
shipping address and attach purchase order and
billing address information.

Signature _____

☐ **PAYMENT ENCLOSED: $**_____

☐ **PLEASE CHARGE TO MY CREDIT CARD.**

☐ Visa   ☐ MasterCard   ☐ AmEx   ☐ Discover
☐ Diners Club
Account # _____

Exp. Date _____

Signature _____

Prices in US dollars and subject to change without notice.

NAME _____

INSTITUTION _____

ADDRESS _____

CITY _____

STATE/ZIP _____

COUNTRY _____ COUNTY (NY residents only) _____

TEL _____ FAX _____

E-MAIL_____
May we use your e-mail address for confirmations and other types of information? ☐ Yes   ☐ No

Order From Your Local Bookstore or Directly From
The Haworth Press, Inc.
10 Alice Street, Binghamton, New York 13904-1580 • USA
TELEPHONE: 1-800-HAWORTH (1-800-429-6784) / Outside US/Canada: (607) 722-5857
FAX: 1-800-895-0582 / Outside US/Canada: (607) 772-6362
E-mail: getinfo@haworthpressinc.com
PLEASE PHOTOCOPY THIS FORM FOR YOUR PERSONAL USE.

BOF96